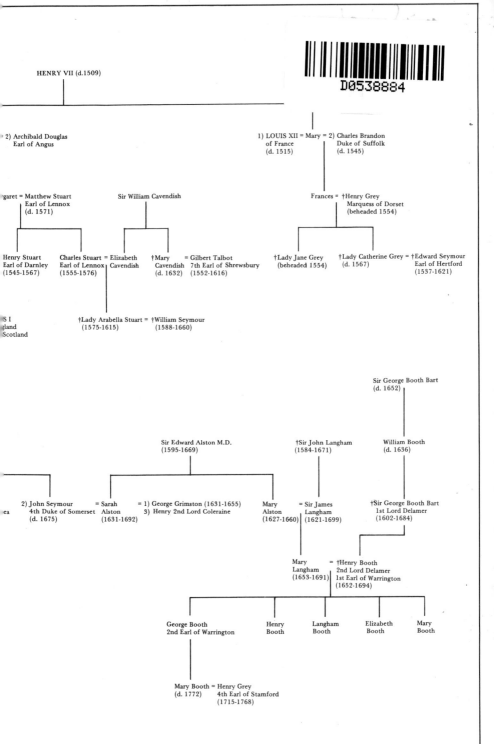

HENRY VII (d.1509)

2) Archibald Douglas
Earl of Angus

1) LOUIS XII = Mary = 2) Charles Brandon
of France   Duke of Suffolk
(d. 1515)   (d. 1545)

garet = Matthew Stuart
Earl of Lennox
(d. 1571)

Sir William Cavendish

Frances = †Henry Grey
Marquess of Dorset
(beheaded 1554)

Henry Stuart   Charles Stuart = Elizabeth   †Mary   = Gilbert Talbot   †Lady Jane Grey   †Lady Catherine Grey = †Edward Seymour
Earl of Darnley   Earl of Lennox Cavendish   Cavendish   7th Earl of Shrewsbury   (beheaded 1554)   (d. 1567)   Earl of Hertford
(1545-1567)   (1555-1576)   (d. 1632)   (1552-1616)   (1537-1621)

S I
gland
Scotland

†Lady Arabella Stuart = †William Seymour
(1575-1615)   (1588-1660)

Sir George Booth Bart
(d. 1652)

Sir Edward Alston M.D.
(1595-1669)

†Sir John Langham
(1584-1671)

William Booth
(d. 1636)

2) John Seymour   = Sarah   = 1) George Grimston (1631-1655)   Mary   = Sir James   †Sir George Booth Bart
ea   4th Duke of Somerset   Alston   3) Henry 2nd Lord Coleraine   Alston   Langham   1st Lord Delamer
(d. 1675)   (1631-1692)   (1627-1660) (1621-1699)   (1602-1684)

Mary   = †Henry Booth
Langham   2nd Lord Delamer
(1653-1691)   1st Earl of Warrington
(1652-1694)

George Booth   Henry   Langham   Elizabeth   Mary
2nd Earl of Warrington Booth   Booth   Booth   Booth

Mary Booth = Henry Grey
(d. 1772)   4th Earl of Stamford
(1715-1768)

ers in the Tower.

A STUART BENEFACTRESS

MR AND MRS M J GUILLE
9 CHALDON WAY
COULSDON
SURREY CR3 1DG
0737 555025

A STUART BENEFACTRESS

Sarah, Duchess of Somerset

by

A. DALY BRISCOE

TERENCE DALTON LIMITED
LAVENHAM . SUFFOLK
1973

Published by
TERENCE DALTON LIMITED
SBN 900963 35 2

Printed in Great Britain at
The Lavenham Press Limited
Lavenham   Suffolk

Contents

Index of Illustrations

Index of Genealogical Tables

6

Acknowledgement

FOR a long time I have had it in my mind to find out more about the life and times of the gracious benefactress who enabled me to have a university career for which I have been ever grateful.

It was not until I retired from general medical practice that I was able fully to pursue this quest. The easily accessible pieces of information from standard books of reference produced very little. Not having undertaken any historical research before I had perforce to seek help from many people. This was always readily given and the number to whom I am now indebted is, in consequence, very large and I could not mention them all.

To those who have guided my search into profitable channels I owe a great deal. One of the earliest to do so was the late Mr Brian Tunstall F.S.A., a friend since undergraduate days. Another contemporary, the Rev. J. S. Boys Smith, Master of St John's College, Cambridge, 1959-1969, kindly arranged for me to have access to certain documents in the College archives. The former Keeper of the Records there, the late Mr F. Puryer White M.A., gave me much help as has his successor Mr N. C. Buck and also Mr M. Pratt of the College Library Staff. Similarly from Brasenose College, Oxford, I was afforded much assistance and particularly by Mr Robin Peedell of the College Library.

These were not the only Libraries which aided me. The congenial atmosphere of St Deiniol's Library, Hawarden, Gladstone's Memorial and the only residential library in the country, provided me with a place to stay and study away from the hurly-burly of our everyday life. The Warden, the Rev. Dr Stewart Lawton made me most welcome on a number of occasions. Other places from which I have received assistance include the Cambridge University Library, the British Museum, and the Seckford Reference Library in Woodbridge where the late Miss Elsie Redstone's knowledge of County history was so readily put at my disposal.

Then there are the Record Offices of various Counties to which I was introduced by Mr D. Charman M.A., former Archivist of

East Suffolk who himself proffered a number of valuable suggestions which uncovered further information.

To Sir John Langham, fourteenth Baronet, I am grateful for some family history and the late Colonel A. Alston Fenn D.S.O. helped me with the story of the Alstons.

Through the courtesy of the Marquess of Bath I was given access to the Thynne Papers and the Seymour Papers at Longleat where the acting Librarian, Lt. Col. H. N. Ingles, gave me much assistance. For help with some Latin translation I am indebted to Mr Ian Munro.

Finally I wish to thank those who undertook the task of typing my manuscript, chiefly Mrs D. G. King, Mrs P. F. Howard Dawnay and Miss K. Warren.

A. Daly Briscoe,
Seckford Lodge,
Woodbridge.   1973.

Dates

	Accession	
Henry VII	1485	1456 – 1509
Henry VIII	1509	1491 – 1547
Edward VI	1547	1537 – 1553
Mary	1553	1515 – 1558
Elizabeth	1558	1534 – 1603
James I (and VI of Scotland)	1603	1566 – 1625
Charles I	1625	1601 – 1649
Commonwealth	1649 – 1660	
Charles II	restored 1660	1630 – 1685
James II	1685 (deposed 1688)	1633 – 1701
William III (joint sovereigns)	1689	1651 – 1702
Mary II		1661 – 1694
William III (alone)	1694	
Anne	1702	1665 – 1714

Battle of Edgehill	23rd October 1642
Execution of Charles I	30th January 1649
Death of Cromwell	3rd September 1658

Sir Edward Alston M.D.	1595 – 1669
Mary Alston (Lady Langham)	1627 – 1660
Sarah Alston (Duchess of Somerset	1631 – 1692
Sir Harbottle Grimston (second Baronet)	1603 – 1685
George Grimston	1631 – 1655
William, second Duke of Somerset	1588 – 1660
William, third Duke of Somerset	1652 – 1671
John, fourth Duke of Somerset	(?) 1630 – 1675
Francis, fifth Duke of Somerset	1658 – 1678
Sir John Langham (first Baronet)	1584 – 1671
Sir James Langham (second Baronet)	1621 – 1699
Sir George Booth (first Lord Delamer)	1622 – 1684
Henry Booth (first Earl of Warrington)	1652 – 1694
Mary Langham (Countess of Warrington)	1652 – 1691
Henry Hare (second Lord Coleraine)	1636 – 1708

9

Introduction

CARE for the unfortunate, the sick and the poor, has been a Christian virtue ever since the story of the good Samaritan. In the Middle Ages the monasteries were the main support and distributers of charity. With their dissolution a great gap was created in the dispensation of largesse. To fill it came benefactions from individuals and an expansion of the Poor Law. In the seventeenth century the difference between the rich and the poor was very great indeed, comparable perhaps to the conditions prevailing in India at the beginning of the present century but over a much smaller population. The whole of England, it has been estimated, contained only about four and a half million people with London in the region of three hundred thousand.

The tremendous upheaval caused in the middle of the Stuart era by the Civil War did not bring about a radically changed society, unlike what happened in Britain after the First World War. The state of the lower classes was not much altered. An awareness of the extremes of poverty however began to dawn upon those who enjoyed the luxuries of life. The possessors of large estates bethought themselves, mostly in their Wills, of helping the destitute by founding almshouses for the aged, and schools or scholarships for the young. Among those with such commendable motives was Sarah, Duchess of Somerset, who gave much thought to the disposal of her wealth. She did not neglect or deny her own kith and kin, but after she had provided for them as far as she considered necessary she proceeded to a liberal philanthropy. She left money to provide almshouses, to train apprentices, to found scholarships and to support and enlarge schools.

In her lifetime she was connected to many prominent people in the City, in Parliament, in the Law and at Court. Her father, Sir Edward Alston, became a distinguished physician and was President of the College of Physicians for over ten years. Her elder sister married the son of an outstanding Alderman of the City of London. She, herself, married three times; on each occasion into a family of some eminence, but she died without any surviving issue. She had no brother and her only sister died young, leaving an only daughter.

This study is intended to be a peep into the lives of those to whom she was related, or with whom she was associated, and so give a glimpse of contemporary life. It is also an investigation into her legacies and benefactions to see how these are functioning after three centuries. Because of the need to keep the book down to a reasonable size these accounts have had to be curtailed. However, if any reader should desire to know more of their history the original manuscript will be deposited in the Library of St John's College, Cambridge.

People in the Narrative

SOME of the prominent personages mentioned in this story were at various times known by different names. This can be confusing and as an aid to identification, the following notes are appended.

Sarah Alston (1631-1692) became the wife of George Grimston (1631-1655). Widowed, she then married Lord John Seymour who later succeeded his nephew as the fourth Duke of Somerset. After his death in 1675 she was married a third time to Henry, Lord Coleraine (1636-1708) but she was granted by Royal Warrant the privilege of being styled Sarah, Duchess of Somerset and this title she used at all times.

Edward Seymour (1537-1621), eldest son of the first Duke of Somerset (Protector Somerset), had restored to him by Queen Elizabeth the titles of Lord Beauchamp and Earl of Hertford which had been forfeited, in addition to the dukedom, when his father was beheaded. He was known throughout his life thereafter as the Earl of Hertford. His son, Edward (1561-1612) was called Lord Beauchamp and his son and heir William Seymour (1588-1660) became successively Lord Beauchamp, Earl of Hertford, Marquis of Hertford and eventually he was restored to his great grandfather's dukedom by Charles II to become the second Duke of Somerset.

The eldest son of this second Duke was Henry, Lord Beauchamp (1626-1654). He died before his father and so the succession to the dukedom devolved upon his son William (1651-1671) who succeeded his grandfather as third Duke of Somerset.

The widowed Lady Beauchamp, the mother of the third Duke married as her second husband Henry, Lord Herbert (1629-1699) who inherited his father's title of Marquis of Worcester and he was subsequently created the first Duke of Beaufort.

Mary Langham (1652-1691) the only surviving child of the marriage of James Langham and Sarah's sister, Mary Alston, married Henry Booth (1652-1694) who succeeded his father to become the second Lord Delamer and was created the first Earl of Warrington. His father, George Booth (1622-1684), inherited his grandfather's baronetcy and was later created the first Lord Delamer at the time of Charles II's Coronation.

Lady Arabella Stuart was the daughter of Charles Stuart, Earl of Lennox (1555-1576). His elder brother, Henry Stuart, Earl of Darnley (1545-1567) was married to Mary, Queen of Scots. Lady Arabella was therefore first cousin to James I. Throughout the book her name is spelt in the modern way in place of the old Arbella.

PART I

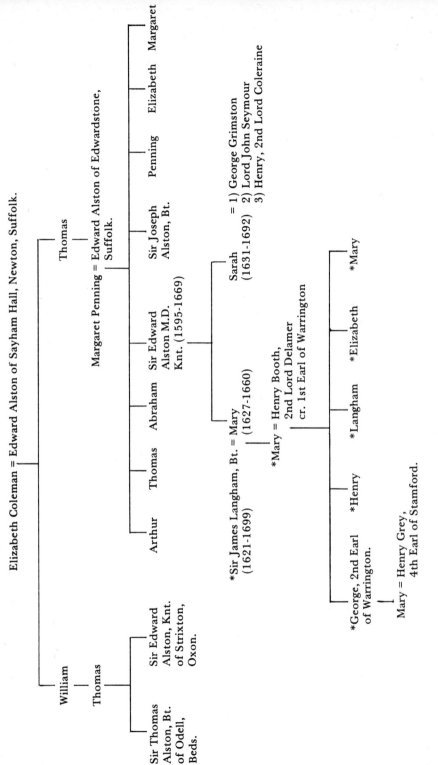

Elizabeth Coleman = Edward Alston of Sayham Hall, Newton, Suffolk.

William

Thomas

Margaret Penning = Edward Alston of Edwardstone, Suffolk.

Sir Thomas Alston, Bt. of Odell, Beds.

Sir Edward Alston, Knt. of Strixton, Oxon.

Arthur

Thomas

Abraham

Sir Edward Alston M.D. Knt. (1595-1669)

Sir Joseph Alston, Bt.

Penning

Elizabeth

Margaret

Sarah (1631-1692) = 1) George Grimston 2) Lord John Seymour 3) Henry, 2nd Lord Coleraine

*Sir James Langham, Bt. (1621-1699) = Mary (1627-1660)

*Mary = Henry Booth, 2nd Lord Delamer cr. 1st Earl of Warrington

*George, 2nd Earl of Warrington.

*Henry

*Langham

*Elizabeth

*Mary

Mary = Henry Grey, 4th Earl of Stamford.

*Mentioned in Sarah's Will.

Suffolk Ancestry

THE early Alstons who appear to have been indigenous in East Anglia for a very long time, would seem to belong to what Stubbs described as "that great body of freeholders, the Yeomanry of the Middle Ages, a body which in antiquity of possession and purity of extraction was probably superior to the classes that looked down upon it as ignoble." Some of these settled down as tradesmen in the cities and formed a link between town and country. When personal extravagance became the rule at Court, the nobility and the gentry gradually lost their hold on land and great estates were broken up. The rich merchant and the City tradesmen then bought the Manor of the impoverished Squire.

In the time of Edward I there was a William Alston living at Stisted in Essex. A descendant of his was John Alston who was the father of William Alston of Newton near Sudbury, Suffolk. In the Subsidy List for 1524 he is assessed at ten pounds but pays five shillings! His heir was Edward Alston who lived at Siam (Sayham) Hall, Newton.*

In feudal times the organisation of military forces rested on the King demanding men from his Barons who selected them from their serfs and henchmen. These men had little if any knowledge of the cause or merits of the war in which they were thrust. The Crown later acted through a "Captain" in every county who, with the Sheriff, exerted authority and raised forces if urgently needed. Henry VIII increased the standing of this position by appointing "Lieutenants and Captain Generals" which led on to the title Lord Lieutenant first mentioned in the reign of Mary. From this grew a policy of keeping a roster of all men between the ages of sixteen and sixty who were considered fit to serve if needed. The 1638 roster for Suffolk described them as *able men* in the certificates delivered by the Petty Constables to the Chief Constable for the various Hundreds. These names excluded the "Trayned Band" and the clergy. There were no less than

---

*Siam Hall was accidentally burnt to the ground in July 1959.

twenty-three such men bearing the name Alston in almost as many villages (seventeen) in Suffolk in that year. The family must therefore have been fairly widespread throughout the county and the name is still well represented today in various parts of Suffolk. This enumeration of able-bodied men also gives some idea of the population for at this Census of men between those ages there were about twenty-four thousand of them on the Suffolk Roll.

Among the great grandsons of the Edward Alston mentioned above three were created knights and two were made baronets. The grandson, also named Edward, who lived at Edwardstone, Suffolk, was a landowner and presumably one of the important and influential people in the district.

One Sunday in the year 1637 when attending Divine Service in the church there was a violent thunderstorm. A lad in the employ of this Mr Edward Alston had just brought up his master's horse for him to ride home, as was his custom, when torrential rain descended. Some of the worshippers seeing the heavy downpour through the open door, beckoned to the boy to take shelter within the porch. The porch, however, was not large enough to accommodate both boy and horse so the horse went into the church itself and was seen by Mr Alston who mounted it while in the church and rode forth "using at the same time some indiscreet words to the Sexton." For this act he was held punishable and it was thought fit that he should do penance by acknowledging his fault in the said church, but in delivering judgment, John Lambe, the presiding officer of the Court, decreed that "as Mr Alston is an ancient gentleman in years and desireth he may rather redeem his penance I accept his offer to pay 20 marks towards the repair of St Paul's Church in London and he is to pay £6.13.4. to the promoter of the suit."

This same Edward Alston in his Will dated 3 February 1649 wrote, "I give to my son Edward Alston, Doctor in Physick of St Mary Hill London, one great gold ring which was his mother's and to his wife forty shillings for a ring and the same amount to his two daughters living." It must be remembered when reading these amounts that the value of money was worth about twenty times what it is today and this must be kept in mind throughout when interpreting sums of money that may be mentioned appertaining to events in the seventeenth century. Doctor Alston's mother was Margaret Penning of Kettleburgh, Suffolk. In the

Visitation of the County in 1612 the Penning family is recorded and an uncle of Margaret, Anthony Penning, was Sheriff of Suffolk in 1607. There were eight children of this marriage, Arthur, Thomas, Abraham, Edward, Joseph, Penning, Elizabeth and Margaret. Edward, the doctor, was knighted in 1660 and Joseph was created a baronet in 1681.

At the age of seventeen the young Edward matriculated as a pensioner from St John's College, Cambridge, in the Easter Term 1612. He graduated four years later and took his M.A. in 1619, receiving his doctorate in medicine seven years after that. He spent some time at Oxford also being incorporated there in the year he took his M.D. At the age of thirty-six he was elected a Fellow of the College of Physicians, subsequently becoming Treasurer and eventually President from 1655 to 1666.

He must have been very proficient in his practice of medicine to reach such eminence. Apart from his skill as a physician he probably possessed sound business acumen for he became a very rich man. He was largely responsible for restoring the fortunes of the College when they were at a low ebb, and he put the administration of it on a sound footing. At the Restoration of Charles II, as President of the College, he kissed hands on 3rd September 1660 and received the honour of knighthood.

Because of the political disturbances of the times, the affairs of the College had fallen into great disorder. The funds were well nigh exhausted, lectures had been suspended and a large number were practising within the liberty of the College without licence. The examinations of apothecaries' apprentices, which for many years had been rigorously enforced, were no longer taking place. In consequence there was much difficulty in restraining the activities of unqualified practitioners and quackery abounded. Some of the unlicensed physicians were known to be able and the problem was to sort out the chaff from the wheat. So Sir Edward busied himself in the correction of the abuses that had grown up during and after the Civil War. He became responsible for the adoption of a method by which the worthy unlicensed practitioners could be embraced by the College which would, at the same time, benefit financially. He proposed that they should be created Honorary Fellows by the payment of certain fees.

It is recorded that at an extraordinary meeting called on 1st September 1664 for the purpose of improving the finances of the

College and for strengthening the authority of the same, it was decided to admit to the College learned and distinguished men with the title of Honorary Fellow. This proposal pleased everyone because there were in London a number of doctors of outstanding character and knowledge for whom an examination would have been a hardship. So those who received a majority of votes from the Fellows, were to become Honorary Fellows and enjoy the freedom of practising medicine within this City and its surroundings.

On the 16th September this Statute was ratified by the majority.

As a result upwards of seventy physicians were elected Honorary Fellows, and the objects aimed at by the new regulations were fully attained, all physicians of repute practising in London being thus brought into the College. The finances were greatly augmented and the College was in a more prosperous condition than it had been at any former period, but not for long.

When the Plague came in 1665, the President and most if not all the officers of the College left London for the country, for the reason generally given that they were merely following their paying patients who had fled from the stricken city. During their absence thieves broke into the College and the treasure chest containing the whole of the funds, including all the above mentioned fees from the new Honorary Fellows, was robbed of its entire contents. Worse was to follow for during the next year the College and the whole Library except for a few unimportant volumes was destroyed in the Great Fire.

The Fellows having no longer a House of their own held their Comitia during the first year in the house of Sir John Langham, a London merchant, one of whose sons, William, had recently been elected an Honorary Fellow. They also met sometimes in Sir Edward Alston's house and in those of others who had the necessary accommodation. Much time was spent on deliberating over the search for a new College House. It is understandable that Sir Edward took a leading part in this, and when eventually a decision was taken to rebuild he offered considerable sums of money and invited others to give freely too. Most unfortunately the Fellows became divided as to where the new building should be sited and the friction developed into a major conflict. In the heat engendered the President took offence and it is said that by his conduct both in and out of the College, greatly upset his colleagues. As a result at the next general election Dr Glisson was elected President in his place. Sir Edward must have felt tremendously affronted by this for he thereupon revoked his promised subscription and never afterwards renewed his proffered help.

Edward Alston married at the age of twenty-eight a widow, Susan Hussey, who according to the church record was thirty-two. The ceremony took place at St Botolph's, Aldersgate, and he is described as of St Mary Abchurch, while her former husband is referred to as a deceased merchant. Her father was Christopher Hudson of Norwich.

Two daughters were born of this union. Mary the elder is mentioned as being seven years old at the time of the Visitation of London in 1634. She married James, eldest son of Alderman Sir John Langham already referred to above, who was Sheriff of London. A little over twelve years later she died leaving an only surviving child, Mary, and was buried in St Helen's Church, Bishopsgate, on the south side of the Altar. The younger daughter, Sarah, married three times but died without surviving issue. Her first husband was George, eldest son of Sir Harbottle Grimston, second baronet, who was Master of the Rolls. The two children born of this marriage both died in infancy, and George Grimston himself died on the 5th June 1653. Her second husband was Lord John Seymour who afterwards became the fourth Duke of Somerset. He died on the 29th April, 1675. Finally she married as his second wife Henry Hare, the second Lord Coleraine, who survived her. Sarah died on the 25th October 1692 and was buried in Westminster Abbey.

By his successful career Sir Edward Alston added to any inherited money he may have received, and is said to have accumulated an ample fortune. He endowed handsomely both his daughters on their marriages (a generous amount would be commanded as they were both espoused to heirs of baronetcies) and later, when Sarah became a widow, Sir Edward gave her an additional £10,000 as a portion on marrying into the family of the Duke of Somerset. In those times it was considered a father's duty to see that his daughter was well provided for when she married; the preliminary negotiations being carried out by fathers who made enquiries to find out who was on offer in their own social sphere. In the Verney papers the efforts to secure a suitable match for Edmund Verney (Mun) is mentioned in April 1661, "meanwhile the heiress hunting for Mun continues", and Anne

Hobart* is referred to as having a widow to recommend, Sir Edward Alston's daughter, who had just thrown over Lord Paget, and was in treaty against her father's wishes with the son of Lord Coleraine. Sir Edward, it was thought, preferred the Verney alliance and was conferring with Dr William Denton who was Edmund's uncle, but nothing came of it. It is, however, an enlightening piece of news as it is clear that Sarah must have been interested in Henry Hare, who became the second Lord Coleraine, before her marriage to Lord John Seymour. It may have been her father's wish that he was passed over in favour of a son of the Duke of Somerset, but when she became a widow for the second time she did marry Lord Coleraine, although neither of these marriages proved to be happy unions. Dr Denton would be well known to Sir Edward for he was a member of the College of Physicians and had been a Court Physician to Charles I.

It can be safely assumed that Sir Edward Alston had a good practice as probably many of the nobility were his patients, there being two recorded occasions when he was called to submit evidence on the state of health of peers who were under restraint. In 1645 Lord Savile had been committed to the Tower in connection with a charge he had made against Mr Holles† and Mr Whitelocke† that they had corresponded with the King's Party at Oxford. He made many applications for release on account of ill health, and a medical report from Dr Alston was taken before the Committee of the House of Lords but no release was granted. Eventually Lord Savile's resolution gave way and he made a full confession to the House of Lords of all he knew in the matter, stating that a letter from Oxford accusing Holles was written by the Duchess of Buckingham. He remained in the Tower until May 1646. In the following year another Peer was in trouble and a certificate was presented to the House of Lords from Dr Alston stating that on account of indisposition Lord Capel ought not to reside in London.

A physician's fees in the seventeenth century were considerable and one as eminent as the President of the College of Physicians must have received a large income from his practice. Sir Theodore Mayerne, who was the King's doctor, died worth £140,000, which represents a figure at today's value of something well over two

---

*Daughter of Sir Nathaniel Hobart, Master in Chancery.

†Denzil Holles (1599-1680) and Bulstrode Whitelocke (1605-1675), Parliamentary Statesmen.

million pounds. Dr Radcliffe's* regular fees were estimated to bring him in an income of at least four thousand a year, and Dr Mead's was valued at between five and six thousand. It is no wonder that Sir Edward was stated to have died very rich.

At the beginning of the century the College of Physicians started a procedure for testing the capacity of candidates for a licence to practise. Those who wished to practise in the country were supposed to be more leniently treated than those who proposed to remain in London. However, after the end of the Commonwealth, efforts were made to raise the standard all round, and some confirmation of this is provided by a certificate signed by Sir Edward Alston as President with other Fellows of the College, stating that they had examined Richard Clampe who had practised medicine in Lynn Regis and had approved of him.

The social side of the College came to life again in the early days after Charles II's return. John Evelyn writes that on 6th October 1664, "I heard the anniversary oration in praise of Dr Harvey† in the Anatomy Theatre in the College of Physicians, after which I was invited by Dr Alston, the President, to a magnificent feast."

Sir Edward Alston lived in Great St Helen's, Bishopsgate, and when he died he left a wish to be buried in the Parish Church. His life ended on Christmas Eve 1669 and he was interred on the last day of December in the Chancel near his daughter Mary who had predeceased him.

His last Will, made during the latter days of November, only ten days before he died, was proved in the Prerogative Court of Canterbury on 24th January 1670. He gave to his wife Susan "the use of all my jewels, plate, goods, chattels and household stuff and an annuity of £200 to be paid by my executors out of the interest of my money." To his granddaughter, Mary Langham, he gave £20 in old gold. Among other bequests there were £100 to Sir Harbottle Grimston, Bart, Master of the Rolls, and £50 to George Lowe of Lincoln's Inn, who were his executors. The rest of the estate was to be disposed as his daughter Sarah "shall desire". There were a number of special legacies which he entrusted Sarah to give to certain persons, including "To a spectacle woman by

---

*Dr. John Radcliffe (1650-1714), Royal Physician who endowed Oxford with its Hospital and Library.

†Dr. William Harvey (1578-1657), discoverer of the circulation of the blood.

Crosby House gate forty shillings. To Sarah my maid twenty shillings and £5 more if she stays with my wife. To Mathew Offly such clothes of mine as are fit for his wear and my velvet coat if he intends to practise Physic, also some of my Physic printed books." He left legacies also to servants of Lady John Seymour and Sir John Langham. "To Mr Norbett, a Brickler (sic) who bricked up my vault and thus preserved my goods in the time of the Great Fire, forty shillings."

Lady Alston did not long survive her husband, for she was buried in the same church and the same grave on 3rd August 1670*.

Reading through the Wills of the Alstons gives the impression of a closely knit family. There is evidence also of affinity with both the Grimstons and the Langhams, into which families Sir Edward's daughters married. As Sir Edward practised in the City and Sir John Langham was a City merchant and Alderman, while Sir Harbottle Grimston was Master of the Rolls, it is more than probable that they knew each other very well. It is noteworthy that Sir Edward remembered Langham's servants in his Will; he must have seen a lot of them. This congenial atmosphere is unlikely to have extended to the Seymours or the Hares, the in-laws of Sarah's second and third ventures into matrimony. In her Uncle Penning's Will an acid note is found when he directs that if his own daughter dies without issue, "I give to my niece, the Lady Sarah Seymour, £2,000 for her own separate use, her husband Lord John Seymour not to intermeddle." This was dated 1667 when Sarah had been married to him barely six years.

Penning Alston was the youngest brother but he predeceased Edward, and he too must have been a wealthy man. He had married Judith Chandler sometime before 1648 and their only child was christened Sarah like her cousin. Apart from the conditional bequest noted above, he gave also "to my niece, the Lady Sarah Seymour £100 for her own use" and probably because he was fond of her and wanted to do the right thing, he left £10 not only to her for mourning, but also a like amount to her husband. To Sir Edward and his lady £10 each, also for mourning. Mourning rings were provided in plenty — "For two hundred rings or

---

*I have learned from Major T. R. Mordaunt-Hare, M.C., that portraits of Sir Edward Alston, M.D., and Lady Alston were lost in an air raid on London when Maples, where they were stored, was hit.

so many of them as shall be used all of them at the price of eight shillings except three at twenty shillings, upon which my coat of arms is to be enamelled, the said three rings be for my brothers, Sir Edward Alston and Joseph Alston and my sister Mrs Elizabeth Gilbert." For preaching his funeral sermon Dr Wells was to receive £3. He wished to be buried in the Parish Church of St Buttolph without Aldersgate "as near my Pew Door as may be." It went on, "I desire that there may be a Velvet Pall and escutcheons of my arms." From the proceeds of a Manor in Buckinghamshire his daughter was to receive £80 per annum for her own separate use — "Edward Skynner of London, merchant, who makes some pretence of contract of marriage with my said daughter shall not inter-meddle with said annuity." His bequest to his daughter was to be void if she is or shall be married to the said Edward Skynner, or if she allow him to receive any benefit from the said annuity or if she marry without the consent of her mother and Sir Edward Alston. If Edward Skynner should die and his daughter remain unmarried or marry without consent, then she was to receive £4,000 as her portion. More was to be added to this on the death of his wife. There were further bequests including £500 to Christ's Hospital and £200 to St Bartholomew's Hospital. Finally he proposed that any residue there might be after paying the legacies outlined should be paid to such poor widows and fatherless children as his trustees should think fit, his own poor kindred to be first preferred. His daughter did not marry Skynner but was wedded to one named Harrington who was mentioned in her mother's Will but without reference to any children. A final moving and intimate touch to the Will was this sentence: "I desire Mr Cole, my brother Chandler, my brother Johnson, Mr Farre, Mr John Mynne, and Mr John Townsend to be pall bearers and to have love scarves and gloves." In this context the word brother means brother-in-law.

This recital of Wills ends with that of another brother, Sir Joseph Alston, Bart. He gave to "Harrington and his wife, sonne of my brother Penning Alston ten pounds apeece to buy them mourning." Here again the word son means son-in-law. Sir Joseph also wrote, "I doe desire Doctor Littleton to preach my funerall sermon upon the same text which he preached upon my former wife's funerall, the thirteenth chapter of the Acts of the Apostles and the nine and thirtieth verse. And I doe give him five pounds for mourning and five pounds for his sermon. And I doe order and appoint that not above three hundred pounds shall be expended in my funerall for rings, mourning and all other charges over and above what I have herein before given and hereinafter doe give."

The customs associated with a death in the family have undergone profound changes since the seventeenth century. Now there is the minimum of mourning and those rings which were distributed to mourners as a remembrance have become just interesting antiques.

City Merchant

SIR Edward Alston's elder daughter, Mary, married into a family with recorded beginnings in the reign of Edward I when one William, son of Henry de Langham, held three carucates of land in Langham, Rutland.

This marriage took place during the difficult time of the Civil War. The licence reads "1647. Dec. 8. James Langham gent, of St. Helen's Bishopsgate, bachelor, 26, and Mary Alston of St. Mary Hill, London, spinster, 20, daughter of Edward Alston of same, Doctor of Physic, who consents."

The bridegroom's father was Alderman John Langham. He was a considerable figure in the City of London, having amassed a fortune by his business ability. He was the son of a linen draper and was born in Northampton, although his father subsequently moved to Guilsborough. His mother became a widow when there were still several small children, and John left home resolved not to return until he had become wealthy. It is said he was left £100 by his father, and with this he apprenticed himself to Sir Robert Napier, a Turkey merchant. He represented Sir Robert abroad as his factor, and on the first occasion made a return which highly pleased his master. He continued in this capacity to his own as well as his employer's benefit, and although in his trading he met with some setbacks he determined to continue until he had gained a great estate. He married the daughter of James Bunce, M.P. for the City of London, and sister of Sir James Bunce. His father-in-law advised him to trade in future with only half his fortune and to leave the other half as a provision against possible catastrophes. His financial wizardry is illustrated by a deal he made with another merchant when between them they bought the entire produce of currants to be imported into the country. They sailed with a fleet of merchantmen but on the voyage home a great storm sank most of Langham's vessels. Ships were scattered but he got home first and did not know how his fellow merchant's ships had fared. When he heard that those which had escaped had reached the Thames he went down to meet them and offered his

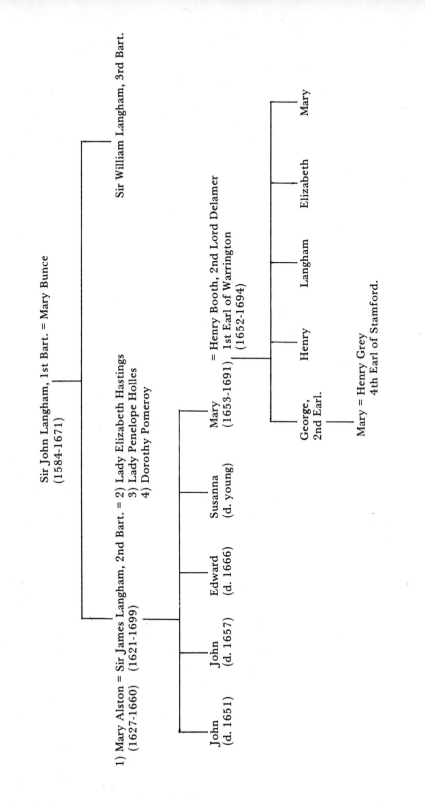

Sir John Langham, 1st Bart. = Mary Bunce
(1584-1671)

Sir William Langham, 3rd Bart.

1) Mary Alston = Sir James Langham, 2nd Bart. = 2) Lady Elizabeth Hastings
(1627-1660)   (1621-1699)   3) Lady Penelope Holles
                                                4) Dorothy Pomeroy

John   Edward   Susanna   Mary   = Henry Booth, 2nd Lord Delamer
(d. 1651)   (d. 1666)   (d. young)   (1653-1691)   1st Earl of Warrington
John   (1652-1694)
(d. 1657)

George,   Henry   Langham   Elizabeth   Mary
2nd Earl.

Mary = Henry Grey
       4th Earl of Stamford.

partner in this deal £30,000 for the whole of his stock. This money he borrowed on short loan and then told his father-in-law what he had done to retrieve his losses, for when it was known that all the currants were held in one hand and that no more would be coming that year he was quickly able to sell them, pay off his loan, and make a handsome profit.

At the beginning of the conflict between King and Parliament many in the City were opposed to the absolute power of the Monarch. As time went on it became apparent that Parliament itself was assuming dictatorial authority, and so the feelings of those sound, reasonable people were roused to resist the substitution of one tyranny by another. John Langham was one of these.

The simmering of discontent was brought to light by a committee appointed to examine witnesses concerning speeches against the Lord General (Cromwell). Silvanus Taylor, Serjeant Major of Sir James Harrington's regiment, denied that at a meeting of the Committee of the Common Council on 18 April 1644 he or any other person present said that by increasing the number of troops in ·the Lord General's army they were putting a sword in their hands with which to cut the citizens' throats, or that Parliament would have reformed the army but for Essex. He merely said he was against the manner of raising 20,000 men. John Langham was one of the witnesses and he stated that he had heard no words of disparagement spoken of the Lord General's army. No doubt they were all cautions.

As the Civil War progressed the City became slowly but steadily more at variance with Parliament. The writer of a letter to Sir Richard Leveson in September 1647 gives a picture of the tremendous rift between them: "The Parliament are upon a new model of propositions; some few of the old ones will be taken and some of the army's proposals; if they continue masters of the army I look for little good by them; if not I look their propositions should break their own necks, for there has been snapping lately in the House between some of the root and branch men and the officers of the army who are members. They have accused the Lord Mayor and four Aldermen with two or three Common Councillors of High Treason. The Aldermen are Bunce, Langham, Cullen and Adams. Some Aldermen have shaken off their furs and say they will serve in that condition no more. I hear the City will lend no money which will cause the army to take violent cause for raising it upon them."

With others John Langham was committed to the Tower. After six months he and his fellow aldermen with the Lord Mayor, Sir John Gayer and Sheriff Thomas Cullum (presumably Cullen above) were charged with having "maliciously and traitorously plotted and endeavoured with open force to compel the Lords and Commons to alter the laws and ordinances of Parliament established for the safety and weal of the realm." This was because they had refused to raise a loan of £50,000 for the army. The prisoners appeared before the Lords and when ordered to kneel at the Bar as delinquents, Langham in company with his companions refused to do this, so they were all tried and sent back to the Tower where they remained until 1648 when the Commons, wishing to improve relations with the City, released them. Public opinion may also have helped to prompt this action, as the following Broadside which was circulated on the impeachment of Sir John Maynard, late M.P. and Aldermen Bunce and Langham, indicates the strength of feeling prevalent at the time.

"The Humble Petition of many well-affected citizens and other free born people of England." It was dated 14 February 1648.

"That on the occasion of the late war was the danger of being enslaved by arbitrary and tyrannical power, and as upon invitation of the House the people have hazarded their lives, consumed their estates, lost their trades, and weltered in blood to defend their laws and liberties against those who in their apprehensions, intend to subvert them, and to introduce an arbitrary government; so the enemy being vanquished they expected according to your promises a perfect enjoyment of all their rights and liberties and the benefit of all their just and wholesome laws which this Honourable House and the Army have frequently and solemnly engaged to reserve to the people. That, nevertheless, the Lords are permitted to assume unto themselves and exercise a power over commoners in cases criminal to summon, impeach, try, adjudge, and censure them as appears in the present case . . . . Wherefore petitioners do most humbly pray that our ancient freedom of the indifferent equitable trials by our equals in all cases whatsoever, may be preserved entire to us and all the commoners of England. And we further desire that Sir John Maynard, Aldermen Bunce and Langham, or any commoners may not be deprived of his or their liberties during pleasure, which is contrary to Magna Carta and many other wholesome laws of the land, but that justice may be dispensed legally and a speedy establishment of all our common rights and liberties be vigorously endeavoured."

There was subjoined, "All well affected persons who are desirous of securing England's peace and their own rights and freedoms are desired peaceably to repair to Westminster on Friday morning next 18 February 1648 to assist in delivering this Petition and to attend the answer of Parliament thereupon, Sir John Maynard being appointed to be carried up to the Lords' Bar upon 19 February. The rule of law is *'Actus non facit reum nisi mens sit rea'* ".

Langham with the others stood firm in his opposition, and in April 1649 he was deprived of his Aldermanry with others for refusing to publish an "Act for the ex heredation of the Royal Line, the abolishment of the monarchy in the Kingdom and the setting up of a Commonwealth." Again he was incarcerated in the Tower.

Some years before all these happenings Langham had acquired Crosby Hall on a 99-year lease. When the Civil War began the mansion underwent a great change for it was commandeered and became a sort of prison for royalists, termed 'malignants', who refused to contribute to the service of Parliament. About thirty-seven eminent royalists were held there while their estates were sequestered.

The records of the Parish of St Helen's, Bishopsgate, show that in 1649 while he himself was suffering, Langham gave thought for those in need, for he arranged for £5 to be expended on bread for distribution to the poor. They were remembered in his Will for he wrote, "I give and bequeath for the use of the poore ffamilyes or widdowes of the same parish, of the best name and ffame, by 20/- a piece every St Thomas's Day for the next five years after my decease."

When Langham was released again is not clear, but in 1654 he was concerned with the problem of import levies, a subject again before Parliament as recently as 1968. Trading then, as now, must have been difficult for merchants. An Act of Navigation stated that "all persons exporting foreign goods and receiving back half the custom should pay the full custom on re-importing them and that the precedent of their re-admission on half custom would be very prejudicial to the revenue." On this matter Langham petitioned the Protector: "On complaint of pressure on my person and estate you ordered the Council of State to hear my counsel about the import from Holland of some silks and cotton yarn, exported hence in the time of my restraint. On encouragement I told my factors beyond seas to send the goods hoping for my order before their arrival; but the time of Council is so taken up that I cannot obtain an audience. Pray grant me license if they arrive, to receive them, on payment of customs, and on bond to stand to the order of the Council without danger of confiscation. With order thereon that the Council will speedily determine the case, but if the goods arrive before may the petitioner receive them on bond on the terms named." The Council answered bluntly No.

From all this it is understandable that John Langham increasingly supported the exiled Charles Stuart, and in spite of the risk he conveyed £500 yearly to him. Time and discontent dragged on until by 1659 there was much unrest. After Cromwell's death those who wanted the return of the King felt the time was ripe, and John, Viscount Mordaunt, was one of those foremost in Charles's service. He had risked his life in keeping in touch with him on many occasions and was concerned with the abortive rising in July and August of that year when, as the leader in Surrey, he and his party found the rendezvous occupied by Parliamentary troops. He was nearly captured but was hidden in the house of Alderman Robinson and eventually escaped to France in September. With consummate courage he returned to England early in 1660 and from London wrote to his wife, "The little interest I left and found here has raised £5,000 without bond termes or conditions, to be imployed in making a purchase may put me in a condition to buye the land I have sold, if it succeed his Majestie will be obliged to Aldermen Robinson and Langham for the money. My expense was only a few courteous words which I shall never reccon to the King in discharge of what I was borne to owe him . . . My escapes are so eminent that I question not God will blesse undertakings and you would wonder to have seen the satisfaction people had when they knew I was come. By Robinson means and Langhams the Citty purce is open to me, if the attempt take, and they promise me a constant supply for the army. If we get Master the King will be restored without termes."

In March 1659 Charles Stuart had appointed Commissioners to inform those in the City who would support them that the King was resolved to uphold the privileges of the City and wished to owe his restoration to it. The Commissioners also had to try to win over to the King's service some officers and men in the army with a promise of pardon, but excluding regicides, a project which Lord Mordaunt considered obtainable because "the officers here (London) have been so often changed that tis but naturall to believe the souldiers are not so affectionate to those that lead them now that they will refuse money from any hand whatsoever." This was where "the citty purce" was to be so valuable.

The Rump Parliament was turned out and a new free one called. Alderman Langham took his seat and when it was determined to bring home the King the expense was estimated at £60,000. During the debate on how this was to be raised, Langham stood up and said that as parliamentary ways take up more time than this occasion would allow, he himself would lend £30,000 if anyone else would lend a similar amount. Forthwith Lord Craven remarked that he would not be outdone by a citizen and was ready to put up a like sum.

It is easy to understand from all this how John Langham came to be chosen as one of the principal citizens nominated by the City of London to wait upon his Majesty in Holland. Wearing his fur gown he met the King at The Hague. His Majesty asked who that venerable gentleman was and upon hearing his name said, "I am more obliged to that man's purse than to any private man in England." He then knighted him and his son James, who was with him.

After the landing at Dover it must have been a rousing journey back to London with the King. This is how it was described by a letter-writer at the time — "Great concourse of people in all the towns through which the King passed from Dover. At Blackheath not less than 120,000 people — all the horses came along with the King to the City — the King's Life Guard and Col. Monck's Life Guard always next to the King's person; and a little before the King came to the City the Lord Mayor and General Monck rode bare-headed before the King all along the City."

Soon after the King's return to England John Langham was created a baronet, the honour he chose after being offered the highest titles of honour. Even so he paid for his baronetcy, a discharge note dated 8 June 1660 acknowledges £1,095 due from Sir John Langham on his creation as a baronet.

He was still, however, always willing to help with his money; for example he lent £10,000 to Sir George Carteret, Treasurer of the Navy, to pay off certain ships and mariners and received as security twelve boxes of silver coins on 24th December 1662.

He was most hospitable and any provisions left over from his table were daily distributed to the poor, as well as bread to several prisons. He was generous to the Clergy. When they were restored to their beneficies after the return of the King, those who had unjustly enjoyed them were reduced to poverty, but Sir John said they must not starve though they were mistaken deluded people, and he gave them a weekly allowance of bread and meat from his slaughter house.

At the time of the Great Fire in 1666 he offered £500 to anyone who would extinguish it before it reached his house. This stimulus brought success and earned rewards. After the Fire, when the poor sufferers were in the fields, some sick and all in need, Sir John put into the hands of proper persons £500 for their subsistence, the second week giving £400, the third £300 and then £200 and £100 until the fields were cleared.

He gave £1,000 towards building a church in Cornhill, £1,000 for building the Grocers Company's Hall, of which he was a Freeman. Another £1,000 he gave towards building the Royal Exchange, as well as many other benefactions. He would sometimes give to a diligent young man sufficient to set him up in his trade and would pay debts for honest poor men to keep them out of gaol.

To every one of his daughters he gave a £10,000 fortune and spent £1,000 in equipping the bride and on the wedding entertainment. When he visited any of them he used to stay about a month carrying with him £100 "to make," he said, "the pot boil".

Another example of his kindness concerned his son, William, who married a daughter of Sir Anthony Hazelwood (Haslewood) of Maidwell. Her dowry was £3,000 but she died six weeks later. Sir John then heard that the money had been borrowed and so he visited Sir Anthony and gave it back to him, an exceedingly generous gesture.

When his servants grew old he would say to them, "Business is now tiresome for you. I will allow you £5 (or £6 or £10) a year for life, it is time you should live free from care and leave serving an earthly master."

His resolution not to see his mother until he was in a flourishing position he kept, although with his first profits he assisted her and his brothers and sisters. When he did visit his mother it was in an equipage suitable to his circumstances.

He endowed the Free School at Guilsborough with £80 a year and he erected a Hospital at Cottesbrook and provided £50 per annum for it. He left £36 a year to maintain six poor widows at St Thomas's Hospital, Northampton. He also gave £25 to Christ's Hospital for placing out yearly six poor children of that House.

In Evelyn's *Diary* there are two letters that serve as examples of the gracious courtesies of the time, at least in letter writing – Sir John Langham to John Evelyn.

"Crosby House
this 30th July 1667.

Worthy Sir,

I presume upon your goodness, though a stranger, so far to trouble you as to make a double enquiry concerning Mr Phillips who lately was entertained in your family. The one how he approved himself to you in learning and behaviour, whom I had long known to be the greatest judge of both; the other where he is now disposed of, and whether in the liberty of receiving an ingenuous employment, if your character of him and my discourse with him shall encourage me to give him a call thereto. One requisite that I am commissioned to be assured of, is his ability of speaking ready and refined Latin; for as to his manners and regular conversation, there lies not a suspicion for anything in them unworthy of the sanctimony of your house, which hath long been venerated as the holiest temple of all virtue and ingenuity. I am sensible how far already I have trespassed upon your consecrated leisures, therefore, lest I should continue the fault I add not more than, I am, Sir,

Your very humble servant,
J. Langham."

John Evelyn to Sir John Langham.

"Sir,

It is from the abundance of your civility that you load me with eulogies, and because you are not acquainted with my imperfections, which are so much the greater by having not had the honour to be known of so deserving a person as yourself. I can say nothing to the disadvantage of Mr Phillips which might not recommend him to your good intentions except it be that I did not observe in him any greater promptness of readily speaking Latin (which I find is one of the principal faculties you are in search of), but it was not for that, or indeed any other defect which made us part, but the passion he had to travel and see the world, which he was made believe he should have had a sudden opportunity of effecting with a son of my lord of Pembroke, who has now three years been under his tuition without satisfying his curiosity as to that particular. Mr Phillips is, I think, yet at Wilton, where my Lord makes use of him to interpret some of the Teutonic philosophy to whose mystic theology his lordship, you know, is much addicted. As to Mr Phillips' more express character, he is sober, silent and most harmless person; a little versatile in his studies, understanding many languages, especially the modern, not inferior to any I know, and that I take to be his talent. Thus, Sir, what I have said concerning Mr Phillips, in the matter you require, I hope I shall not abate your value for him, or the honour and promise in receiving your future commands, who remain, Sir,

Your very humble servant,

J. Evelyn."

Sir John died at Crosby House in Bishopsgate on 13th May 1671 at the age of eighty-seven, and he was buried at Cottesbrooke in the county of his birth. He was succeeded in the baronetcy by his son James, already a knight, who had been M.P. for Northampton and the county previously. His marriage to Mary Alston was productive of five children but only one survived beyond childhood. Of three sons and two daughters, just one daughter, christened Mary after her mother, reached womanhood. When her mother died she was only seven years old. Lady Langham's death must have been a grievous blow coming so soon after the happiness of the Restoration and the knighting of her husband and of her father.

The register of her burial at St Helen's Church reads "1660 Sep. 12 Dame Mary, wife of Sir James Langham, Knight, in the Chancell of the Church." At the end of 1800 the Chancel was restored and the grave of Lady Langham was opened. It was found that she had been buried in a leaden shroud which was somewhat destroyed, but the body was in good preservation. The Plate on the leaden shroud read —

Here Lyeth
the Body of Dame
Mary Langham wife
of Sir James Langham
of Cottesbrooke in ye
County of Northamp
ton Knt daughter and
co heir of Sir Edward Alston
of London Knt by Dame
Susan his wife. She
departed this life
the 3rd September
ANNO DOMINI 1660
aged 32 years.

The funeral sermon was delivered by Dr Reynolds, rector of Braunston, Northants, and afterwards Bishop of Norwich. In her youth "she had a propensity to Atheism but as she advanced in years and understanding she became a christian upon sound principles and rational conviction. . . no woman of her age was more religious or less superstitious. She was equally a stranger to the moroseness and flights of bigotry and displayed a constant cheerfulness which rendered her a most agreeable and amiable woman in proportion as she was a better Christian."

In those days mortality was high and infant mortality very high. The same pattern was to be found in many families. It is not uncommon to find identical christian names for more than one child in a family because of such early deaths in an attempt to perpetuate a particular name. Of the three sons born to this union two were called John. The eldest was buried on 3rd January 1651 at Cottesbrooke. His coffin is still in the family vault at the furthest end on the left hand side. It is of lead shaped to the body and the top forms an effigy of the child; under it are two similar ones, probably his brothers, the second John and Edward. Leaden shrouds such as these were fairly common at that time. The lead is somewhat decayed and there are a few holes in it, but the inscription can easily be read:

"John eldest son of James son & heir of
John Langham, Alderman of London
Born April 25 1650 Died Dec. 28 1651."

Sir James married as his second wife Lady Elizabeth Hastings. In less than two years she also died, but during that brief spell of married life she was so kind to her two stepchildren (Edward Langham did not die until 1666 when he was ten or eleven) "that it was wholly impossible for any but those which knew otherwise not to have mistaken her for their natural mother."

As the sole surviving child and heiress to her father's estate it was likely that Mary Langham was much sought after in marriage. When she was sixteen a marriage contract was very nearly concluded for her to marry the Earl of Huntingdon, who was brother to her stepmother. She was devoutly religious and she used to repeat by heart sermons she heard to Lady Elizabeth, who instructed her so well in memorising the spoken word that she was able to analyse a sermon containing thirty or forty particular heads with most remarkable enlargement upon them.

In April 1667 Sir James Langham married for the third time. Mary's second stepmother was Lady Penelope Holles who was also deeply religious. When she died Sir James married, fourthly, Dorothy Pomeroy, but all these marriages were childless.

At the time of the proposed betrothal to Lord Huntingdon, Sir James was prepared to give £20,000 as her dowry with even further expectation. The plan, however, came to nought, but in 1670 when she was still only seventeen Mary Langham was married to Henry Booth, eldest surviving son of Lord Delamer. Like his father he was destined to have an exciting life at the very hub of the nation's affairs. She, after bearing him several children, died before her fortieth year and in the lifetime of her father, who lived on until 1699. Her aunt Sarah, Duchess of Somerset, also outlived her by eighteen months.

Sir James Langham was a Fellow of the Royal Society which was founded in 1660. The fee for admission was ten shillings and a further subscription of one shilling per week. The members were bound to constant attendance at meetings, which were held in Gresham College. He was well known as a classicist and Bishop Burnet described him as "famed only for his readiness of speaking Latin which he had attained to a degree beyond any man of his age: but he was become a pedant with it and his style too poetical and full of epithets and figures." Luttrell in his diary under date 24th August 1699 records that "Sir James Langham, eminently known for his being well versed in the Latin tongue died lately at his house in Lincoln's Inn Fields and was much lamented."

He was succeeded by his brother William, to whom reference has already been made. He graduated at Cambridge and then studied medicine at Leyden and gained a degree at Padua.

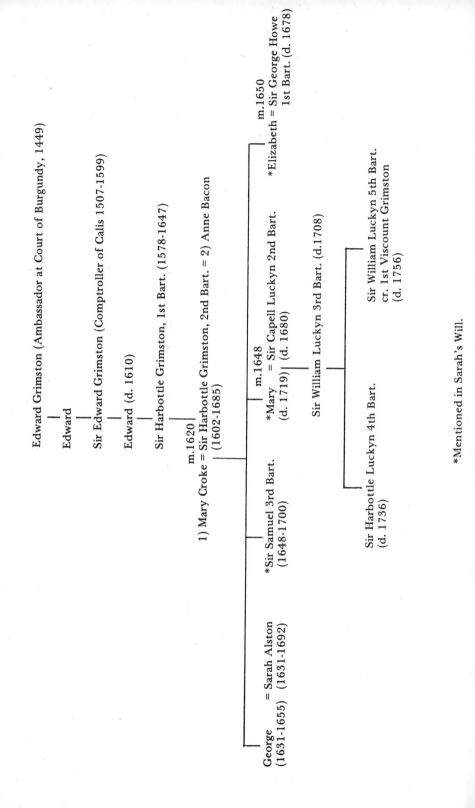

Edward Grimston (Ambassador at Court of Burgundy, 1449)

Edward

Sir Edward Grimston (Comptroller of Calis 1507-1599)

Edward (d. 1610)

Sir Harbottle Grimston, 1st Bart. (1578-1647)

m.1620

1) Mary Croke = Sir Harbottle Grimston, 2nd Bart. = 2) Anne Bacon
(1602-1685)

George = Sarah Alston   *Sir Samuel 3rd Bart.
(1631-1655) (1631-1692)   (1648-1700)

m.1648   m.1650
*Mary = Sir Capell Luckyn 2nd Bart.   *Elizabeth = Sir George Howe
(d. 1719) (d. 1680)   1st Bart. (d. 1678)

Sir William Luckyn 3rd Bart. (d.1708)

Sir Harbottle Luckyn 4th Bart.
(d. 1736)

Sir William Luckyn 5th Bart.
cr. 1st Viscount Grimston
(d. 1756)

*Mentioned in Sarah's Will.

i)   Sarah, Duchess of Somerset.

By kind permission of the Master and Fellows of St John's College, Cambridge.

(ii)   John, fourth Duke of Somerset.

By kind permission of the Master and Fellows of St John's College, Cambridge

ii)   William, second Duke of Somerset. After R. Walker.
        By courtesy of the Courtauld Institute of Art, from the Collection of the Marquess of Bath.

(iv)   Henry Seymour, Lord Beauchamp, by Lely.
       By courtesy of the Courtauld Institute of Art, from the Collection of the Marquess of Bath

(v) William, third Duke of Somerset, by Lely.

By courtesy of the Courtauld Institute of Art, from the Collection of the Marquess of Bath.

(vi) Lady Mary Langham. *Engraving from Harding's Biographical Mirror, 1796.*

(vii)   Sir James Langham, second Baronet, by Carlo Dolei.
        By courtesy of the Courtauld Institute of Art, from the Collection of Sir John Langham.

(viii)   Sir John Langham, first Baronet, by Soest.
By courtesy of the Courtauld Institute of Art, from the Collection of Sir John Langham.

3   An Essex Family

SIR Edward Alston's second daughter, Sarah, married firstly
George Grimston, eldest sòn of Sir Harbottle Grimston, the
second baronet. George did not live long enough to implant his
image on posterity like his forebears. The brief details of his life
are that he was admitted to Brasenose College, Oxford, on 1st
May 1649 at the age of eighteen. No doubt it is in memory of him
that towards the close of her life Sarah founded scholarships there.
From Brasenose College he proceeded to Lincoln's Inn where his
father had been before him.

The marriage was arranged by a tripartite Indenture, made on
1st November 1652, between Sir Harbottle Grimston, Dame Ann,
his wife of the first part, Edward Alston of the City of London,
doctor in physic, of the second part, and George Grimston
Esquire "sonne and heire apparent" of Sir Harbottle Grimston
and Sarah Alston, younger daughter of Edward Alston of the
third part. The deed "witnesseth whereas a marriage by God's
permission is intended to be had and solemnised between George
Grimston and Sarah Alston before the fifth and twentieth day of
December commonly called the feast of the Nativity of the Lord
Christ next ensuing." This document settled land in Essex upon
George Grimston and Doctor Alston contributed six thousand
pounds of lawful English money for their "joynture."

During their short married life two sons were born but both
died in infancy, and when her husband died in 1655 Sarah was
left a childless widow at the age of twenty-four. She must have
got on well with her father-in-law for she entrusted him with her
affairs and after his death her husband's younger brother
Samuel became an executor and was concerned with the
administration of her estate.

The Grimstons had been in the public eye for generations. The
earliest notable member of the family was Edward Grimston who
was Ambassador to the Court of Burgundy in 1449 and whose
portrait by Peter Christus is the oldest surviving documented

painting of an Englishman. His great grandson, Sir Edward Grimston, Knt. was Comptroller of Calais in 1558 when it was captured by the Duke of Guise. He was closely held in the Bastille and a high ransom was placed upon him. Meanwhile in England he was indicted, in his absence, for high treason, accused by some of making a private agreement with the French King to surrender Calais, although he had reported earlier the poor fortifications of the place. After nineteen months confinement he made his escape from the Bastille in dramatic fashion. With a file he cut the bars of his window; he then changed clothes with his servant who, with a pair of scissors, cut off his beard. By tearing his sheets into strips and knotting them together he let himself down. Said to have passed as a Scot, he eventually reached England in mid November, only to find himself in disgrace. He was arrested and put into the Tower, which must have been a devastating experience, after all the vicissitudes of his escape. However, he did not have long to wait for justice because he was arraigned at Guildhall on the first of December and there acquitted by the Jury, and at once discharged. He was a strong anti-papist and this antipathy to Roman Catholicism and High Church practices was transmitted down to his great grandson, the father of George, who was a staunch Presbyterian. He has already been referred to as the second baronet. It was the first Sir Harbottle on whom a baronetcy had been conferred in 1611. He lived at Bradfield in Essex and was M.P. for Harwich. He became much concerned with the state of the fortifications of that port in 1643. Fearful that an attempt would be made by foreign forces to seize the place, he tried to persuade Parliament to supply guns, muskets and men to guard it and later in the same year he warned Parliament that alarm was felt at the presence of Danish ships and other rovers and pirates and thought a bare fifty men could take the town. He asked for money to make bullets and swords at Ipswich, and demanded that Captain Richard Hawkins'* Commission be sent "for no one will obey him, being without authority and the town not watched and the works not guarded." He got in touch with his son, who was now M.P. for Colchester, saying that ten great guns were needed to furnish new works. He was more fortunate than his ancestor at Calais and did manage to get things stirring for at a later date Captain Richard Hawkins and others wrote to Mr Speaker Lenthal thanking him for

---

*Appointed Commander of the Garrison.

sending Sir Harbottle Grimston among them, for his care of the town of Harwich had been abundantly manifested and no part of England had been more vulnerable to invasion. They now had twelve great guns mounted with sixty "musquetts" and sufficient powder.

This Harbottle Grimston had been elected to Parliament for the County of Essex in 1626, but in the following year, on refusing to contribute to a forced loan, he was committed to prison. However, by 1628 he was back in the House again. Parliament was in their blood for his father, Edward Grimston, was M.P. for Eye, so three successive generations served in the House of Commons. It was this Edward Grimston who married a granddaughter of John Harbottle and inherited the Bradfield estate. He died a year before his son's advancement to a baronetcy and the following verse was composed in his memory.

> "The sonne paied to his father's part increase
> Wittie and wise he was, us'd lawe for peace.
> What first he chus'd for good he changed never
> His care was temperate, his zeale fervent ever
> And theise fayer gifts yt heare his power did give
> Did make the father in the sonne to lyve
> What truth hath writt that envie cannot blot
> The name of Grimston cannot be forgot."

The second Sir Harbottle was the second son of his father and was born in 1602 at Bradfield Hall near Manningtree. It was quite in keeping with the inherited religious principles of the family that when the time came he went up to Emmanuel College, Cambridge, which was intended by its Puritan founder for the education of youth "in all piety and good learning but especially in sacred and theological learning" and the oath taken by the Fellows described "the true religion of Christ" as "contrary to Popery and all other heresies". From there he entered Lincoln's Inn and was called to the Bar, but on the death of his elder brother abandoned the idea of practising. He then fell in love with the daughter of Sir George Croke, Knight, one of the Justices of the Court of Common Pleas. Sir George refused to give his consent to the union unless he returned to the law; this he did and they were married on 16th April 1629 at St Dunstans in the West. Eleven years later he was elected to Parliament and understandably with his Presbyterian outlook, he stood against the Court. He was soon in the fray and spoke with considerable invective on a motion concerning the conduct of Archbishop Laud. He gave his reasons for proceeding beyond a mere sequestration. "Mr Speaker," he said "long introductions are not suitable to weighty affairs. We are now fallen on that great man, the Archbishop of Canterbury; look upon him as he is in his highness, and he is the stye of all pestilential filth that hath infected the state and Government of this Commonwealth. Look upon him in his dependencies and he is the man, the only man, that hath raised and advanced all those that together with himself, have been the authors and the causes of all our ruins, miseries, and calamities we are now grown under. . . . who is it, Mr Speaker, but he only that hath advanced all our Popish Bishops? . . . . and there is scarce any grievance or complaint come before us in this place where we do not find him mentioned and as it were twined with it; like a busy angry wasp his sting is in the tail of everything." By the Commons Laud was condemned; he was sequestrated and committed to custody but his end on the scaffold did not come for just over four more years.

In another debate on the Bishops in the following year there was an entertaining battle of words between Harbottle Grimston and John Seldon:

HG.   That bishops are JURE DIVINO is a question; that archbishops are not JURE DIVINO is out of question. Now if bishops which are questioned whether JURE DIVINO, or archbishops who are out of question are not JURE DIVINO, should suspend ministers that are JURE DIVINO I leave to you, Mr Speaker.

JS.   That the convocation is JURE DIVINO is a question; that Parliaments are not JURE DIVINO is out of question; that religion is JURE DIVINO is no question. Now, Mr Speaker, that the convocation which is questionable whether JURE DIVINO and Parliaments which are out of question are not JURE DIVINO, should meddle with religion which questionless is JURE DIVINO, I leave to you Mr Speaker.

HG.   But archbishops are not bishops.

JS.   That is no otherwise true than that judges are no lawyers and aldermen no citizens.

Grimston was quoted as saying "that the Judges have overthrown the law and the Bishops the Gospel."

Religious feelings were running high in 1642 and at Colchester an ugly riot occurred. The garrison commander wrote an account of it to Harbottle Grimston who was now Recorder of Colchester as well as its M.P. Word had got about the town that a store of arms had been taken to the house of Sir John Lucas, a Royalist supporter, and it was thought that he also intended sending horses to the King, so a watch was put on the house. Later, rumour that there were a hundred men in arms at the place sent the town into an uproar so that with drums beating, the trained band and volunteers turned out to surround the house. The mob following, with women and children, was about five thousand strong and as the situation was out of hand the Garrison Commander summoned the Aldermen and the Justices to his aid who made proclamation charging the people to go home, the mob ignored this and they eventually broke into Sir John's house in the early morning. They took away eight or nine horses and found much armour and many pistols and carbines ready charged. The whole house was then rifled and Sir John and his mother and servants were put into the Moot Hall. By now the angry crowd was so roused that they set upon and nearly killed the aged vicar of Holy Trinity Church, and then poured out of the town towards the country house of the Roman Catholic Countess of Rivers, who fled for her life to London.*

It speaks a great deal for the integrity of Sir Harbottle Grimston that Lady Rivers made him one of her executors when she made her Will in 1644. It is also of interest that she wished to be interred near her daughter, Susan Darcy, in the Church of Holy Trinity, Colchester, desiring that her body should be borne to the grave by four poor persons of the parish. Contrary to the custom of the time she directed that no sermon should be preached at her funeral and that there should be no eating or drinking, usual on such occasions, and that no mourning should be given for her. Instead she bequeathed £20 to the poor of the parish. She also directed that her executors were to give the sums of money which she had tied up in little bags to the several persons whose names were labelled on them.

Later in the Civil War Colchester, which had been taken by the Royalists, was besieged and when, after a dour and lengthy struggle

---

*She was aided in her escape by Sir Robert Crane, who although a 'Parliament man', risked arranging a safe journey for her.

of endurance, the garrison surrendered, ammunition had been reduced to a barrel and a half of powder and provision to two horses and a dog.

Although at the beginning of the conflict Sir Harbottle's sympathies lay with Parliament, yet as Cromwell took increasing control his leaning veered away from a new form of exercise of arbitrary power.

In 1647 after Cornet Joyce had taken care of the King for the Army, Sir Harbottle rose in the House of Commons and accused Cromwell of plotting to destroy Parliament. Two witnesses related how he would use the Army to purge the House, whereupon Cromwell fell on his knees and vowed before Heaven that no man was more faithful to the House than he. His vehemence prevailed and Grimston was silenced, but the fear then expressed became a reality just over a year later.

The Presbyterian majority in Parliament wished to negotiate with the King. In September 1648 fifteen Commissioners were chosen by both Houses of Parliament to meet the King on the Isle of Wight with reference to the Treaty of Newport, Grimston and Holles* were among them and these two being fully alive to the danger of military intervention, knelt before Charles and entreated him to yield at once all that was possible without wasting more time in useless discussions. It was a tragedy that Charles disdained this appeal. In the event the army did seize the King and brought him back to the mainland.

The House of Commons met at the beginning of December to protest against the King's removal without their consent or knowledge. The following day a majority thought there was good ground for further negotiation with Charles. That was too much for Cromwell. Early in the morning of the next day Colonel Pride with a body of musketeers arrived at Westminster. He dismissed the usual guard and then, as members arrived, Lord Grey of Groby, who was standing beside him, whispered the names of the Presbyterians as they approached. Sir Harbottle was one of the forty-one who were hurriedly taken to a neighbouring tavern where they passed the night in two upper chambers, resting as best they could on benches and chairs. By what law, they asked, were they detained? The answer returned

---

*Denzil Holles was head of the Presbyterians.

was "It is the Law of Necessity, truly, by the power of the sword!" Four others were later added to their number and a further ninety-six were excluded from the House. The purge predicted by Sir Harbottle Grimston had indeed now taken place. Eventually the prisoners were set free on giving their parole that they would not attempt to return to the House. Sir Harbottle thereupon retired into private life.

At the time of the King's trial, however, his influence with the people and some of the army was considered to be so great that he was again put into confinement. He was only released on the very day of the execution by the order of Lord Fairfax, having given an undertaking not to do anything to the disservice of Parliament or the Army. Following this he prudently went abroad and resigned his Recordship of Colchester.

When he felt the time ripe he returned and was elected to the newly modelled Parliament of 1656 as one of the members for Essex, but he was not allowed to take his seat. He protested that the assembly was not representative of the country, but no heed was paid to him so he quietly returned to his legal work until better times.

On the abdication of Richard Cromwell after his father's death, he was a member of the Committee appointed to summon a new Parliament, and after the re-admission of the secluded members he was elected to the Council of State. When after a general election in March 1,660 a new Convention Parliament assembled a month later, Sir Harbottle Grimston was chosen as Speaker. This is recorded in the Journal of the House of Commons under date Wednesday, 25 April 1660.

> "The Parliament being summoned to meet at Westminster this present day; the members of the House of Commons repaired about ten of the clock in the forenoon to Margaret's, Westminster to hear a sermon which was preached by Dr. Reignolds: And that being ended they repaired to the Parliament House, went in and sat in their places. Edward Birkenhead Esquire, formerly Serjeant at Arms, attending at his Place within the Door of the House.

> "Whereupon William Pierrepont Esquire rose up and put the House in Mind that their first work was to choose their speaker; and that there was a worthy Person of the Long Robe in his Eye, whom he conceived well experienced and

every way qualified for the Trust; and by the leave of the House proposed Sir Harbottle Grimston Baronet who was fully approved of by a General Call of him to the Chair.

"He standing up in his place, offered his Excuse in Respect of the weakness and indisposition of his Body and Mind; and that there being many others amongst them of the Long Robe more fit and worthy than himself he desired the House to pitch upon one of them to serve them as Speaker.

"But being generally called on by the House; he was by the Lord General Monck, Mr. Holles, and Mr. Pierrepont conducted to and placed in the Chair, the usual place for the Speaker: where being set, the Mace was called for and brought in by the Serjeant and placed on the table."

Later in the Proceedings messengers from the Lords said that they had been "commanded by the Lords to desire the House will concur with them to keep a Fast on Monday next to seek the Lord for a Blessing". This was agreed and that day was appointed a Day of Fasting and Humiliation and all were to attend at St Margaret's, Westminster.

As Speaker he received Sir John Grenville on the 3rd May. Sir John brought a letter from the King and in the House of Commons he read his reply —

"I need not tell you with what grateful and thankful hearts the Commons now assembled in Parliament have his Majesty's gracious letter, *Res ipsa loquitur,* you yourself have been *auricularis et ocularis testis de rei veritate.* Our bells and our bonfires have already begun the proclamation of His Majesty's goodness and of our joys. We have told the people that our King, the glory of England, is coming home again, and they have resounded it back again in our ears, that they are ready and their hearts are open to receive him: both Parliament and people have cried aloud in their prayers to the King of Kings. Long live King Charles II."

On 8th May Charles was proclaimed King, both at Westminster and in the City of London, and in the procession of coaches from the one place to the other Sir Harbottle rode with General Monck.

Charles II landed at Dover on 25th May. In the Banqueting Hall, Whitehall, four days later, it fell to Sir Harbottle Grimston to make a fulsome speech of welcome to His Majesty. Charles repaid the compliment by visiting him and taking supper with him in his house in Lincoln's Inn Fields a month later. The following November he was made Master of the Rolls and Records in Chancery.

In the midst of all this activity it is pleasing to find him giving support to a poor relation, one Alice Smith, a widow, who had been unable to obtain payment from the Admiralty Commissioners of money due to her. He wrote entreating them to help as she was "loaded with actions" (presumably for debts) and otherwise would be ruined.

His feeling for legal tradition and proper procedure is illustrated in the case of a petition by Robert Prescod who held the office of prothonotary* of the Court of Chancery. Prescod appealed to some of the Judges and Heralds to be allowed to sit in Court covered and next to the Clerk of the Crown. This was a matter of status and the Master of the Rolls gave it as his view that there was a right to this privilege as that office was one of dignity and held directly from the Crown by eminent persons. Its rights had fallen into abeyance because the duties had too often been carried out by deputies.

One of the lesser perquisites of the office of Master of the Rolls at that time was an annual allowance of one tun of Gascony wine. The Treasury paid £6.13.4. for this to Sir William Waller, who was a Custom farmer of the Prizage and Butlerage. Wine similarly anciently allowed was to go to the Provost and Fellows of Eton as granted by Edward VI — three tuns of red Gascony wine at £5 a tun payable to the Chief Butler of England.

Bishop Gilbert Burnet in his *History* of his own times gives the following picture of Sir Harbottle: "I lived many years under the protection of Sir Harbottle Grimston, Master of the Rolls, who continued steady in his favour to me tho' the King sent secretary Williamson to desire him to dismiss me. He said he was an old man, fitting himself for another world and he found my ministry useful to him; so he prayed that he might be excused in that. He was a long and very kind patron to me. I continued ten years in that post, (settled preacher at the Rolls and sometimes lecturer at St Clemens), free from all necessities, and I thank God that was all I desired. But since I was so long happy, in so quiet a retreat, it

---

*The name given to the Registrar in the Courts of Chancery, of Common Pleas, and of the King's Bench.

seems but a just piece of gratitude that I should give some account of that venerable old man. He was descended from a long lived family for his great grandfather lived till he was ninety eight and himself to eighty two. He had to the last a great soundness of health, of memory, and judgment. He was bred to the study of the law being a younger brother. Upon his elder brother's death he threw it up, but falling in love with Judge Crook's daughter, the father would not bestow her on him unless he would return to his studies, which he did with great success. That Judge was one of those who delivered his judgment in the Chequer Chamber against ship money which he did with a long and learned argument. And Sir Harbottle's father, who served in Parliament for Essex lay long in prison because he would not pay the loan money. Thus both his family and his wife's were zealous for the interest of their country. In the beginning of the London Parliament he was a great asserter of the laws and inveighed severely against all that had been concerned in the former illegal oppression. His principle was that allegiance and protection were mutual obligations and that the one went for the other. He thought the law was the measure of both; and when a legal protection was denied to one that paid a legal allegiance the subject had a right to defend himself. He was much troubled when preachers asserted a divine right of regal government. He thought it had no other effect but to give an ill impression of them as aspiring men; nobody was convinced by it; it inclined their hearers rather to suspect all they said besides. It looked like sacrificing their country to their own preferment; and an encouragement to Princes to turn tyrants. Yet when the Long Parliament engaged in league with Scotland he would not swear the Covenant. And he discontinued sitting in the House till it was set aside. Then he came back and joined with Holles and other Presbyterians in a high opposition to the Independents and to Cromwell in particular. And he was one of the secluded members that were forced out of the House. He followed afterwards the practice of the law, but was always looked upon as one who wished well to the ancient government of England. So he was chosen Speaker of the House of Commons that called home the King; and had so great a merit in that whole affair that he was soon after, without any application of his own, made Master of the Rolls, in which post he continued till his death with a high reputation as he well deserved. For he was a just Judge; very slow and ready to hear everything that was offered without passion or partiality. I thought his only fault was that he was too rich. And yet he gave yearly great sums in charity discharging many prisoners by paying their debts. He was a very pious and devout man and spent every day at least an hour in the morning and as much at night in prayer and meditation. And even in winter when he was obliged to be very early on the bench he took care to rise so soon, that he had always command of that time which he gave to those exercises. He was much sharpened against Popery; but had always a tenderness to the Dissenters tho' he himself continued still in the Communion of the Church. His second wife whom I knew, was a niece of the great Francis Bacon and the last heir of that family. She had all the high notions of the Church and the Crown in which she had been bred but was the humblest, the devoutest and best tempered person I ever knew of that sort. It was really a pleasure to hear her talk of religion. She did it with so much elevation and force. She was always very plain in her clothes and went off to jayls to consider the wants of the prisoners and relieve or discharge them, and by the meanness of her dress she passed but for a servant trusted with the charities of others. When she was travelling the country, as she drew near a village, she often ordered her coach to stay behind until she had walked about it, giving orders for the instruction of the children and leaving liberally for that end. With two such persons I spent several of my years very happily."

Sir Henry Chauncy, another contemporary, says of the Master of the Rolls that "he was of free access, sociable in company, sincere to his friend, hospitable in his house, charitable to the poor, and an excellent master to his servants."

By his first wife he had six sons, one only of whom survived him, and there were two daughters, the elder of them married Sir Capel Luckyn. Sarah, Duchess of Somerset, remembered in her Will both Lady Luckyn and her son.

He married secondly Ann, daughter of Sir Nathaniel Bacon and relict of Sir Thomas Meautys, by whom he had one daughter.

He died on the 2nd January 1685 about four in the morning of apoplexy after a sickness of five days.

Some idea of the scale of funerals of persons of eminence and substance at that time is indicated by the list of charges submitted by Sir Harbottle's Steward.*

---

*See Appendix II.

He remembered his servants in his Will and his steward left "A Note of those of the Masters Legacys as are paid" and these ranged from "Mrs Berkley £200 to Ann in ye Kitchen £5. Also Wm. in ye Kitchen £5. The poor of St Michael's £20 and myself (Mr Bressey) £50." The total came to £800.

In Latin, Sir Harbottle wrote a small book, later translated into English, entitled "A Christian New Year's Gift or Exhortations to the Practice of Virtue". It was originally written as a guide for his eldest son, George, for the conduct of life, and as it was not published until years after he and other sons had died, it is addressed to his only surviving son, Samuel Grimston.

"Dear Son,

This book being dedicated formerly to your brother (who was snatched hence by an overhasty death) appeared first in publick without my knowledge or approbation. And now I have exposed it to open view myself though I could not finish it (as I intended) being diverted by publick employment; nevertheless I have added one Chapter more viz concerning travelling, because I designed you should see some forrain nations which though you have not yet accomplished (by reason of some occurrences that happened) yet I made that small addition that if ever your inclinations should bend that way, you might have some directions, not altogether incommodious. And I shall think it a sufficient recompence for my labour if you diligently observe these precepts which are chiefly intended for your welfare; and if any others are benefited or grow better thereby, I shall account that as clear gain. And seeing we live in an age that cries up virtue and still acts it down that exclaims against all vice and yet will admit of no remedy; I will not, nay, I cannot be silent, and suffer my own bowels to perish. Son, it is in your power, to beautify and adorn this token of your father's love; by living up to the rules thereof; and if you would recommend it to others, be sure to study and practise it first yourself; that so, when God shall have multiplyed, and blessed you with a numerous offspring, they may read and imitate, not so much this book, as yourself; and both you and they become venerable to posterity; which is earnestly desired and hoped for,

By your most loving father,

Harbottle Grimston.

Evidence of Sir Harbottle's great interest in Lincoln's Inn is brought to light by a minute of the Council held on 26th January

1674 when it was "ordered that Sir James Butler (and others) be desired to wayte on the Master of the Rolls to give him thankes for the favour of the statue he hath declared he will give the Society and to invite him to dinner on the Grand Day".

He was succeeded by his only living son who became Sir Samuel Grimston Baronet and who acted as one of the executors of the Duchess of Somerset from whom he also received a legacy. Sir Samuel married firstly Elizabeth, eldest daughter of the Earl of Nottingham, and secondly Anne, sixth daughter of the Earl of Thanet. He was M.P. for St Albans on two occasions. During the reign of James II he remained in private life being, it was said, much disliked by the King who expressly excepted him from pardon in the manifesto he issued when he contemplated landing in England in 1692.

A reference to one of his daughters' wedding is contained in a letter from Lady Gardiner, "I have had a world of company with mee daly, bot not my lady Ann Grimston for Miss Grimston was not marayed on Monday morning but at night being a mode amonxt the great ons and yesterday they all dined at my Lord Notinghams". This daughter had married the second Marquis of Halifax.

Sir Samuel died in 1700 aged fifty-seven years and the baronetcy became extinct, but the large estates devolved upon his nephew, the son of his sister.

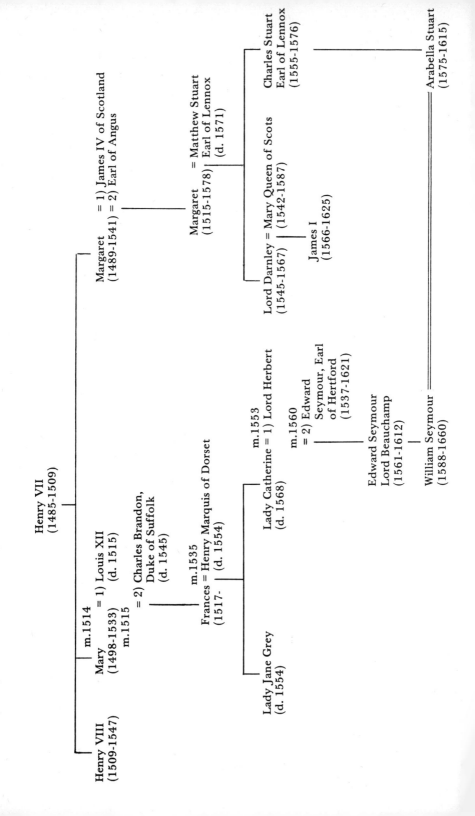

Henry VII
(1485-1509)

Henry VIII
(1509-1547)

Mary   = 1) Louis XII
(1498-1533)   (d. 1515)
            m.1514
            m.1515
            = 2) Charles Brandon,
                 Duke of Suffolk
                 (d. 1545)

m.1535
Frances = Henry Marquis of Dorset
(1517-   (d. 1554)

Lady Jane Grey
(d. 1554)

Lady Catherine = 1) Lord Herbert
(d. 1568)
            m.1553
            m.1560
            = 2) Edward
                 Seymour, Earl
                 of Hertford
                 (1537-1621)

Edward Seymour
Lord Beauchamp
(1561-1612)

William Seymour
(1588-1660)

Margaret   = 1) James IV of Scotland
(1489-1541) = 2) Earl of Angus

Margaret   = Matthew Stuart
(1515-1578)   Earl of Lennox
               (d. 1571)

Lord Darnley = Mary Queen of Scots
(1545-1567)   (1542-1587)

James I
(1566-1625)

Charles Stuart
Earl of Lennox
(1555-1576)

Arabella Stuart
(1575-1615)

4   A Royal Servant

Two Clandestine Marriages

SARAH had been a widow for six years when she married again. The information culled from the Verney papers shows that her father was concerned to find a husband for her and he may have had a good deal to do with her entry into the Seymour family. Her new spouse was the youngest son of the second Duke of Somerset, that distinguished man whom Charles II honoured immediately on his return by investing him at Canterbury, when on his way to London, with the Garter. He was then the Marquis of Hertford, but in a little over three months he was restored to his great grandfather's Dukedom as if the attainder in King Edward VI's reign had never been made. On passing the Act on 13th September 1660 the King addressed the House in person and added fresh honour to the dignity by the terms in which he spoke of the services he wished to acknowledge. "I cannot", he said, "but take notice of one Particular Bill I have passed, which may seem of an extraordinary nature, that concerning the Duke of Somerset; but you all know it is for an extraordinary person, who hath merited as much of the King, my father, and myself as a subject can do; and I am none of those who think that subjects, by performing their duties in an extraordinary manner, do not oblige their princes to reward them in an extraordinary manner. There can be no danger from such a precedent; and I hope no man will envy him because I have done what a good master should do to such a servant."

This nobleman had a remarkable career. He was a younger son of the grandson of Protector Somerset, the first Duke, and was born in 1588, the year of the Armada. His father, Lord Beauchamp, died in 1612 and his elder brother in 1620 without issue. From then onwards he was heir to his grandfather's title of Earl of Hertford.

William Seymour, by which name he was known in his youth, had an aptitude for study and entered Magdalen College, Oxford, at the age of seventeen. Unlike many young men from aristocratic families who just whiled away some time at the University, he worked and obtained a degree. A little before this there was a rumour that Lady Arabella Stuart was going to marry into the Seymour family, and it is possible that while he was at Oxford he met and came to know her, for she was then at Woodstock and was also of a studious nature.

It is accepted that the pair plighted their troth on 2nd February 1610. The knowledge of this leaked out and soon William was summoned before the Privy Council, for Lady Arabella was first cousin to James I and in line of succession to the throne. In his statement William said he had first imparted his desire to marry her on Candlemas Day, but they had decided to wait for His Majesty's most gracious favour. The King refused consent.

Lady Arabella was an orphan, her father Charles Stuart, Earl of Lennox having died of consumption in the year after her birth, and her mother when she was seven. She had been brought up by her grandmother, the remarkable Bess of Hardwick, and by her mother's sister, the Countess of Shrewsbury.

There was much disparity in their ages as William Seymour was twelve years her junior. She had some two years earlier been granted her own house in Blackfriars where, in Henry VIII's reign, there had been a Dominican Monastery. Soon after she moved in she became very ill with smallpox. She survived, but generally those who were fortunate to do so were left with some disfigurement.

Despite the gap in years there must have been some infatuation, and four months later, tired presumably of waiting for a royal change of heart, they made a clandestine marriage. William with his friend Edward Rodney* went down by river to Greenwich Palace where Arabella had been given apartments. They arrived at midnight and by previous arrangement were let in. A priest had been engaged and the ceremony took place in the early hours of the morning. The witnesses were Lady Arabella's gentleman-in-waiting, her usher, and her two waiting women. Three weeks later it was no longer a secret and retribution followed very quickly. William was sent to the Tower and Arabella put under restraint

---

*He was already related, for one of Rodney's ancestors had married a daughter of Sir Henry Seymour, brother of the first Duke of Somerset.

in the care of Sir Thomas Parry, Chancellor of the Duchy of Lancaster. Sometime later because it had been disclosed that they had managed to communicate with each other it was decided that she should be sent to Durham, to be placed in the care of the Bishop there. This so distressed her that she became ill and for many weeks did not leave her bedroom and so the move never happened. When she began to recover thoughts of escape took shape, aided by her aunt, the Countess of Shrewsbury. Her Chaplain's wife helped her to disguise herself in a man's habit with a long wig which partly hid her face. She proceeded on foot to an inn where her faithful servant had horses ready. At Blackwall they were met at a rendezvous by her former gentleman-in-waiting and her waiting woman and from there they went on to Woolwich and took boat for Tilbury; from there to Leigh, a little fishing port, which they reached by daylight the next day. Eventually they found the French ship that had been chartered to take them across the Channel.

While this was taking place William, who was in the Tower, induced his barber to help him. He provided a common man's clothes and William, wearing them, and putting on a black wig and beard, walked out of the gate by following a cart. Thus he reached a river landing place where Edward Rodney was waiting with a boat. Timing had gone slightly awry, however, and they arrived at Leigh far behind Arabella's party. The skipper of the French boat had not waited because a storm was brewing and had set sail, much to Arabella's distress.

Unable to find the Frenchman, Seymour, with Rodney and two servants managed to persuade, by means of £40, the master of a collier to take them over. The storm was severe and he had to land them at Ostend. From there they travelled to Bruges and on to Brussels, where they stayed at an unfrequented inn.

It was not long before the escape was discovered, and it came about thus — Rodney shared lodgings in London with William's younger brother Francis. When he left to accompany William he felt obliged to leave some note for Francis. This he did and when Francis received it the next morning he became so alarmed that he set off at once for the Tower. There he found only the barber in his brother's quarters. So perturbed was he that he decided he should let his grandfather know, and this he did by letter:

My most honourable and dear Lord and Grandfather,

Lately (I may say unfortunately) is my brother escaped out of the Tower. He went disguised in mean apparel as I hear since about four o'clock in the afternoon upon Monday being the 3rd of June. His lady also went the same night at six o'clock, disguised in man's apparel. Whither they are gone it is not certain. My cousin Edward Rodney is gone with them. Who besides is gone I know not but there are missed Edward Reeves one of my brother's men, and a gentlewoman of hers and Mr. Crompton. Edward Rodney left a letter behind him to be delivered to me which letter I received upon Tuesday following at eight o'clock. He desired me to excuse him in he did not acquaint me with his unfortunate business (as I may well term it) besides that they had resolved to tell it none by which means they might the better keep it from your Lordship knowing your Lordship would presently have acquainted the King therewith.

Your Lordship's most obedient child,

F. Seymour.

To the Rt. Hon. my very singular Good Lord and Grandfather The Earl of Hertford.

Lord Hertford received this letter at night when it was brought to his bedroom while he was undressing. He became greatly agitated and after much mental turmoil he wrote to the Earl of Salisbury.

My lord, this last night at eleven o'clock, ready to go to bed, I received this letter (enclosed) from Francis Seymour which I send to your lordship. A letter no less troublesome to me than strange to think I should in these my last days be grandfather of a child that, instead of patiently tarrying the Lord's leisure (lessons I learnt and prayed for when I was in the same place, the Tower) he would not tarry for the good hour of favour to come from a gracious and merciful King, as I *did* and enjoyed in the end (though long first) from a most worthy and noble Queen, but hath plunged himself further into his Highnesses just displeasure to whose Majesty I do these lines "earnestly pray your Lordship to signify most humbly from me how distasteful this his boyish and foolish action is to me. And that as at first upon his exam^n. before your Lordships and before his Majesty afterwards, nothing was more offensive to me misliking altogether the unfitness and unsuitability of the match and the handling of it afterwards worse so do I condemn this as the worst of all in them both. Thus, my lord, with an unquiet mind as before — to think I should be grandfather to any child that hath so much forgotten his duty as he hath now done and having slept never a wink this night (a bad medicine for one that is not fully recovered of a second great cold I took) I leave your lordship with my loving commendations to the heavenly protection.

From Letley this Thursday morning at four of the clock the 6th of June 1611.

> Your lordship's most assured loving friend,
>
> Hertford.

P.S. As I was reading the letter (Francis Seymour's) my sise* took — as your lordship may perceive — with the bottom of the letter.

No wonder his hand shook and the letter nearly caught fire. It must have brought back his own past vividly to him. In so doing instead of producing a feeling of compassion, as might be expected, for the intrepid courage of youth, it raised in him such ire that he at once denounced his grandson's action in the strongest terms. Although his own behaviour had been so similar many years before, yet it angered him to see a grandson treading the same path even more dangerously.

To recount the story of his own youth entails going back in time to the first Duke. His sister, Jane Seymour, had married Henry VIII as his third wife. She died soon after giving birth to a son destined to be Edward VI. At this young Prince's christening his Uncle Seymour had the privilege of carrying Princess Elizabeth, and he was created Earl of Hertford. The ducal honour did not come until the first month of his nephew's reign when he had been chosen Protector. In 1551 he was accused of high treason and although he could not be proved guilty, he suffered at the block on Tower Hill, an innocent man. Shortly after his death he was attainted by Act of Parliament. When Elizabeth I came to the throne in order to show her feelings and her gratitude for kindnesses she had received at his hand, and perhaps in some way to right the wrong that had been done, she decided to restore his eldest son Edward to the titles of Baron Beauchamp and Earl of

---

*Described as a six sized wax light. Original French syse meaning a wax candell (1530).

Hertford. To support the title he was granted £20 a year out of the customs of Southampton.

All then seemed set fair for the Seymours but within two years Lord Hertford brought upon himself the royal wrath. He fell in love and married secretly the Lady Catherine Grey, younger sister of Lady Jane Grey. She had been betrothed when only thirteen to the son of the Earl of Pembroke. After the execution of her elder sister and of her father, the Duke of Suffolk, Lord Pembroke was worried about the future of himself and his son so he procured an annulment of the marriage which had never been consummated.

During the latter years of Mary's reign Lady Catherine had been in the care of the Duchess of Somerset and no doubt when she was living with the family her attachment to Lord Hertford began. After Elizabeth came to the throne Lady Catherine Grey and Lord Hertford's sister, Lady Jane Seymour became Maids of Honour.

Fearful of approaching Elizabeth for her consent, the young lovers decided to get married without it. Early one morning towards the end of 1560 when the Queen was to leave her palace at Whitehall for Eltham, Lady Catherine was reported to have toothache and asked to be excused from taking the journey, Hertford's sister requesting permission to stay behind with her. As soon as the Queen had left, the two girls made their own exit unobserved. They made their way to the house where Hertford was living in Westminster, and he himself let them in. As the priest assigned had not arrived Lady Jane Seymour went off to find another, and when she returned the ceremony took place in the bedroom. When it was over, the priest having left and their health having been drunk, Jane, observing that they wished to go to bed, went downstairs. Later in the day the two young ladies returned to Whitehall, and sat down to dinner with the Lord Comptroller as though nothing had happened.

During the subsequent weeks Hertford visited his wife on pretence of going to see his sister who arranged for them to be alone together when "he used her as his wife". Sometimes Lady Jane went with her to her brother's house in Cannon Row and while Jane waited in another room they "had company".

In March of the following year this blissful arrangement came to a sudden and tragic end by the death of Lady Jane Seymour who was only nineteen. She died on 23rd March and was buried three days later in Westminster Abbey.

After this Catherine could only put trust in her waiting maid, which proved too big a strain for she left never to be heard of again. Sometime in April Hertford was asked to accompany Sir William Cecil's son on a visit to France. Catherine then broke it to him that she thought she might be having a baby. "If you are with child, I will not leave you," he said, but as she was not sure he told her that if she would let him know he would return at once. In July she wrote, "I am quick with child, I pray you therefore to return and declare how the matter standeth between us." Soon her pregnancy was discovered and the Queen sent her to the Tower. Hertford returned and was arrested at Dover, put into the Castle there for the night and then taken to London the next day, and likewise incarcerated in the Tower. On the 21st September it is recorded that Lady Catherine was brought to bed of a son.

They were in a hopeless position now. Not only had they incurred the Queen's great displeasure, but they had no one to substantiate their plea that they were in fact husband and wife. The only witness had been Lady Jane Seymour, who was now dead, and the priest whom they did not know either by name or place of residence. They could only describe him "a well complexioned man with an abram* beard of a mean stature in a long gown faced with budge† the collar turned down." Mrs Leigh, Catherine's waiting maid, had vanished into thin air and although search was made for her she was never traced. They were separately both subjected to considerable interrogation and as one was lodged in the Bell Tower and the other in the White Tower there was no collusion. In spite of many examinations their answers were always the same but still their union was not conceded.

Their descriptions of the ceremony were closely similar. Hertford said he did not provide the priest but his sister fetched him. He said the minister used such words and ceremonies as set forth in the Book of Common Prayer. The priest had stood by the window of the bedchamber and he and Lady Catherine faced him, that he was a man of average height, fair complexion with an "abram" beard and of middle age and wore a plain long gown

---

*Abram denoted a brownish colour.

†Budge was lambskin dressed with wool outside, a fur used for academic gowns.

of black cloth faced with budge and a "falling collar". He said he gave nothing to the minister but Lady Jane told him afterwards she had given him "Tenn pounds for his labour". When she was questioned Lady Catherine replied that the minister who was fetched by Lady Jane wore no surplice, that he was a well complexioned man with an "abram bearde" with a long gown faced with budge the collar thereof turned down; that he "chargdged them both that, if they knew any impediment of ether of there partes, they shold staye from proceedinge any further:" that their backs were towards the bed and their faces towards the Minister, and his back toward the window; that the "words of matrymonie they both spake th'one to the'other, as the saied Priest did declare to them by the Booke of Service wherein he redd."

The Earl said that immediately after the Solemnization they went into bed in the same room, he somewhat before her he thought; that nobody helped "either to unarrange them to bedd or to make them readie after there arrysinge" and that Lady Catherine "was in attyringe and arrayinge herself abowt half a quarter of an hower and noe more." She confessed that after the ceremony "shee had companie and intercourse with the Earle divers tymes in the house at Channon Rowe" and after the Solemnization of matrimony "she was by the Earle gotten with childe". She further answered that "shee dressed herself without the helpe of any others". In another interrogation of the Earl he said that intercourse first took place after the marriage ceremony at his house in "Channon Rowe" and he likewise confessed that he "begatt the said Lady Katherine with child but not unlawfullie."

Both continued to be kept in the Tower but as time passed surveillance of their movements became less strict. In some way they managed once more to enjoy each other's company. Catherine became pregnant again and another son was born to them while they were both prisoners. A London diarist of the time notes the event thus: "The x day of February 1563 was browth abed within Towre with a sunne my lade Katheryn Harfford wiff to the yerle of Harfford and the godfathers wher ii warders of the Towre and ys named was called Thomas."

This time Queen Elizabeth was really furious. Hertford was brought before the Star Chamber and fined £15,000, which was made up of £5,000 for having seduced a virgin of the blood royal in the Queen's House, £5,000 for breaking prison and £5,000 for having again visited her. Strict security was imposed upon them both and Catherine was doomed to nearly another five years close guarding before she pined away, dying at Cockfield Hall, Yoxford, Suffolk, where she had finally been put under the charge of Sir Owen Hopton.

The Duchess of Somerset tried hard to obtain their release by appealing to the Queen. She also wrote to Sir William Cecil whose son Hertford had looked after abroad, and pleaded for his helping hand "to end this tedious suit," adding, "how unmeet it is this young couple should thus wax old in prison, and how far better it were for them to be abroad and learn to serve." It was of no avail.

At her death Lady Catherine's body was embalmed so that she might lie in state as became the grand-daughter of a Queen, and for three weeks she remained in the church at Yoxford. Sixty years later she was re-interred alongside her husband in Salisbury Cathedral.

After her death the Earl of Hertford remained under restraint but was allowed to live in various country houses instead of the Tower. Eventually he was given his freedom and he married Frances, daughter of Lord Howard of Effingham as his second wife. Years later, in 1595, thinking the time was due, he petitioned the Queen to have his first marriage recognised. This upset her so much that he was again committed to the Tower, and she ordered that his son who had been known by the courtesy title of Lord Beauchamp should henceforth be called Mr Seymour. One reason for this was that John Hales wrote a little book in favour of the House of Suffolk in which he proclaimed the entitlement of Lady Catherine's son to the Crown if Queen Elizabeth died without issue. When this became known at Court Hales was imprisoned in the Tower.

Lapse of time once more assuaged the royal anger and Hertford was allowed his liberty again. His second wife died and further trouble was in store. It seems incredible that he would once more risk royal displeasure, but in fact he married a third time without letting Sir Robert Cecil know for the Queen's information. He may have had some reason for doing so. His third wife was the widow of Henry Pranell and the daughter of Viscount Howard of Bindon, and was said to have been courted by Sir George Rodney. Here may lie the explanation for the absence of banns, omission of licence, and marriage in Hertford's own house. He was in great disgrace again and so was the priest who had married him. This Divine was Thomas Montford S.T.P. who for so irregular an act of conducting a clandestine marriage without asking of banns, without licence or dispensation, without the parish church but in the private house of the Earl and according to the form of public prayers, was suspended from his function for three years. Hertford yet again went to the Tower. In the next year after humble supplication, the Queen intimated that it was her pleasure that the Earl should be removed from the Tower to the custody of the Archbishop of Canterbury (Whitgift). He was to be "at his own charge and in his private chamber."

All this past history must have profoundly affected him when William's trouble burst upon him. He himself had suffered over nine years imprisonment and although at last he was now on good terms with Salisbury, yet he could not but wonder how this debacle would react upon his family.

To go back now to the discovery of the escape of the two unfortunate prisoners, William Seymour and Arabella Stuart; a Proclamation was issued warning all persons against giving any assistance to them. Everyone in any way connected with them was interrogated and Sir James Croft, who at that time had overall responsibility for Arabella, was committed to the Fleet prison, the minister's wife, Mrs Adams, was put in the Gatehouse and the barber, Batten, thrust into a dungeon. Shortly afterwards, the Countess of Shrewsbury was arrested and sent to the Tower. The Earl of Northampton told the King that Lady Shrewsbury was the contriver of this "bedlam opposition" to the King which had been exhibited by the Lady Arabella. It was said that the latter had been given £850 by Lady Shrewsbury for some things she had that had belonged to Mary, Queen of Scots, and this had helped to finance the operation.

The route of the escape was traced and Sir William Monson in the *Adventure* was sent in hot pursuit, it being considered they were making for Calais. The French ship in which Arabella was travelling, was indeed offshore near Calais but she wished to wait for William and so the boat hove to, which enabled the *Adventure* to catch up with them. Monson ordered the French ship to stand to, but the Master attempted to escape. Thirteen shots were then fired, the command was obeyed, and Arabella was captured. She said she was more concerned for William than herself, and when Monson called off further search for him she rejoiced.

The ill-fated Arabella was taken to the Tower and with her aunt, the Countess of Shrewsbury, there she stayed. Later Lady Shrewsbury was brought before the Star Chamber, but she was intransigent and so was sent back to the Tower. Another year went by and a plot to escape by means of duplicate keys was afoot. Lady Arabella had been given a "kye quherof she did take a print in waxx and caused one uther bye it." This was discovered and was admitted but "in the discoverye of the uther matters that has bein in hand her Ladyshipe keipes a lytill too closs, yet I think it wil be in the end gottin out."

This took all the remaining spirit out of Arabella. She became increasingly depressed and took to her bed. She refused all medicines and became extremely melancholic. Death came on 25th September 1615 when she was just forty years old.

The death in the Tower of any important person, and particularly a political prisoner, for that is what she really was, always raised the question of an unnatural cause. It is not surprising therefore to find Sir Ralph Winwood, the Secretary of State at the time, writing to the President of the College of Physicians on 27th September:

> "Whereas the Lady Arabella is lately deceased in the Tower and it is His Majesty's pleasure, according to former custom upon like occasions when prisoners of great qualitie die in that place, her bodye should be viewed by persons of skill and trust, and thereupon certificate to be made of what disease she dyed as to their judgment shall appear. These are therefore to will and require you to appoint some three physicians of your Societie of good reputation as well as for their learning as otherwise, who together with the physicians of the said Arabella shall presently repayre unto the Tower, and there view and search the corps of the said Ladie and to return joyntly their opinion unto me of the nature of the disease whereof she died, that we may acquaint His Majesty therewithal."

The next day the physicians reported that they went at eight in the morning. The cause of death was a chronic and long sickness, the species of disease was *"illam jaundin producem cachexiam"* which increased as well by her negligence as by refusal of remedies (for a year she would not allow doctors to feel her pulse or inspect her urine). By long lying in bed she got bedsores and a confirmed unhealthiness of liver and extreme leanness and so died. The report was signed by Tho. Moundeford (President of the College), Guil Paddy, Ed. Lister, Ric Palmer, Jo Argent, Matt Gwynn.*

She was buried in Westminster Abbey beside Prince Henry (James's eldest son) in the vault of Mary, Queen of Scots. It is said the ceremony was performed privately at night.

Her aunt continued in the Tower but on Christmas Day she was allowed to leave to nurse her dying husband. After his death she had to go back and in 1618 she was sentenced by the Star Chamber to life imprisonment and a fine of £20,000. She remained in the Tower until 1623 when she was released.

A Wanderer in Europe

Just when William Seymour heard that Arabella had been captured is not clear. It cannot have taken long because a correspondent from Paris writing to William Trumbull, the English Ambassador in Brussels, under date 15th June 1611 says "the lady has been taken back to London and we have no news of Seymour but suppose him harboured in some of your towns under the charitable shadow of the Spanish wing which is like to prove an 'irritamentum' between England and those provinces." By then Trumbull had learned of his whereabouts and hearing that he was about to leave for Liege went to see him himself. He was concerned lest "some Jesuit or other ill-affected Englishman should seize upon Seymour and by his enchantments lead him blindfold to his perdition." This expressed the anxiety that William and Arabella would be persuaded to join the Roman Catholic Church and so be supported by the Catholic following of whom one of the leading figures was the Countess of Shrewsbury. Seymour assured Trumbull that "he did not desire to live any longer than he should continue a faithful subject." He was desperate to know what had become of his lady and Trumbull must have told him.

William now became a political refugee, a wanderer and an outcast. He was living in the domain of the Archduke Albert and some pressure was exerted to persuade him to arrest William and

---

*Lady Arabella's body was embalmed by Duncan Primrose, one of the King's surgeons, for which he was paid £6. 13. 4.

deliver him over to James. Seymour, however, was well treated by the Archduke who refused to take any action. Nevertheless his position was uncomfortable and uncertain and the very means for living had to be found. Sir Dudley Carleton, the Ambassador at Venice, wrote to Trumbull at the end of June "I think young Seymer will quickly wish himself back in the Tower where he was well provided for and I know no danger to be feared by him unless our Jesuits make him a stale for their practices." From Brussels he went to Liege and on to Spa. At this time Trumbull received a letter from London, "Our tongues and ears have been so long busy about the Lady Arabella and your wandering esquire that now we care no more about the subject. His wandering into Germany is here little regarded for the greatest harm he can do is to slip in again from whence he went. The Lady Shrewsbury (who has amassed a great sum of money we know not to what ill use)* is in the Tower perhaps for as long a time as her niece."

Whitehall continued to press for news, and a month later Trumbull received a letter that "Lord Salisbury would have you taken occasion yourself to know the Archduke's resolution which his Majesty doth now expect because Mr Seimer doth remain within his dominions."

The Embassies were all interested to know what was taking place. From Venice Sir Dudley Carleton in August was asking for a word "where Seymour is and what are his purposes" though he is "little to be esteemed as the poorest fugitive yet, knowing the arts and practices of Rome." He continued to be much worried by the Jesuits and then recounts instances of violence, much of it due to religious intolerance: "An officer of one of the Courts stabbed his wife and a priest found with her but both escaped. A

---

*The Countess of Shrewsbury was in fact putting some of her money to very good use by spending it on building the Second Court at St John's College, Cambridge, part of which is now known as the Shrewsbury Tower. In a niche of this there is a statue of her with a shield below showing the arms of Talbot and Cavendish impaled. This was given by her nephew William Cavendish, Duke of Newcastle.

She had promised to give £3,400 which was nearly the entire contract price of the whole of Second Court (£3,665) but because of her imprisonment and heavy fine she could only manage to subscribe £2,760.

Some time after the Master of the College, Dr. Clayton, died in 1612 his successor received a letter from Robert Booth which stated that the late Master's sister, Mrs. Ashton, had taken away as part of his property "a picture of my Lady the Countess of Shrewsbury which her House at my humble suit bestowed upon the College, and desired that Dr. Clayton would cause it to be hanged up in the gallery there". Dr. Gwyn the new Master was urged "to use all good means for the recovery thereof for the College behoof" and went on, "if it shall be needful, I will at all times be ready to testify upon oath that it was bestowed upon the College and that Dr. Clayton only made suit for it for that purpose".

secretary to Cardinal Capponi sent on private business was murdered by his own servant a few days since, and was dead a week before he was discovered. At Florence at a supper of our countrymen one Cartwright was slain in a sudden quarrel at the board — Sir John Hambden a bankrupt knight is condemned to the galleys for having an old quarrel with him and a swaggering Captain Skidmore to the gallows for giving the blow.''

Towards the end of August Lord Salisbury wrote to Trumbull, "I will leave these (matters) to come to the honest care and vigilance you have expressed in the business of Mr Seymour who by his remove to France hath ridden you of much trouble but left such a proof of your industry as cannot escape His Majesty's approbation.''

In September Trumbull hears from Paris, "Mr Seymour is arrived within this sennight and will spend the winter here . . . He doth give out to have left the Low Countries out of respect to his Ma^{ty}, being advised by friends that his stay there increased his Ma$^{ty's}$ indignation.''

A month later Sir Thomas Edmondes, Ambassador in Paris sends Trumbull this information, "I forgot before sealing my other letter to tell you that Mr Seymour being arrived here sent Mr Rodney to let me know that he desired to see me and that he was retired out of the Low Countries because he understood from friends in England that his lying in that place increased his Ma^{tys} displeasure. I answered that I was sorry he had so much forgotten his duty towards his Ma^{ty} as that I could not admit him to come to me. The said gentleman told me that he meaneth to reside here all this winter. I have not yet made any motion here for the staying of him, not knowing whether his Ma^{ty} thinks him worthy of that consideration.''

John More from London passed on current news to Sir Ralph Winwood at The Hague. "The Archduke's Ambassador hath carried himself very strangely since his arrival . . . and he hath brought a letter from the Archduke in favour of Mr Seymour no less strange than the rest that his Majesty would be pleased to pardon so small a fault as a clandestine marriage and to suffer his wife and him to live together.''

The weary trek for an agreeable resting place went on. Luxembourg Jan. 14th 1612 — Monsieur de la Voye to William Turnbull — "Last Thursday the gentleman left this town who

68

married the lady said to have some claim to the Crown of England and who was caught when trying to escape and brought back to London. The gentleman was accompanied by two other young gentlemen and by a third about 40 who serves as interpreter and guide. He is a very short and solemn person with a fair beard, his doublet of grey English fustian with a plain silver hem. They all called themselves merchants trading by sea and land; but having heard speak of them and of their flight last summer I had my suspicions that it was they. Although I have never seen them before I could easily judge them from their physiognomy and their way of doing things that they were other than they said. For news of them you should apply where the posts of Luxembourg arrive and ask where four men with a servant who arrived last Saturday have gone to lodge. You can then do as you think fit. This is all I have to tell and I may say it has not helped the despatch of my affairs. P.S. Note that they are all English. The husband of the lady is about 28 with a black beard, a very fair skin, and of quite medium height."

From there back he went to Paris where he was allowed by the King to stay, but after a year lack of financial help added to his troubles. In the early summer of 1613 he is found in Bruges from where he writes on 26th June to William Trumbull, "Though the occasion of my move from Paris and from all those parts where I might be liable to the action of creditors be too notorious, yet being now resident in a country where you are his Majesty's public instrument I thought I would become me to crave your advice and assistance. Hitherto I have foreborne because I know not how it might stand with your liking, and I hastened out of Bruxells lest my presence might have drawn out such visits and conversations as would have made me subject to a doubtful construction. I also deferred writing that you might have time to learn from Paris what would give me better access to your belief. My only desire is to avoid disgrace in the country I left and repair unto merchants with whom I have yet some credit, to support my necessary expenses, and to be near to England from whence only I seek and hope relief. I trust you will not disallow of my proceedings but favour my truth in the just interpretation of my actions which are and ever shall be such as may become a most humble and loyal servant of his Majesty, howsoever it pleaseth God to lay these crosses on my youth. Yet I cannot despair but one day I shall obtain that grace both of God and my Sovereign that all these trials and afflictions will but turn to my good and even this enforced residence of mine, where temptations may be offered will be but further argument of a zealous constancy. Craving such favour at your hands as unto such a disposed subject belongeth."

From this next letter it can be assumed that William Trumbull accepted this approach and gave what advice he could. "1613. Aug. 9. Sluice. Sir Henry Peyton to William Trumbull. I have not lately heard from Mr Seymour but I learn that he receives much comfort by your friendly acceptance of his letter and from your good counsel. Though he be well enough inclined of himself and well counselled by his friends I wish he had such supply from home as might enable him to return to his former and safer station. His letters and mine to his grandfather plead for it but I do not hear his lordship's resolution."

The Earl of Hertford's heart was however beginning to soften.

Thomas Floyd to William Trumbull.

"1613 Oct. 18. Paris. Mr Seymour is arrived here and hath obtained a favourable letter from my ld his grandfather. Of late he has fallen sick of smallpox and is in great danger."

Like Arabella he survived this scourge of the time. Now he was restored in favour with his family and so presumably his material needs were catered for but he remained in exile.

After he had received the news of Lady Arabella's death he decided after a suitable interval to make submission to the King. On New Year's Day 1616 he wrote:

"Vouchsàfe dread Sovereign to cast your merciful eyes upon the most humble and penitent wretch that youth and ignorance have thrown into transgression, and shut not up your mercy from him to whom nothing remains but the hope of your princely mercy and forgiveness."

He did not have long to wait for an answer. The Privy Council despatched their decision to him on 5th January. "We have of late received a letter from you wherein we are very glad to observe that you acknowledge your fault and high offence unto his Majesty with a repentance (as we hope) unfeigned and sincere. We do therefore let you know that according to your humble request, we have interceded for your return unto his Majesty, who is graciously pleased, upon this your sorrow and humble submission to extend his favour and mercy towards you, and is contented that you may freely and safely come into your country again as soon as you think good; for which this letter shall be your warrant."

And so the outcast returned, after nearly five years of wandering on the Continent, to his homeland. He arrived in London on the 10th February 1616 and on the following day he was received by the King who granted him his pardon and restored him to favour.

His grandfather was still alive but his father had died and his elder brother Edward died about 1618 without issue. William thus became heir to his grandfather. The old Earl of Hertford lived on until April 1621 dying at Netley. In his lifetime he had managed to get his marriage to Lady Catherine Grey accepted. It had taken him forty-six years to win that battle and so establish the legitimacy of his children and ensure the inheritance of his title.

The Dawn of Service at Court

After William Seymour's return to England in 1616 he soon established himself as reliable and responsible. In the following November he was created a Knight of the Bath at the same time as the young Prince of Wales.

In the following March he again essayed matrimony. This time, although his bride was the elder daughter of Robert Devereux, Earl of Essex, favourite of Queen Elizabeth, who nevertheless ended his days on the block on Tower Hill, no suspicion or objection was raised at Court. During the previous month a letter writer to Sir Dudley Carleton had said, "Sir William Seymour that married Lady Arabella is in some forwardness to marry the Earl of Essex's Sister." The future would find him and his brother-in-law in opposite camps during the Civil War. On the occasion of this marriage his grandfather, the Earl of Hertford, is said to have settled £3,000 a year on him.

Some time later he must have assumed the title of Lord Beauchamp as heir to his grandfather because in 1620 under that name he was elected M.P. for Marlborough. On his grandfather's death in the following year he became Earl of Hertford and left the Commons for the Lords.

The usual problem of money soon presented itself in settling up the estate. Three years after he inherited the title he and his brother Francis (now knighted) succeeded in getting an Act passed by the

House of Lords to enable them to convey certain lands for payment of debts and for establishing other lands in lieu thereof and of better value.

Property that was held "in chief" and involved feudal rights to the Crown came under scrutiny on the death of any tenant in chief. Such *Inquisititiones post mortem* were returned to the Court of Chancery. These enquiries were held by the escheator of the County in which lands were held, and answers to the following questions had to be given:

1 Of what lands the deceased died possessed
2 Of whom and by what service the same were held
3 The date of his death
4 The name and age of the heir-at-law

The escheator summoned a jury who gave a verdict on oath. The report was sent to the Court of Chancery and finally a copy was forwarded by the Chancery to the King's Exchequer so that feudal dues could be collected.

Two such *Inquisititiones* were held on the lands in the possession of Edward, Earl of Hertford, at Marlborough in April and September 1626. The law moved even slower then! John Foyle esquire was escheator for Wiltshire and he had a jury of fifteen who on oath said what the Earl was "seised of". An impressive list of manors and lands and advowsons follows. Against some, additional details are recorded, for example, "the premises aforesaid without the woodland are held of the King in chief by the service of the tenth part of a Knight's fee and are worth per annum clear £19.17.7. and the third part of the said woodland is held by Knight's service, but by what part of a fee the jurors know not and is worth per annum clear forty shillings."

The answers therefore to 1 and 2 above were long and complicated, 3 stated that the Earl died 6th April 1621 at Netley, Southampton, and 4 that William, his grandson and heir was aged 33 years 7 months and 5 days at the time of his death.

Much enquiry had likewise to be made into family settlements and any trusts affecting them apart from the Will itself.

The new Earl quickly took his place in public affairs. In February 1628, along with twenty two other Justices, he signed a reply to a letter from Charles I. This showed statesmanship in advising His Majesty to a better course of action than the one he proposed for the levying of a benevolence. The signatories wrote that they were unable to do it for the following reasons:

1 They conceive it impossible to tax each particular man according to the truth of his estate.

2 His Majesty's present occasions would be sooner supplied by a parliamentary course, for what may be given in Parliament can be presently levied, but in this way, though men were willing to give, they would take their own time, and if they refuse, the Justices know no legal cause to force them to pay it.

3 Upon the last loans the Lords then employed upon that service assured them that His Majesty would not press his people anymore in this nature which was confirmed by Proclamation upon which assurance the Justices engaged themselves in like manner.

4 The charges upon the country for billeting and conducting soldiers and relieving the infected City of Salisbury have been so great that by reason of the poverty of the country the said charges already lying upon them can hardly be gathered."

This document is endorsed "Never sent by reason of the King's countermand and somons of Parliament." Had the Earl or someone else perhaps spoken into the King's private ear? On that occasion at least wise counsel had prevailed.

The practice of instant duelling to settle some dispute was still common. Everyone carried a sword and quick-tempered men drew on slight provocation. Less hot blooded men who felt affronted issued challenges for duels at set times and places. Two accounts follow of how the Earl of Hertford became involved in such an event.

George Rawdon in a letter to Viscount Conway:

"1636. 26 May. There happened a quarrel on Monday at Mr Osbaston's tennis court. Mr Uvedale and another gentleman looking on, a gentleman of the Earl of Hertford, Mr Brooke, came between them, where at Mr Uvedale took exceptions. Mr Brooke answered he knew not why he might not stand there, some other words passed, Mr Uvedale struck him with a ca(ne), Brooke requited with a — which caused Mr Uvedale to bleed. (He) spoke big words and Brooke told him he knew him not but his name was Brooke, and he was found at the Earl of Hertfords. Afterwards Mr Uvedale spoke some words of the Earl which came to his ears, who was then in the ground. So his Lordship and Mr Uvedale went presently to the Park. Mr Cary, suspecting a quarrel, sent up after them. His keeper found them putting off their spurs whom they spying drew on him, but the longstaff beat down their swords, Mr Uvedale's out of his hand and so no hurt was done. The Marshall's messenger has Brookes but Mr Uvedale is not found."

Authority did not turn a blind eye on such contests and if the participants were caught they were proceeded against.

For another more colourful description of what occurred, which must have aroused considerable interest, there is a letter from Robert Robotham to Sir Gervase Clifton.

"1636. 26 May. Darby House. On Monday last was a duell betweene the Earle of Herford and young Uvdall. Sir Lewis Dives was second to the Earle and Sir Ed. Griffith to young Uvdall; and second to the second was the Earle of Essex and one Brooke, and to the other one Chapman and another . . . Two bouts or passages they had and then the Earle closed with him and had him downe at his mercy: the other partyes of Uvdall's offring to releive him, was interposed by the other and then they begann to buckle to it, Dives and Griffith, Essex and Chapman, Brooke and the other. This was in Marybone Park, which being heard by Mr Cary the keeper supreme there, very fortunately took the Earle of(f) Uvdall and parted them and prevented ensewing mischeife which was fallinge upon the others. This hath drowned the quarrell and duell between Lord Wentworth and Lord Berry (?) and what course the King will take in these thinges as yett I know not, nor canne heare; but it seemes my Lord of Hertford was infinitely abused and provoked."

Only a few years later serious conflict developed between King and Parliament. Hertford was one of those who tried hard to guide Charles I towards a better understanding. In August 1640 twelve English peers, of whom the Earl of Hertford was one, submitted a petition to the King in this form:

"Your Majesty's most loyal and obedient subjects on behalf of themselves and divers others, most gracious Sovereign, the sense of duty and service which we owe to your realm of England have moved us in all humility to beseech your royal Majesty to give us leave to offer your princely wisdom the apprehension which we and other your faithful subjects have conceived of the great distempers and dangers now threatening the Church and State and your royal person, and of the fittest means by which they may be removed and prevented. The evils and dangers whereof your Majesty may be pleased to take notice are these:

1 That your Majesty's sacred person is exposed to hazard and danger in the present expedition against the Scottish army and by occasion of this war your revenue is much wasted, your subjects burdened, and disorders committed in several parts of your realm by the soldiers raised for that service and your whole Kingdom become full of fears and discontents.

2 The sundry innovations in matters of religion. The oath and canons lately imposed upon the clergy and other your Majesty's subjects.

3 The great increase of Popery and the employing of Popish recusants and other ill-affected to the religion of law established in places of power and trust especially in sundry counties of your realm, whereas by the law they are not permitted to have arms in their own houses.

4 The great mischief which may fall upon this Kingdom if the intentions which have been credibly reported of bringing in Irish and foreign forces should take effect.

5 The urging of Ship money and prosecution of some sheriffs in the Star Chamber for not levying it.

6 The heavy charges upon merchandise to the discouragement of trades, the multitude of monopolies, and other patents whereby the commodities and manufactures of the Kingdom are much burdened to the great and universal grievance of your people.

7 The great grief of your subjects by the long intermission of Parliaments and the late and former dissolving of such as have been called without the happy effects which otherwise they might have procured. For remedy whereof and prevention of the dangers that may ensue to your royal person and to the whole state they do in all humility and faithfulness beseech your excellent Majesty that you would be pleased to summon a Parliament within some short and convenient time whereby the causes of these and other great grievances which your people lie under may be taken away; and the authors and Councillors of them may be brought to such legal trial

and condign punishment as the nature of their several offenses shall require and that the present war may be composed by your Majesty's wisdom without blood in such a manner as may conduce to the honour and safety of your Majesty's person, the comfort of your people and the uniting of both your realms against the common enemies of their reformed religion . . . ."

In the following May the King appointed the Marquis of Hertford, advanced in rank as a reward for his services, to be Governor to the Prince of Wales. In August he was one of seven to act for the King during his absence in Scotland as a Commission for Custos Regni. By October the House of Commons had resolved that the Prince should live constantly at Richmond and that the Marquis of Hertford, his Governor, should be present when anyone came to see him lest any evil counsels might be given him. For this Mr Pym gave sundry reasons in debate.

At this juncture both King and Parliament respected Hertford and placed their confidence in him. As time went on the struggle for power became fiercer and then the final break came. Hertford made his choice by continuing to serve his royal master unswervingly.

On 12th July 1642 he wrote to his wife:

"Deare Lambe,

I have been these 3 or 4 days with the King. . . .He hath commanded me to goe into Summersetshier. I tooke my leave of him yesterday and came last night hither to York and within a day or two (God willing) I intend to sett forward towards ye West. Wells is like to be the place of my abode. I have sent this bearer, James Paytie to you with this letter fearing it might otherwise miscarry. I must entreat you to send my Sonn Robin to Wells to me, with all possible speede, I would have no body come with hym but Mr Richard and his owne servants and this bearer who shall wayt on hym all the way. I hope when you have donn with the Waters I shall see you there to, the journey is much easier than to Yorke. In the meantime I shall pray for health and commit you and all ours to God's holy protection and and now remayne.

Your most faythfull and most affectionate husband,
Hertforde."

Close to the Throne.

In August 1642 an Ordinance of Parliament was issued declaring the Marquis of Hertford a delinquent and orders were issued for his apprehension. The reason for this was a Declaration by him and other Commissioners for Somerset addressed to the people of that county in these words:

"You have been summoned to hear such things as the Commissioners think necessary to be publicly known that you may not be deceived by the malicious suggestions and deceitful pretences of those men who disturb the peace of the Kingdom and endeavour to bring in great changes in the Church and State against the King's consent and just authority. For the better effecting their wicked designs they have cast all manner of slander upon those men they know are ready at all hazards to oppose them in their mutinous and rebellious enterprises. They give out that the Commissioners are papists and popishly affected, whereas it is known that they had lived and are resolved to die as their fathers have done in the practice of the Church of England. While these men are known to despise the Common Prayer Book and to favour Brownists, Anabaptists, and other disturbers of all order and government. They also give out that the Commissioners have power to take what they please of any man's estate, which is as foul an untruth as that of their being papists, since the Commission was only to review the arms of the subjects, to see them muster and to take care that no person of ability should be without arms; this commission they are resolved to put in practice until it be better liked and understood. The quarrel which these men have with the commission is, that they would have gladly found all men unarmed but their own faction for the more easy effecting of their wicked purposes, which manifest themselves in their levying armies against the King to the terror of all good subjects. The Commissioners therefore pray and require your assistance against such traitorous and rebellious practices."

Parliament had reacted strongly to this and an order for the Impeachment of William, Lord Marquess of Hertford, and others was issued by the House of Commons. The charge was of having summoned His Majesty's subjects together at Sherborne in the County of Dorset in August and of having incited them to take up arms, and also for having published a paper containing malicious scandals against Parliament.

The country now began to divide itself into opposing camps. The King appointed the Marquis of Hertford Lieutenant-General of the West with power of levy such a body of horse and foot as he found necessary for His Majesty's service. From then on he continued a most loyal and steadfast supporter of the royal cause.

Meanwhile passions were running high and very ugly vandalism took place in Canterbury Cathedral. It is described in a letter from one of the dignitaries there:

"We have found much trouble from the troopers sent among us. Colonel Sandes arriving here with his troops on Friday night caused a strict watch and sentinels to be set upon the church and upon several houses to the great affrightment of all the inhabitants. This done Serjeant-Major Cockin came to me and in the name of Parliament demanded to see the arms of the Church and the store of powder of the county which I showed him and he then possessed himself of the keys and kept them in his own custody. The next morning we were not permitted to enter the Church for the performance of divine service, but about eight o'clock Sir Michael Livesey and Captain Player attended by many soldiers came to our officers and demanded the keys of the Church to be delivered to one of their company. Then they departed and the soldiers entering the Church giant-like began a fight with God himself; overthrew the communion table, tore the velvet cloth from before it, defaced the Goodly Screen or tabernacle work, violated the monuments of the dead, spoiled the organs, broke down the ancient rails and seats, with the brazen eagle that did support the Bible, forced open the cupboard of the singing men, rent some of their surplices, gowns and bibles and carried away others; mangled all our service books bestrewing the whole pavement with leaves. A miserable spectacle to every good eye. But if this were too little to satisfy the fury of some indiscreet zealots (for many did abhor what was done already) they further exercised their malice upon the arras hangings in the choir (representing the whole story of our Saviour) and finding a statue of Christ in the frontispiece of the Southgate, they discharged at least forty shots against it, triumphing much when they did hit it in the head or face. Nor had their fury been thus stopped had not the Colonel and some others come to the rescue. They then departed for Dover from whence we expect them this day (Aug. 30. 1642) and are afraid that upon their return they will plunder our houses, unless steps be taken to prevent the same, as they have already vilified our persons and offered extreme indignities to one of our brethren. I am confident that the Houses of Parliament being rightly informed herein, will provide against the like abuses and impieties in other places."

This letter was followed by another which gave the information that Sir Michael Livesey had apologised in the presence of the Mayor and others for what had been done and expressed himself as overwhelmed with sorrow for what had happened. It was later confirmed that only after Sir Michael had departed on the day in question that a Captain Baynes and his men had entered the Church and committed the outrages which included much violation also of the monument of Archbishop Chichele.

After the Restoration Sir Michael Livesey was said to have "gotten into the Low Countries." There by chance in October 1660 he met a gentleman he had formerly "highly abused" in Kent. The latter forthwith demanded satisfaction of Sir Michael, but the Knight refused to own his name, whereupon the gentleman told him to draw or else he would run him through. A duel ensued and Sir Michael was soon disarmed. When people came running up to ask the cause of the quarrel, the gentleman said he was one of the murderers of the King. The "Dutch boors" thereupon cut Sir Michael to pieces and trod his body in the dust — a grim end.

Throughout the fearful times of the Civil War Hertford was often and for long periods close to the King, and when it came to the parley over the Treaty of Newport in the Isle of Wight, he was appointed by Charles with others to wait upon him when he met the Commissioners from both Houses. He must therefore have come to know Sir Harbottle Grimston, one of the Commissioners to whom reference on this occasion has already been made, whose daughter-in-law was later to marry his own son John after she had become a widow.

The Marquess of Hertford continued his service to the very end. Four noblemen, the Duke of Richmond, the Earls of Southampton and Lindsey, with the Marquess offered their own lives to save the King's. All that was allowed to them was permission to bear their Sovereign to his grave. After the execution of Charles on 30th January 1649 his body was exposed to view in a room in Whitehall. It was then embalmed and carried in a coffin to St James's. It was decided he should be buried at Windsor. The four of his bedchamber, the Lords already mentioned, were allowed to perform "the last duty to their dead master and to wait upon him to his grave." The body was carried privately to Windsor and the same night placed in his chamber there. The following afternoon the four peers went to Colonel Whichcot, the Governor of the Castle, and showed him the Order from Parliament acquiescing to their presence at the burial. When they desired that the King should be buried according to the Book of Common Prayer, by the Bishop of London, who had accompanied them, the Colonel refused to allow it. He said it was not lawful, that the Book had been put down, and he would not suffer it to be used in his garrison. So they went into the Church to choose a place for the burial. Although they were well acquainted with the building it was all so altered inside that they could not find their usual landmarks. Then a kindly resident of the town came forward and showed them where King Henry VIII and his Queen were buried. They then asked for a grave to be dug as near that place as could be. Into it the King's remains were lowered without word or ceremony. During the interment the Governor watched; he then had the Church locked up again and took the keys.

During Lord Hertford's devoted service he had advanced considerable sums of money for the King and he continued to subscribe large amounts to sustain his son in exile. All this was in addition to the very large fine imposed upon him on the surrender of Oxford in 1646 when he was permitted to stay in the country by compounding in the sum of £8,345; his younger brother Francis had to pay £2,725, with Sir John Thinn of "Longleace" who was mulcted of £3,100. These were the three highest figures for Wiltshire.

After the execution of the King the Council of State considered Hertford's case and they allowed him to stay in his house at Netley on the surety of recognizances of £20,000 on his own behalf and of £10,000 from two others. He was to be of good behaviour and appear when necessary. This permission to live in one of his own houses in the country was reviewed every so often. In March 1651 the Council of State wrote that on 1st April the privilege was due to expire and "we conceive it will not tend to the peace of the Commonwealth and security of those parts if you continue there any longer and therefore remind you of the expiration of the time and desire you to remove your family to your house (at Amesbury) in Wilts. (and give security to do nothing prejudicial to the State). As we are informed that many dangerous and disaffected persons resort to your house and that several of your servants are such, we desire that such resort must be discontinued and that such of your servants as are within the Act for Confinement of Delinquents keep themselves within the limits. The like to be observed by all those who resort to your house."

Six months later from 'Totnam' he addressed a letter to his wife "Deare Lambe (under date October 5th 1651)

It is noe small comfort to me that you are so well. I hope you shall continue so. Whereas the Doctor feares that my returninge to the place where my disease began may againe renewe it I assure you he is much mistaken if he thinkes it to be Netley. This was the place (as those of my chamber well knowe) where it first begann though I concealed whilst I was with you in London in the Strand thinking it woulde have gon away of itselfe however till I see myselfe free to dispose of myselfe, I shall take noe resolution for my winter abode but wherever it be, if I be at liberties I will not fayle (God willing) accordinge to my former promises to visite you. In the meantime committing you to the protection of the Almightie I rest.

Your most faythfull and most affectionate husband,

Hertforde."

By astute management he continued to live unmolested during the eleven years of the Commonwealth while still keeping in touch with Charles II beyond the sea and supplying him with money. The sums lavished by Lord Hertford from his own purse for the service of the Crown were prodigious. He is said at one time to have brought for the King £60,000 contributed by himself and some of his friends, and he supplied the necessities for Charles II during the fifteen years of his exile with nearly £5,000 annually.

After Cromwell's death and his son's Abdication the Lords in April 1660 resolved "that they owne and declare that according to the ancient and fundamental lawes of the Kingdome the Government is and ought to bee by King, Lords and Commons." By the end of the next month the Restoration was to be an accomplished fact. On the 26th May Charles II landed at Dover and within three hours he was at Canterbury. Among those who made the journey to greet him there was the Marquis of Hertford who had hastened to kiss his hand. Thereupon he was invested with the Order of the Garter.

Among the number of distinguished people who accompanied Charles II on the ride to London were three who, by marriage, became connected to Sarah, Duchess of Somerset. They were the Marquis of Hertford, the father of her second husband; Alderman John Langham, the father of her sister's husband, and Sir George Booth, the father of her niece's husband.

During the ensuing weeks Charles sought to reward those who had served the royalist cause loyally throughout all the weary years. He had it in mind to restore the Dukedom of Somerset to the Seymour family. There was, however, a difficulty in that his father in 1645 had promised this title to the Marquis of Worcester, and he had actually issued an instruction for this in the following terms:

"To our Attorney or Solicitor General for the time being. Charles R. Our will and pleasure is that you prepare a bill for our signature for creating our Right Trusty and entirely beloved cousin, Henry, Marquis of Worcester, Duke of Somerset, to him and his heyres male of his body issueing, with all the priviledges and immunities thereunto belonging and with a grant of an annuity of fifty pounds yearly to be paid to him and them out of our customs of Swansea in our County of Glamorgan for the support of the said dignity, for which this shall be your sufficient warrant.

"Given at our Court at Oxford the sixth day of January on the twentieth yeare of our reigne   Charles R."

It was not surprising, therefore, that the right to the Dukedom was disputed. Andrew Newport writing to Sir Richard Leveson tells how it was settled —

"1660 Aug. 23. . . . The Marquis of Hertford and the Earl of Worcester both pretend to be Duke of Somerset; Hertford by restauration, the other by patent from the late King; yesterday a committee of Lords sate upon it; Worcester produced his patent, but withall said the King gave it him with some conditions which he acknowledg'd were not by him perform'd and therefore referred himself to the King."

In a later letter dated 4th September the same writer tersely records, "Lord Hertford will carry the Dukedom of Somerset." The Act authorising this and Charles II's speech thereon have already been mentioned. Thus was the injustice which had rested upon the Seymours for a number of generations reversed and rectified. The Marquis of Worcester was at a later date created Duke of Beaufort.

The Duke of Somerset did not live long to enjoy his honour. In October he began to fail. Lord Chancellor Hyde, in reply to a letter from the Earl of Winchilsea, son-in-law to the Duke, wrote on the 14th. . . "I have your Lordshipp's favour of the 10 and can hardly yett believe that you will leave Englande without seinge London agayne; you heare of the sadness at Essex House, for the death of my poore Lady Awdry, and the extreme sickness of My Lord Duke of Somersett much increased it; I doubte he cannot hold out longe, the Kinge was this afternoone to see him".

Heneage, third Earl of Winchilsea, had married Lady Mary Seymour in 1653 and they had seven sons and four daughters before she died a little less than twenty years later. He was about to take up an appointment under the Foreign Office in the Middle East. On 3rd January, 1661 he was at Smyrna from where he addressed himself to Lord Treasurer Southampton, "I cannot but condole with your Lordship our mutual losse of the Duke of Somerset, whose owne worth and merits might make his death lamented by all his relations and the whole kingdome; but more especially, it is to be resented by mee, who have lost one by whose assistance and authorities my interest and memory might in my longest absence (have) beene preserved. And truly now I have cause to fear that at a distance I may be reckoned also among the dead unless your Lordship will remind the King that he has a minister in these parts of the world who hopes to live nearer under the shadow and refreshment of his Majestie".

Lord Winchilsea had supported the monarchy throughout their misfortunes and had contributed to the return of Charles II. He hoped to return to England one day to serve his Majesty at Court and the letter continued ". . .that I might be one of the gentlemen of the bedchamber. The King gave me some hopes of this, but as it is not probable that either he or Lord Bath will remember me in the matter, I pray you to continue me in his Majesty's memory".

Three months later he sounded somewhat melancholy when he wrote in the middle of April to Dr Wedderbourne from Pera, "Though I am at this greate distance from you that before I can expect an answer wee may bee in another world, yet we must not want hopes of often returnes and of meeting againe in England; though I confesse were it not for the Duchesse of Sommersett, my Lord Treasurer, and some few other friends of myne, I should seldome thinke of England, unless it were of my master (whom God preserve). . . .for I have received deep wounds there, in the losse of the Duke of Sommerset who was a reall father to mee".

On 20th October Andrew Newport wrote, "The Duke of Somerset is like to die," and on the 26th Mr Secretary Nicholas communicated with the Chancellor of the Order of the Garter, "The Duke of Somerset died at Essex House on Monday (24 October) of a general decay of nature." He was in his seventy-third year.

Many years later Lady Gardiner writing to her brother, Sir Ralph Verney, records that "My lady Seymore* told me the old Duck of Somerset wch was her Lords brother was very inclinable to an apooplex above twenty years before he dyed, and did often indanger his life, and after taking many things of severall physitians was advised by a friend as had helped many of that complant to ware ould cloth at the bottoms of ther feet between their and ther feet it might be next ther skin: and after my Lord wore this, hee never had any aparplexicall fit: so I have sent you down some in case you ware it, tis held of drawing much from the head wch is imputed to prevent thes fits."

Clarendon described the Duke as "a man of great honour, interest and estate, of an universal esteem over the whole kingdom, as one who had carried himself with notable steadiness from the beginning of the Parliament in the support and defence of the King's power and dignity." He was no doubt steadfast also in his religion. The Bishop of Salisbury (Bishop Duppa) said, "the good Marquess of Hartford" had told him what comfort he had derived from repeating the 57th Psalm and particularly the sentence "under the shadow of thy wings shall be my refuge, till this tyranny is overpast."

By his second wife, Frances, who survived him, he had nine children, but of his five sons only one outlived his father, John the youngest, who in the year following his father's death married Sarah, widow of George Grimston. The other sons had all died earlier, the eldest, William, in June 1642, when about the age of twenty-one, of consumption. The second son, Robert, died in January 1646, presumably of a similar infection at the age of

*The wife of Francis Seymour who was created Lord Seymour of Trowbridge.

twenty-three. Neither had been married. The third son, Henry, then became heir apparent. He was born in 1626 and married Mary, daughter of Arthur, Lord Capel of Hadham, famous for the defence of Colchester, but who because of it, ended his life on the scaffold with consummate heroism. Two children, a boy and a girl, were born of this marriage and these were expressly mentioned in the Duke's Will. He wished them, during the lifetime of his widow, to be brought up and educated "in such sort and by and with such persons as the said Lady Marchioness, my wife, shall well like and approve of and not otherwise." These directions were soon to cause trouble, as will be related later.

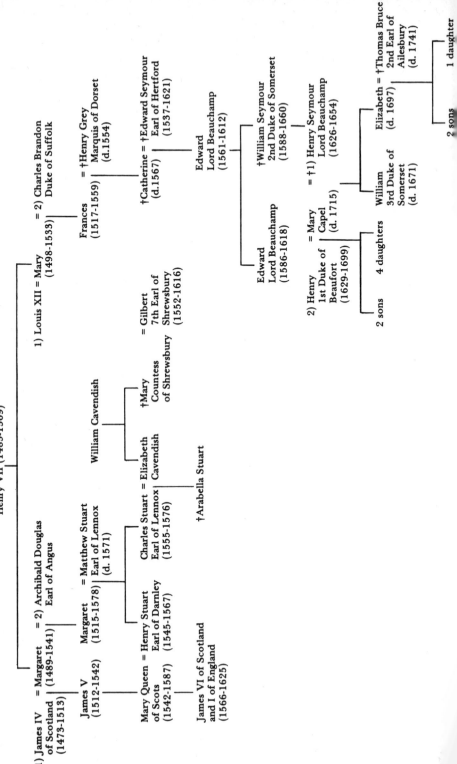

High Promise Doomed

O N THE death of the second Duke the title passed to his only grandson, the son of Henry, Lord Beauchamp. When a very young man Lord Beauchamp had joined his father in the field on the King's side. He was well thought of by his elders, but as his health was not good it was decided that he should go abroad to try to improve it. This was difficult at that time because he would have to pass through the lines of the Parliamentary forces. However, no doubt on account of the relationship of the Earl of Essex (who was his father's brother-in-law, and therefore his Uncle, and who was a Lord General on the other side) a pass was obtained which permitted him to travel to France with two servants and a Monsieur Richante, his tutor. Advantage was taken of this by Charles I who decided to entrust the young Lord Beauchamp with a letter for the Earl of Essex, through whose quarters he would have to pass to get to Plymouth for embarkation. This missive written in the King's own hand under date 6th August 1644, suggested that they should try to find a way of settling the dispute. The Earl of Essex is stated to have received his nephew with great kindness, but after reading the letter declared that "I could have no treaty with the King, having received no warrant for it from Parliament; that the best counsel he could give the King was to go to his Parliament."

Almost two years later his father wrote to the young Beauchamp in July 1646, while he was still abroad, "Harry, I hear you are now in Paris, I likewise understand you have a great desire to go for Italy but for many reasons not fit to be expressed I desire you to leave the thoughts of that journey and to repair hither to London (where I am now) with all the possible speed and secrecy you can. Show Mr Richard* this letter and I doubt not he will readily help you and direct you in your journey hither. So with my blessing I rest your most affectionate father."

What business his father had in mind for him can only be conjectured. He was then about twenty and old enough to take part

*Presumably Monsieur Richante.

in affairs. In just over two years he was married and two months after that his father-in-law Lord Capel was taken prisoner at the fall of Colchester. This family tragedy must have been heartrending to his wife. Her mother, Lady Capel, broke the news to her in a letter dated 31st August 1648 in which she wrote that she had heard only the day before of the surrender of Colchester. She went on to say that her great affliction was that her dear Lord had fallen into such merciless hands. She had, however, obtained leave to go and see him.

Early in the following month Lord Capel wrote himself to Lady Beauchamp from Windsor where he was held prisoner — "My good daughter — The gentilman that commands heere doth not refuse mee the visitt of my friends, and I do not apprehend others but that hee is like to use that respect to mee as may stand with the discharge of that trust hee is imployed in, and therefore I cannot discourage that resolution which your Lord told mee you had to give mee a visitt. My affectionate service to your Lord. God bless you both. I rest your affectionate father, Arthur Capell."

Later he wrote again, "Your letter was a very great comfort to mee and the contentment I receive to hear how happy you are in your Lord is an unspeakable joy to mee", and then again, "My deare daughter, I pray send this encloser to my wife this afternoon — about 4 of the clock I remove from hence to the Tower — the other business uppon trial will not doe. God bless thee. Your most affectionate father, Arthur Capell. My service to your Lord."

And then a letter from Lord Beauchamp to his wife on 25th September just letting her know of his safe arrival at Bagshot and then on to the King — "You may be confident and I shall omitt noe opportunity to give you newse, my deerest heart, your ever affectionate husband, Hen. Beauchamp."

He was evidently accompanying a party on their way to join the King in the Isle of Wight probably acting as aide to his father in the parley with the Commissioners appointed by Parliament. Four days later he writes from Newport, "I am confident you have heard of the King's passing the first proposition and yesterday he gave his answer to all the rest." All this was to no avail and the following year saw the execution of the King and of Lord Capel.

It has already been mentioned that subsequently the Marquis of Hertford was confined to his house at Netley, from where he wrote in March 1650 of the pleasure he felt at the prospect of his son and his wife coming to stay with him, "I am confident you will find it neither unpleasant nor unsafe if any place in England be safe, for all are now alike, but this has something the advantage being out of all roads." He went on to say he was sending his coach for them.

From then onwards there developed what is now called an underground movement, and sometimes there were minor risings or skirmishes.

On 31st May, 1650, Lord Beauchamp wrote to Charles in exile, "May it please your Majesty, since I had ye honour to receyve your Majesties commands it hath been my onely study how with advantage to your service to employ y^t trust which your Majesty was pleased so far above my merrit to impose in mee. To give testimoney of my faithfull endeavours in it, I shall thinke my life most happily sacrifised in obedience to your Majesties commands. I have advised with your Commissioner of each county, who are ready to embrace the first opportunity of appearing your Majestyes faythfull subjects; but findinge ye countreys soe extreamly awed yt, though theyre affections are generally loyall, they will hardly move without some assistance from abroade, they have obleged to joyne theyre most humble request with myne unto your Majesty for two thousand foote with which wee doubt not in a short tyme to give your Majesty a very good account of all ye West; without it, our endeavours wee feare, though never so faythfull may prove fruitlesse. . . . Your Majestyes most humble and faythfull subject.

H. Beauchampe."

In the following year he was a prisoner in the Tower and there he received the following letter from his father, now at Amesbury.
"Deare Harry, I am very gladd toe heare that you have your health soe weel in the Towre. It seems it is a place entailed upon our famylie, for wee now have helde it five generations, yeat toe speake the truth I like not the place soe well but coulde be very well contented the entayle should be cutt off and settled upon some other familie that better deserves it. I wish you here (Wiltshire) with all my harte, the place being very pleasant at this season . . . and therefore with my blessing to yourselfe and your wife, I rest, your most affectionate father that entirely loves you,

Hertforde."

It was on the 4th April that the Lieutenant of the Tower was given a warrant to receive Lord Beauchamp, eldest son of the Marquis of Hertford, to keep him a close prisoner for ten days for high treason. At the expiration of that time he was sent for and examined by an appointed Committee and was permitted to see his physician in the presence of the Lieutenant. A further concession was made the next day for he was allowed a servant to attend him, provided he was such as the Lieutenant approved of and not one of his Lordship's own servants. He was, however, still to be kept a close prisoner for another week and then re-examined. This next interview gained him a little more favour, for on 28th April Lady Beauchamp with one maidservant was permitted to join him, and he was given leave "to take the air within the Tower with his keeper." During the following month Lord and Lady Beauchamp were allowed one more man and one more maid-servant to prevent the servants from going in and out once they were admitted to the Tower.

After a few months his health began to deteriorate. At the end of July his father wrote that he was very glad he was endeavouring to get his liberty for a month because of the state of his health, and Lord Hertford believed that Epsom waters would do him good. He went on to say that he thought July was the worst time of all to be in the Tower.

The Council of State meeting in Whitehall were moved by the doctor's report and gave restricted permission for a change of scene:—

"Upon reading the petition of Henry, Lord Beauchamp, now prisoner in the Tower with the two certificates of Doctor Wedderborne, and Doctor Paggot setting forth his sickly condition and that it is necessary for the recovery of his health that he should be at liberty to drinke the waters of Epshame for the space of a month. It is therefore ordered that the Lord Beauchamp giving Bond to the keeper of the Liberties etc. himselfe in ten thousand pounds and two sufficient securities in five thousand pounds each conditional that he shall render himselfe again prisoner in the Tower upon the former warrant or sooner if the Council shall require it, and that in the meantyme he shall not act anything to the prejudice of the Commonwealth that thereupon he be at libertie for that tyme, and that a warrant be issued to the Lieutenant of the Tower for that purpose."

Presumably this respite did him good. Two years later his father, writing again in the month of July, shows his pleasure that "you are so well come off with your waters of Epsom though for a while after I hear they did disturb you." Maybe he was allowed more than one visit.

This improvement in his health did not last, and after a further decline, anxiety returned. It all suggests that he may have been the victim of the consumption which had carried off both his elder brothers. The news of his state of health reached Charles II in exile, and on 1st March 1654 he wrote, "I should have thanked you for my gloves before this time, if I had mett with a conveniency of sending — I am very much concerned in your health and therefore have given orders to an honest fellow to stay with you in the country and to give me frequent accounts how you do: take heed of melancholique, I keepe myselfe from it as well as I can, and so must you. Remember me to all your friends and be confident I shall allwaies be hartily yours."

Further weakening followed and presumably he must have been released, on the grounds of his health, from the Tower. A month after the King wrote he was dead. Hyde, in exile too, described the event as, "An unspeakable loss in England by the death of Lord Beauchamp, who was a most excellent young man." One of Dorothy Osborne's letters records that Lord Beauchamp was an extraordinary person and remarkable for being an excellent husband and that he left a fine widow. Another correspondent states "My Lord Beauchamp, the only blossom left that looked like anything of tru nobility is wither'd away, in a time when there was most need of him."

It is not surprising that his death was received at Charles II's court abroad with great sadness. Charles wrote himself to Lady Beauchamp. "If the part I have borne in your late losse could have given you any ease, much of your greefe would be abated for indeede I have beene exceedingly troubled at it, nor can I have many more such losses; you will beleeve I will do my part to repayre what can be recovered and to preserve what is left and that I can never forgett what I owe to you and yours who shall always be as much with my particular care, as the wife of such a husband and the daughter of such a father, ought to be, to whose memories more regards cannot be payd than is dew from, Madam, your very affectionate and constant friend, Charles R."

He also wrote personally to the Marquis of Hertford saying he would do all he could for the preservation and support of a family which had deserved so very much from him but that he could not yet do legally or formally what he desired. He could only promise, he continued, that if Lord Hertford should die before his Restoration, then whatever request he left the King would see that it was punctually granted. This letter he signed in duplicate with the names of persons to be trusted and it was put in safekeeping.

About this time Sir Edward Nicholas wrote to Hyde, "certainly the King had a very great loss in the death of Lord Beauchamp; and by that loss the West will be much unprovided. But some others may be thought on; and if once things were ripe for it, I am confident the Marquis of Hertford, tho' he be old, would not be idle."

Lady Beauchamp too must have continued after her husband's death to do what she could in the King's cause. At a Quarter Sessions (Wiltshire) one William Dory was informed against for using bitter and uncomely speeches against a Mr Edward Mitchell because he would not consent to Dory having a licence to sell drink, saying that he was very unfit to be a justice for he was a high Cavalier and one that frequented the house of Lady Beauchamp and carried thither all the tidings of state affairs.

When he died, Henry Seymour, Lord Beauchamp, left two small children, a boy, William and a girl, Elizabeth.

After the death of Lord Beauchamp his parents became concerned about the health of their remaining son John. Three letters from Lord Hertford to his wife touch on this; the first in May, 1655 said "I am glad to hear that our son John is so well and so near his return. God send him a good passage" − he had probably been sent abroad for the benefit of his health. A year later ". . .I am likewise joyful that you and our son John have reaped so much benefit from your physic". This was followed after only a week's interval on 18th May, 1656 by a further reference, "It is a great comfort to me that our son John's physic has wrought such good effects, yet I am sorry that one of his youth should need it. For the remedies you prescribe, encouragement, subsistance, and liberty I know not what you mean. I have not been wanting to him in any of these. As to any good matches for him, I should be glad they were propounded to me". He was not to marry until after his father's death.

6   A Sheltered Youth

THE widowed Lady Beauchamp married in 1657 Henry, Lord Herbert, Marquis of Worcester. Three years later, therefore, her husband and her father-in-law were contestants for the Dukedom of Somerset. This was resolved as recounted earlier. Lord Worcester waited over twenty years for his elevation in rank when he was created Duke of Beaufort.

There was some chatter about this marriage as might be expected. Edward Hyde, writing at the time from Brussels where he was living with the exiled Court, wondered what would be said. "Sure," he penned, "my Lord Hertford cannot like it." There was no doubt however that she had been a loyal and loving wife to her first husband. In years to come it was conceded that she had also made her second choice completely happy for forty two years.

It is probable that Lady Hertford had been a demanding and possessive grandmother before her daughter-in-law's second marriage. Within four months of Lord Beauchamp's death his widow wrote to her, "It shall be my constant endeavour to make my dear children sensible of their duty to My Lord and your Ladyship for the tender care you please to take of them. Betty* being very well this week I have weaned her".

From other letters there are some indications of the tussles that were to ensue. They appear to have been delicate offspring. A few years later their mother wrote to Lady Hertford, "I am 'joyed' to hear by Dr Hearst of my dear son's† good condition. The doctor saw Betty and hopes she has recovered from the ricketts. He wishes me to leave the rollers off her knees. She swings twice a day".

Into the contest for the care of these two children then strode the other grandmother, Elizabeth Lady Capel. Perhaps she had

---

*Elizabeth Seymour.

† William Seymour.

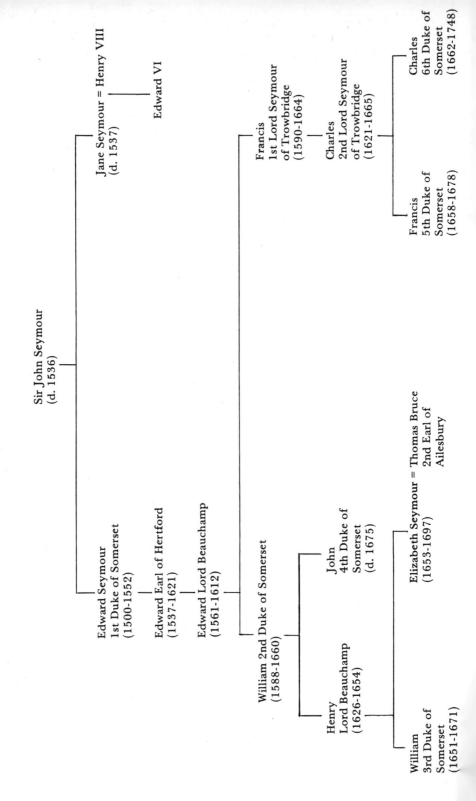

Sir John Seymour
(d. 1536)

Jane Seymour = Henry VIII
(d. 1537)

Edward VI

Edward Seymour
1st Duke of Somerset
(1500-1552)

Edward Earl of Hertford
(1537-1621)

Edward Lord Beauchamp
(1561-1612)

William 2nd Duke of Somerset
(1588-1660)

Francis
1st Lord Seymour
of Trowbridge
(1590-1664)

Charles
2nd Lord Seymour
of Trowbridge
(1621-1665)

Henry
Lord Beauchamp
(1626-1654)

John
4th Duke of
Somerset
(d. 1675)

Elizabeth Seymour = Thomas Bruce
(1653-1697)   2nd Earl of
                   Ailesbury

William
3rd Duke of
Somerset
(1651-1671)

Francis
5th Duke of
Somerset
(1658-1678)

Charles
6th Duke of
Somerset
(1662-1748)

failed to influence the Marchioness of Hertford because she addressed herself in a letter to the Marquess. . . "Understanding by my daughter Herbert your intention of removing to Netley for the winter and that Will is to go with you, I am obliged both in duty and affection to motion that you would leave the dear jewel to his mother's care for that time, for questionless, it is a very unhealthy air and I myself, saw that five weeks I waited on you there that the little maid did daily decline and if I mistake not, never bred a tooth all the time which she did before and after; besides I have often heard Lord Beauchamp say, it is a particular charge on my daughter that his children should never go there. Knowing your great affection for this precious jewel I need say no more but leave it to your consideration."

It is a common experience that inheritance often brings in its train dissension and dispute. The Seymours were no exception. The first troubles arose over the custody of the new Duke and during the month following his grandfather's death, the young boy's mother was in conflict with his grandmother who would not give him up, so in November 1660 his mother submitted a Petition for his return. She wished to know the reason why the Duchess of Somerset was keeping her son, the young Duke, from her or, alternatively, that she should be given permission to recover his guardianship by law. She went on to say that it was an unspeakable affliction not to have him under her eye and she wished to give him an education, which was her responsibility as the surviving parent.

So the battle between mother and grandmother for the possession of this boy of eight began within a month of his succession to the title. Apart from any emotional feeling there may have been on both sides, there was in addition the question of wardship. Henry VIII had created a Court of Wards for the purpose of controlling their affairs. During the Commonwealth this had been abolished, because it was felt that children of the aristocracy who had been left orphans could be legally exploited by the Crown for financial ends. It was decided to continue this abolition by an Act of Parliament after Charles II returned but although this was already in process, it did not in fact become law until the end of December.

The case here then was that on the death of Lord Beauchamp, the Marquis of Hertford had said that he was willing for his grandson to remain under the tuition of his mother only so long as she was a widow. On her marriage to Lord Herbert he had obtained a promise from the King, then in exile, to grant him, as far as he could, the wardship of his heir. He left in his Will* a large property to his wife on condition she retained the wardship. It was further stated that the whole estate was burdened with debt but that the boy's grandmother was willing to educate him at her own expense.

In December, Frances, Duchess of Somerset, described as relict and executrix of William, Duke of Somerset deceased, brought a Counter Petition with the aid of Francis, Lord Seymour†, her husband's brother, Sir Orlando Bridgeman‡, Sir Robert Hyde§, and other trustees of the estate of the late Duke. The preamble was that, following on the death of Lord Beauchamp, his widow had lived under his father's roof until her intermarriage with Lord Herbert, since which time the infant had been in the custody of and living with the late Duke who, by his Will, assigned the custody and estate of the infant to the Duchess of Somerset, and he made it a dying petition to His Majesty to grant it accordingly. It went to say that as the law then stood it was in the power of His Majesty to dispose of the body and lands of the infant at his pleasure, but by the Bill for the taking away of the Court of Wards the custody thereof would devolve upon Lady Herbert as guardian in soccage, though married again, and it would be out of His Majesty's power to grant the late Duke's dying request. This Bill, it is interesting to note, was to provide recompense to the King for the loss of income from the Court of Wards by voting him £100,000 a year in lieu.

The Duchess realised that time was against her, so further mention was made of the great debt upon the estate and that if Lady Herbert had the custody it would be prejudicial to the infant to the value of £20,000, and probably of an additional £100,000 and the trustees were not prepared to take upon

---

*". . . . . and I do hereby further declare my will and meaning to be that the said William Lord Beauchamp and Elizabeth Seymour, my grandchildren, shall be educated and brought up during the life of the said Ladie ffrances, Marchioness of Hertford my wife in such sorte and by and with such persons as the said Ladie Marchioness my wife shall well like and approve of and not otherwise".

After the conferment of the Dukedom a postscript was added that he William Duke of Somerset "do ratiffie and confirm this my Will. . . ." and dated the 4th day of October 1660. One of the witnesses was Sir Orlando Bridgeman.

†Francis Seymour had been created Lord Seymour of Trowbridge.

‡Sir Orlando Bridgeman (1606-1674), Lord Keeper.

§Sir Robert Hyde (1595-1665), Judge of the Common Pleas, died suddenly on the Bench 1665.

themselves the trust which also concerned provision for Lord John Seymour, and Lady Jane Seymour, children of the late Duke, and Elizabeth Seymour, daughter of Lord Beauchamp by Lady Herbert. This appeal was presented to the King for him to think, in his wisdom, most agreeably both for justice and the good of the infant.

Dame Mary Herbert then answered that near the time of his death her late husband had, in the presence of the late Duke of Somerset, made a last and earnest request that his children should never be taken away from their mother, to which the Duke had agreed. She went on that before she entertained any thought of marrying again she had been advised and was satisfied by counsel that remarriage could not in the least prejudice the right she had in the education and custody of her children. Since her intermarriage with Lord Herbert she had, at the request of the late Duke, permitted her children for the most part of the time to continue with him, which he had always acknowledged as her courtesy. She said she had been informed that the Duchess of Somerset had proposed a proviso to be inserted into the Bill for taking the Court of Wards which would gain for her the custody of the now Duke of Somerset, and this would debar the young Duke's mother from the common benefit extended to all the people of England and intended by the Bill to be continued. She prayed that their Lordships would not alter the fundamental laws of England which had always been grounded upon the best reason.

This dispute called for a judgment of Solomon, but Charles, having just resumed his seat on the throne, could not act unconstitutionally. So the Act was passed and Lady Herbert obtained possession of her son again. This did not solve the money troubles. The second Duke's Will provided particularly for the future of his three daughters, Frances, Mary and Jane (the one named Arabella after his first wife had died), and his granddaughter and for this purpose he had bequeathed various Manors to them. Many debts of the Duke must have remained outstanding for a long time because on 24th March 1662 the draft of an Act was placed before the House of Lords to make provision for the speedy payments of the debts of the late Duke of Somerset — a note appended thereto says, "read this day, committed but not proceeded with." Six months later the Duke of Albemarle (Monck) wrote to the Duchess and informed her that he had to know the value of Peers' estates and he wanted a return from her. Some of the repercussions of this financial tangle rebounded upon the Duke's only surviving son, Lord John Seymour. He was forced to submit a Petition himself to the Earl of Clarendon, Lord High Chancellor, in December 1663 in these terms –

"That the Petitioner exhibited his bill to have the reversion of the Manor of Madgehill settled on him and £600 a year for his maintenance and £1,000 to pay his debts according to the Will and settlements made by William, late Duke of Somerset, petitioner's father. The defendant, William now Duke of Somerset, being first served with the Chancellor's letters and after a Subpoena to appear and answer and the other defendants Henry, Lord Herbert of Raglan and Mary his wife (in whose custody the said Duke, her son, being an infant, now is) set in Contempt. Petitioner has used all civil applications but by this day he is deprived of his subsistence and debarred his liberty for want of money to pay his creditors. He thought it his duty to make the Chancellor acquainted herewith before he proceeds in ordinary course against a person of so great honour and eminence."

In spite of this matters did not improve and in January 1666 just over two years after the above petition Sir Orlando Bridgeman wrote to Lady Herbert a *cri de coeur*, "My Lord John Seymour's condition is very sad, having not one farthing but the portion which his lady brought to him and nothing out of his father's estate. There is now behind to him about £4,000 for his annuity and a legacy of £1,000. His debts do so pinch him that he is a continual prisoner, and a close one to his chamber whilst the privilege of Parliament protects him." (He was M.P. for Marlborough).

Lady Herbert continued to have complete control over the young Duke and his inheritance. As the years went by thoughts of a suitable marriage for him began to take shape. The Earl of Essex*, who was Lady Herbert's brother, having been advanced in rank assumed the title previously held by the Devereux family, made enquiries to this end. He approached the Earl of Bedford† who was said to have received favourably the proposal for a treaty of marriage for his daughter and the young Duke, but for some reason it did not materialise.

---

*Arthur Capel, first Earl of Essex (1631-1683).

†William Russell, fifth Earl, later created first Duke (1616-1700).

The young man was now beginning to move in Society. He was seen at a meeting of the Royal Society, which was then much patronised by the nobility. Pepys, who was present, noted among others "Lord George Berkeley and the Earl of Carlisle and a very pretty young man, the Duke of Somerset.

Early in 1671 he was approaching his nineteenth birthday and the Bedford alliance having fallen through another match was sought. The Countess of Northumberland, widowed just about a year and left with a young daughter and considerable estates, was a most desirable attachment, and so he was let off his mother's tight rein to court the lady. She, however, would not be persuaded to marry a suitor who was five or six years her junior.

About this time the Earl of Thanet wrote to his grandmother. . . "If the Duke of Somerset, your grandchild be not already engaged, there is a nobleman who offers £20,000 as a portion for his daughter, who is virtuously and discreetly bred, of an excellent disposition and very young" but nothing came of this either.

As a result of the release from restraint he indulged in the social round of gaiety then to be found in London, and revelled in his new freedom, mixing with company unsuitable for his immaturity. Two letters throw some light on this —

Lady Mary Bertie to her niece Katharine Noel:

"1671 Feb. 23. Westminster. I was on Munday at Court to see the grane ballett danced. It was so hard to get room that wee were forced to goe by four o'clock though it did not begin till nine or ten. They were very richly dressed and danced very finely and shifted their clothes three times. There was also fine musickes and excellent sing, some new song made (on) purpose for it. After the ballet was over several others danced as the King and Duke of York, and Duke of Somerset and Duke of Buckingham. And the Dutchesse of Cleveland was very fine in a riche petticoat and halfe shirte and a short mavis coat very richly laced, a periwig, cravatt and a hat: her hat and maske was very rich."

Jo Pennecke to John Rogers:

"1671. the last of Feb. London. The Parliament not like to rise by Easter though the bill for subsidie gonee by to the House of Lords, and preparing of another bill for an additional exercise which will not reach to private families; the first will fall heavy enough on them which are to pay 12^d in the pound out of their just value . . . I can not learn of any fleet going out this summer, public money never scarcer and so I think private also tho' the vanities of this place are as much as ever: everybody in coach & cloak endeavouring to surpass one the other, and the actions of both sexes, I think, never worse. There was a great ball to be at Whitehall last night but 'twas suspended on what score I know not. Saturday night at night was killed a beadle, the constable's assistant, for attempting a house in or near Whetstone Park, a scandalous place where the Duke of Monmouth, the Duke of Albemarle and the Duke of Somerset with others at a very unseesonable time. At the same time though in another place was killed my lord Hollis's eldest son by a groom which had married my Lord Cullies' daughter which indignity he thought to have avenged; and also in some other place was one of the Life Guards killed in a duel by one of his fellows."

This sort of company meant burning the candle at both ends and apart from other hazards needed a robust constitution to sustain it. In December the young Duke became desperately ill. One of the Thynnes wrote from London, 12th December 1671, "We are like to lose another Duke who is taking a longer journey, the Duke of Somersett; he is fallen ill of the small pocks the infection whereof is so malignant that they appear rather in purple than red spots. The Phisitians have given him over to the universal griefe of the Towne." Within a week he was dead. A fuller account of it occurs in a letter to Sir Robert Paston —

"1671 December 16. Here died on Wednesday last at Worster House the Duke of Somerset, a youth of great beauty and hopes, aged about twenty, he was lately let go out of his mother's constant care and inspection. . . This occasion gave him the acquaintance of the chief young men about the town, and introduced him into libertys before unknown to him; some little disorder the Thursday before began such a fermentation in his blood as produced a violent malignant fever, the meazelles or small pox were expected the first three days; but there never appeared any evident signs of either, so that most now think that if any of that numerous company of doctors that attended had prevailed to have let him blood it had saved his life; which is so much the more deplorable in that the title and estate go to his Uncle, the Lord John, who is never like to have children and after him the honour will go to his Uncle Trowbridge's* children and the land among the ded Duke's daughters."

*Francis Seymour, Lord Seymour of Trowbridge.

Letting blood was, of course, considered the panacea for all illnesses, and the doctors were prone to be blamed if it was not done. The first writer mentions purple spots whereas the second says that for the first three days none appeared at all. Usually the spots of smallpox appear on the third day and in the case of measles on the fourth. The description of the spots indicates an extremely severe infection which could have been either a fatal form of smallpox, *purpura variolosa,* or haemorrhagic measles. So died the third Duke, eleven years after his grandfather and like him he was buried at Great Bedwyn in Wiltshire.

It must have been a sad cortege that left Worcester House in the Strand. The journey was accomplished in two days with an overnight stay at Reading. An account of it was sent by Thomas Gape to the Dowager Duchess of Somerset, who had now outlived her husband, four sons and her grandson. First in the procession was Colonel Cooke's mourning coach then the Marquis of Worcester's coach drawn by six horses, and about eight or ten horsemen attending the hearse. The following morning they left Reading between five and six and reached Hungerford at noon where the gentry of the country met them. These included Sir Francis Popham with his coach of mourning and six horses (but Sir Francis was in a light greyish suit), Sir John Elwes, and many others together with his late Grace's servants, tenants, farmers and bailiffs. After eating, the procession moved on towards Bedwyn and arrived there about three in the afternoon. The coffin was covered with black velvet and a silver plate nailed to it bearing an inscription with titles described thereon. Superimposed on this was a black velvet cushion with a ducal coronet placed thereon. The chancel was hung round with black baize, and escutcheons, with the Duke's coat of arms pinned thereon. After the corpse had been let down into the grave the Herald spoke all the Duke's titles of honour and dignity, Colonel Cooke, who was the Chief Mourner, presumably representing the family. The writer goes on to say, "There was much rudeness of the common people amongst whom none suffered that I hear of but myselfe, I having above a yard of cloth of my long black cloake cutt and rent off in the crowd at my going into the church."

The Duke had executed a Will on the 11th December 1671 in the presence of five witnesses. It was very short and simple —

"In the name of God Amen. I, William, Duke of Somerset, do make and declare this my last Will and Testament. First I commend my soule into the hands of my Blessed Saviour and as to my goods, chattels, and Personall Estate (my full debts being first satisfied) I do give and bequeath the same to my most honoured and dear Mother, the Lady Mary, Marchioness of Worcester, whom I do hereby nominate and appoint and do make and ordain my executor of this my last Will and Testament."

Burdened by Debt

THE premature and unexpected demise of the young Duke made Sarah a Duchess. She had been married to Lord John Seymour about ten years and his financial worries must have been a source of anxiety and annoyance to her. Even when he had succeeded as fourth Duke there was little to support the title and his mother was still alive.

Before he was married Lord John Seymour stood for Marlborough in the election for a new Parliament in April 1660. His father had been one of the burgesses in James I's reign and his uncle, his father's younger brother, had represented it in the reign of Charles I. The town had seen a lot of fighting during the Civil War and at one stage Sir Francis Seymour's house had been surrounded, with Lady Seymour and her daughters held prisoners. In spite of the influence of the Seymours, who were great landowners in Wiltshire, the townspeople were in the main Parliamentarians and Puritans. Marlborough sent two members to Parliament at that time. There were three candidates, the other two being a Mr Grove and a Mr Daniell. The election was a very close thing, and if three supporters of Mr Grove had not been persuaded to transfer their allegiance to Lord John, he would not have been elected with Mr Daniell. He got in by one vote!

In October 1666 he was admitted at Gray's Inn and became a Bencher in the following January. He was also appointed Recorder of Lichfield.

He appears to have been largely dependent upon his mother for money and records of various sums appear among receipts in the Seymour papers —

"December 15th 1666. Received then of my mother the Dutches of Somerset by the hand of Mr Thomas Gape the summe of one hundred pounds in part of last Michaelmas quarter: I say received by me John Seymaure".

Nearly a year later there was a similar acknowledgement —

"26th November 1667. Received then by the hands of Mr Gape, the sum of foure hundrid and seaventy pounds in money and one

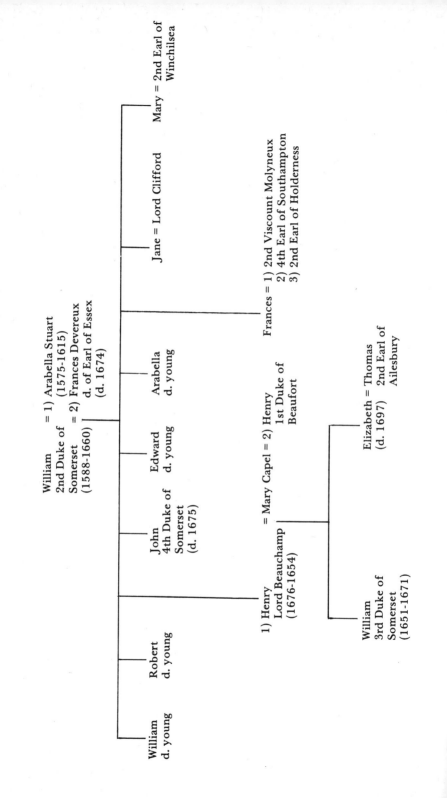

Bond of the penalty of £400 wherein Thomas Randes Esq. and and Francis Bramston Esq. are bound to pay unto me the sum of two hundred pounds upon the fourth day of February next in part of payment of the Arrears of the annuity of £600 p.a. and of a legacy of £1,000 given to me by the late Will and Testament of the Duke of Somerset my late father deceased; I say recd. in money and by Bond as foresaid the sum of £670.

by mee,

John Seymaure."

Mr Gape was his mother's steward.

It would appear from subsequent receipts that he was always kept waiting for his legacy. Under date 12th December 1671 there was written "Received then of my mother, the Dutches of Somerset by the hands of her servant Mr Timothy Whitfielde the summe of two thousand pounds in part payment of the arrears of one annuitye of £600 per annum and of a legacy of £1,000 given me by the last Will and Testament of the Duke of Somerset my late father deceased, I say received as aforesaid the summe of £2,000.

by mee,

John Seymaure."

Only just over a week later and a mere four days after he had succeeded to the title as fourth Duke of Somerset there is another receipt dated 20th December 1671. This is also by the hand of Timothy Whitfielde "The summe of seaven hundred pounde which with one hundred pounde received the 7th day of November last is in full for one yeares present maintenance due to mee from my said mother at Michaelmas last 1671". This is signed "John Sommerset". It was as though he had not become accustomed to the accepted form of signature and still used his Christian name. Subsequently he signed himself "Somerset".

After succeeding to the Dukedom he received his commission in August 1672 to be Lord Lieutenant of Wiltshire. Very shortly afterwards the King noticed that the name of Thomas Thynne was not in the list of Deputy Lieutenants submitted for continuance; this surprised His Majesty, who wished his name to be added. Probably Thynne was not *persona grata* with the Duke, as he acted in the capacity of adviser to his mother, the Dowager Duchess, from whom he could get no money.

Mr Thynne had married the Duke's niece, Frances Finch, daughter of his sister Mary. This sister had been concerned about her brother's behaviour many years earlier, sometime before he was married, and her anxiety was disclosed in a letter to her mother shortly before she was leaving the country with her husband who had been given a diplomatic appointment abroad. It was addressed to the Marchioness of Hertford:— "I wrote from Essex House in such haste that I forgot to mention my brother John. I could give no very good account of him for, though he dined at Essex House he went out afterwards, whispering to My Lord* that he had business in the town but would be back within an hour. But he went with three gentlemen in a coach (this Mr Beaumond, Mr Biron, and another) and though we stayed for him till nearly 6 o'clock and his men looked for him everywhere, we were forced to go without him. As we were taking coach he sent to his men to bring horses to the bridge but arrived too late to venture. Next morning he was with us at Dartford before we left the Inn. My Lord* and I were extremely troubled that he should break his word and I think have made him sensible of it. He would not confess that he had played at all. He has been very orderly since."

The legal adviser to the Dowager Duchess was frequently in difficulty over the need to raise money to pay off debts. He wrote to her on 25th June, 1666 "I must profess that my reason is not convinced that what is now resolved will answer those ends for which it is designed. The money to reimburse your Grace and to satisfy Lord John's arrears cannot be raised but by granting leases or making sales, neither of which can be good unless all the trustees join in." Another communication two years later — "I have paid Lord John £200 of Sir John Monson's money and I never knew him or his Lady more thankful. . . .", and again shortly afterwards ". . .I have paid Lord John Seymour £100. . . .I shall do nothing about liveries for your servants until you give orders and as to their wages I hope God will provide means to defray them".

Relations between Sarah and her husband had been strained for some time because of his debts, and within a year of his inheritance of the title the break came, and the news was scattered about as hot gossip always is. Lady Mary Hastings

---

*The Earl of Winchilsea.

wrote to her brother, the Earl of Huntingdon on 24th October 1672, "The Duke of Somersett and his lady are parted and (as 'tis feared) irreconcileably. He discovers very much his own weakness by making public to the world all the quarrels that have passed between them and many weak complaints too long to relate."

He was still very much weighed down by debts and in November sought a solution by sale of land. To the Dowager Lady Fanshaw he wrote, "I have received your letter proposing to purchase Hewish Farme, allowing its value £1,000, out of the moneys I owe concerning the planting of young trees, I shall readily comply with your ladyship's proposals, I being never scrupulous in trifles. Ryder has promised me to pay in the remainder of your moneys betwixt this and Christmas, which will afford me that satisfaction that I am so much nearer being out of debt. If you will send your servant to Mr Thomas in Gray's Inn he will draw up your lease and I will send it without delay."

There may have been some degree of eccentricity in his nature, although not too much should be read into letters between friends, as when Sir R. Burbogne sought information from Sir Ralph Verney:— "It is earnestly desired by a friend of mine and a servant of yours, in this house, that he may know how it stands between Lord Arlington and Lord Clifford, how it is with his old Mr D. of Bucks, and whether the gentleman of the horse to the mad Duke of Somerset be a place worth harkning after an acceptance, whether of profit or reputation."

It was likely that all the publicity of his marriage break-up and of his debts was becoming too unpleasant, as one of the Thynnes reported from a correspondent that he had gone to Paris, with no clue as to why or for how long. It may have been just to get away from it all for a while, particularly after his wife had petitioned the King to use his influence.

About this time, his brother-in-law Lord Clifford informed his mother "My Lord Duke is so insensed against My Lady that he cannot hear her name with patience. He came to meet me at Marlborough but next day when My Lady came, within an hour he took me along with him to Totham. He told me the reason of his great hatred was her miserableness and her endeavour to govern him. Besides, he has not forgotten her ill useage of him in the time of his restraint".

This is how she set out her case:

Sarah wife of John, Duke of Somerset to the King.

Petition praying him to interpose with her husband to allow her maintenance since he will not cohabit with her having been married to her 11 years ago with a portion of £10,000 and having lived in a condition below her rank to assist in paying off his debts but of late he has by evil instigation refused to live with her or to allow her to enter his houses, leaving her destitute of apparel, meat, drink and maintenance.

Case of Sarah, wife of John, Duke of Somerset.

That she was daughter and heir of Sir Edward Alston, President of the College of Physicians and widow of George, son of Sir Harbottle Grimston, by whom she had two children since dead; and the now Lord Keeper* negotiated her marriage she having £10,000 portion, that after her marriage she found her husband greatly in debt; his mother, the Duchess Dowager of Somerset refused on a quarrell to pay him £600 a year left him by his father and turned him out of her house whereupon she took lodgings for him in Gray's Inn and after ten years care paid off his debts except £1,000 lost by him at play, and set him at liberty; that the Dukedom falling upon him by death of his nephew he got into fresh debt by furnishing Salisbury House which they took, and she refused jewels etc. till this new debt was paid though he told her that she had long suffered for him, and should now be the better for him; but some ill people who got about him persuaded him that she had water put in his wine, and governed his affairs too much etc. so that he treated her harshly, and pretending she had taken away his Will etc. he having forgotten where he put them and he will not communicate with her or her friends she is forced to appeal to the King.

Case of John, Duke of Somerset, in reply.

That his wife knew of his debts before marriage, and was asked to let £4,000 of her portion go to pay them but refused and gave her whole portion to his mother; that his debts since coming to the titles were chiefly contracted by her and for her satisfaction, his wife suffering less than he, having the management of £800 a year the residue of his estate; that having ordered her to stay at his house in London fearing she might convey away the residue

---

*Sir Orlando Bridgeman, Lord Keeper of the Seal.

of his fortune as she had done his plate, deeds, etc.; that she has still £600 a year, has had the disposal of his moneys till of late, and he has offered her more on her giving an account of his plate, deeds, etc.

Reply of Sarah, wife of the Duke of Somerset, to his Answer.

That she was never informed of his debts before marriage, that her whole portion was paid to his mother because she insisted on having it; that she was to have £300 of the £800 per annum settled by his mother for her own use and she had only £500 per annum to manage for him, which was always at his disposal; she admits his debts were paid of the arrears of the £600 per an. paid by his father's trustees and a legacy, but that would have been spent but for her extraordinary care; that she was not ordered to stay at Marlborough and came to London only to tell him where he had deposited his Will etc. which she was accused of purloining but which were deposited with the Master of the Rolls who sent him word thereof: his plate was sent partly to his goldsmith and partly to the Rolls for security there being but one porter in the house: his moneys have been used to discharge his bills etc.: he has offered her £400 a year in addition to her £600 but she does not think that suitable to his condition and her fortune.

Sarah's efforts to try to control her husband's gambling are displayed by the following document which was among the papers at Gorhambury:

On the outside cover is written:

"A true Coppie of the Release that Mr William Howell gave to my Lord when hee pd him the Gameing debt he thus delivered into mee, my Lords Bond, and gave my Lord such a release as this besides.

And all other gamesters shall do the same
When my Lord pays them any monye
This release was drawn by the Master of the Rolls direction."

*   *   *

"Know all men by these presents that I . . . . for and in consideration of the summe of good & lawfull mony of England to mee in hand paid by the right honourable the Lord John Seymoure the receipt whereof I do heerby acknowledge have remised released and for ever quitt claymed and by these presents doe for mee my heires executors and administrators and every of us clearly and absolutely remise, release and forever quit claime unto the said Lord John Seymoure his heires executors and administrators all and all manner of actions cause or causes of actions suits quarrells debts dutys judgments Statutes Recognizances Bonds bills writtings obligatorys reckonings accounts and demands whatsoever which against the saide Lord John Seymoure I ever had now have or which I my executors or administrators or any of us att any time hereafter shall or may have for or by reason or means of any matter cause or thinge whatsoever from the beginning of the world untill the day of the date of these presents. In witness whereof I have hereunto set my hand and seale in the two and twentieth yeare of the raigne of our Soveraigne Lord Charles the Seconde by the Grace of God of England Scotland France and Ireland King Defender of the ffaith Annoye Domd 1670."

Attached to the above was this additional note, "To pay to Mr Hender Robarts (my Lord Robarts son) twenty pounde in full for his gameing debt of fortye pounde and if hee hath had any bonde or note of my Lord for it hee must deliver it unto you upon payment of the mony, And also give my Lord a generall Release under his hand and seale in full of all debts bills Bonds Judgments and all accounts demands whatsoever."

In 1671 various properties in Wiltshire were mortgaged to Sir Harbottle Grimston to ease financial embarrassment.

He took his seat in the House of Lords on 10th February 1673. The dispute with his wife went on and only two days after his admission to the Lords he was represented by his brothers-in-law, the Earl of Winchilsea and Lord Clifford at a hearing before the Lord Chancellor, Lord Treasurer and the Earl of Arlington, and gave them instructions as follows:—

"1 That since my wife has left me and conveyed away a great quantity of plate and household stuff etc. I resolve never to co-habit with her, so I give no authority for any treaty.

2 That upon her delivery of all my silver plate, bonds of money due to me, and an account of what she has received of mine, I give you leave to promise her an allowance not exceeding £1,000 a year."

A memorandum stated that she already had £300 for separate maintenance settled on her marriage, and £300 settled above a year ago, which £600 must be part of the £1,000 maintenance.

A month late, on 16th March 1673, he acknowledged the help the Earl of Winchilsea had been: "I thank you for your care in my concern with my wife. I have perused the particulars of their Lordships the referees' resolves and well approve them. I am informed that your Lordship proposed the restoration of the plate and that the Master of the Rolls engaged the restitution of it. I desire this additional trouble that you remind my Lord Chancellor to perform this that I may be in a better position to keep my house and return to London".

The wrangle went on. To Lord Winchilsea he wrote on 15th April, "I have lately received some demands of my wife's which I neither can, nor will, grant. If their Lordships shall please to pronounce the results formerly sent me, which were £1,000 a year present maintenance, her chamber plate, and £500 a year more on the fall of either of the jointures, she surrendering the pretended settlement of land of inheritance, I shall then make good the other and immediately expect the restoring of my plate."

When his mother died on 24th April 1674 there were more disputes. Three days after her death Dr William Denton wrote to his nephew, Sir Ralph Verney: "The Duchess of Somerset is dead. She left a Will with Codicil at the tail (to which I hear Lord Bridgeman was not privy) not at all to Mr Thynne's disadvantage." What a kettle of fish was here! Sir Orlando Bridgeman had been adviser to the family in legal matters for years and he was a trustee of the old Duke's Will. Now he was Lord Keeper of the Seal and must have felt unhappy at this new turn of events. Was the old Dowager the source of most of the difficulties? We know she was at loggerheads with her daughter-in-law, now Marchioness of Worcester, and clearly she had little time for her son John. This last fact casts some further light on the omission of Thynne's name from the D.L. list submitted by the Duke after becoming Lord Lieutenant. He was probably acutely aware of Thynne's influence over his mother.

The Thynnes and the Seymours had been connected in their affairs for some generations, ever since Sir John Thynne had acted as Secretary to Protector Somerset, the first Duke. He had been knighted after the Battle of Pinkie in 1547. He managed to amass a great fortune and this sudden wealth was so envied by a great Earl and Privy Councillor that he contrived a summons against Thynne, who had to explain to the Council how he had come by so much money. Sir John Thynne calmly answered with unassailable details of how he had married well and taken great care of his fortune ever since. "For the rest, my lords, you have a good mistress, our Gracious Queen; and I had a good master, the Duke of Somerset." That settled the questioners and he was troubled no more by such sniping. He built Longleat, which took twelve years to complete, and was said to be the first well-built house in England.

Thomas Thynne* mentioned in the Will had married Lady Frances Finch, who was a granddaughter of Frances, Duchess of Somerset, by her deceased daughter Lady Mary, Countess of Winchilsea. He had been appointed by the Duchess as one of her executors, the others being Sir Orlando Bridgeman and Sir William Gregory.

There was no doubt about the Codicil which was signed four days before death. Here it is:

"Whereas the greatest part of my jewels are now in Pawn for the sum of £400 and my Will is that the said jewels shall be redeemed by the first moneys that shall be (paid) out of my estate."

She directed her executors to convey the Manor of Drayton in Co. Warwick and Stafford to her grandson, Thomas Thynne, for £10,000 instead of £12,000, because she had forgotten two rent charges that were payable out of the said Manors £18 a year to the poor of Lichfield for ever and £14 to the poor of Tamworth for ever.

Her lands in Ireland and Herefordshire she settled on her grandson, Thomas Thynne and his heirs. And all goods, chattels and personal estate whatsoever at Drayton in Staffordshire she gave and bequeathed entirely to her grandson Thomas Thynne freed from all debts. She further wished him and his wife, the Lady Frances (her granddaughter) to continue in the apartment in Essex House which they were then using. They were also to have the use of the stable and coach house for a space of six months after her decease and likewise use of all the furniture for a similar period.

---

*Cousin of Tom of Ten Thousand, to be mentioned later.

To her granddaughter, Lady Frances, she left her white damask bed and curtains with all things belonging thereto. She was also to receive the portrait of the Lady Arabella, "My dear Lords first wife", which was hanging in the Dining Room, and she was also to have the picture of "Queen Jane Grey now hanging in my chamber." To her daughter Jane, Lady Clifford, she gave the picture of "my son, Beauchamp, now hanging in my chamber."

She wished mourning to be given to all her domestic servants, both at Essex House and Walton.

To her page, Charles Temple (?) £100 to be settled for his use and benefit by her executors and not to be able to dispose of it until twenty-one years of age.

This Will generated increasing alertness in the opposing camps in their struggle for shares of the Seymour cake. A month later, in May, Charles Price wrote to Lady Worcester about a deed that was supposed to have been forged touching the descent of the Duke of Somerset's estates. In the following January Lady Worcester indemnifies Thomas Thynne and William Gregory from any damage accruing to them by reason of their delivering to Charles Price for her use one green damask coach of which she was possessed in the lifetime of her mother (in-law) the late Duchess of Somerset.

The anxiety of the legatees is displayed in a note addressed to Mr Thynne from Badminton on December 14th 1674 from Lady Worcester's daughter. "I desire those pictures and ye other legacies given me by my grandmother's will may be delivered to the Bearer Mr Price and I will own whatsoever he shall give his Receipt for as received by

Your servant,

E. Seymaure"

Lady Worcester had now become very vigilant and another of her emissaries, evidently a lawyer, one George Johnson, was sent down by her, in March 1675, to gain information of the fourth Duke, who was said to be in poor health. In the middle of the month Johnson wrote, "I came from the Duke of Somerset on Friday last. I did not think that he was then in a dangerous condition, his disease being turned to an ague. He did not speak to me about altering his Will and I am confident he had no such intention although some persons about him would, if they dare, persuade him to give his estate to my Lord Seymour*, and they have been very earnest with me to persuade him to it, but I will advise nothing to your daughter's prejudice."

The Duke's health must have been giving some concern, and although the above report was favourable he was, in fact, on the verge of a terminal illness. Lord Seymour was his first cousin's son and he was now the heir to the dukedom.

On the first of April John Verney noted that the Duke of Somerset was sick. Before the end of the month he was dead. This is how one of her informants let Lady Worcester know. "I have certain information that the Duke of Somerset died this morning (29 April). I hear he has made a Will and the Lord Coleraine is his executor. I conceive you will think it prudent that some person or more of quality will go to Amesbury betimes to be informed of his Will and what settlement he has made and to prevent any foul dealing which may be suspected among such people." The next day George Johnson wrote from London to confirm it. "Here is a messenger sent on purpose to acquaint me that the Duke of Somerset died yesterday at 10 o'clock in the forenoon and I am desired to come down, having his Will in my study in the country, but it so falls out that I cannot possibly stir till we have acquitted my Lord Treasurer of all those exhibited against him in certain articles of impeachment. I conceive it is for my lady Elizabeth to take care about the funeral she being the Duke's heir at law."

Lady Elizabeth Seymour was the niece of the Duke and sister of the third Duke. She had been granted the place and precedency which she would have enjoyed had her father, Lord Beauchamp, survived his father, the second Duke.

Within a week of his last letter George Johnson wrote again, this time to the Marquis of Worcester.

"1675 May 4. London — We have now voted that there is no ground to impeach my Lord Treasurer† upon any of the articles exhibited against him. I therefore intend to wait on your Lordship about the middle of next week at Badminton. What makes me stay longer here is a report that the Duke made another Will about two or three days before he died giving all his estate to Lord Clifford. I confess I do not believe it because I had two letters from his

---

*Grandson of Francis Seymour, the first Lord Seymour of Trowbridge.
†The Earl of Danby.

servants who did not mention it, besides Lord Clifford denies it and I am informed he was not compos mentis since the first fit of apoplexy. If the report be false I intend to come out on Monday in a Bath coach and hope to wait upon your Lordship on the Thursday following."

Lord Clifford, who was also known as Viscount Dungarvan, was the son of the first Earl of Burlington and had married the Duke's youngest sister, Lady Jane Seymour, on 7th May 1661, it was said very privately. There had in fact been no last-minute Will and the one that was proved was dated 17th June 1674.

The Duke was, like his great-grandfather, buried in Salisbury Cathedral. On his death the Marquessate of Hertford became extinct, but the dukedom passed to his young cousin, Francis. At once the Marquis of Worcester bought the late Duke's estate at Amesbury for Lady Elizabeth Seymour. An account of it says that many trees had been planted during the previous year — forty-six apricots, twenty plumtrees, twenty cherry trees, thirty vines, sixty peach trees, two hundred lime trees, three hundred elms and laurels, also a bowling green of 67 yards square. Three men were employed and two weeding women and there was a cart to draw water to preserve the trees. The men were already doubtful about their future employment as no one promised to pay them. There was also the Duke's butler, who was described as a very able man and "sufficient to be butler and housekeeper for any noble person in England, he is a very solid man in his life and conversation, and it is almost as great a wonder as Stonehenge to see him without the gates and also to see him drink any strong liquors, he is so temperate. He desires to be at any Lord's disposal."

With only one year between the Dowager Duchess's death and her youngest son's the affairs of the former and the disputes with Mr Thynne had not been resolved. The processes of the law moved exceedingly slowly then, as sometimes now.

Frances, Countess of Southampton, who was the elder of the surviving daughters of the Dowager, wrote in July 1675 to the Marchioness of Worcester, her sister-in-law.

"I was in hopes at my first coming to town to have dispatched our business with Mr Thynne .... we cannot come to an end till all our witnesses are examined, I am resolved not to leave it, being above £2,000 a year. We may be caught at (out) if we do not our uttermost to show his fraud. I thought it fit to acquaint you that Mrs Matthews not coming to town puts a great stop to my niece Betty's concern."

When the fourth Duke made his Will, in the year before he died, he described himself as being "of perfect memory and also of good health of body". He expressed a desire "that his body should be decently interred according to my Quality in the Cathedral Church of Sarum in and unto the place where my great grandfather Edward the late Earl of Hertford lies buried." He asked his executor to expend £1,000 of good money on his funeral.

To his two surviving sisters, Frances, Dowager Countess of Southampton, and Jane, Baroness Clifford, he gave £1,000 on the Feasts of Candlemas and of St Michael the Archangel.

To his nephew Heneage Finch, son of his other sister, Mary, the same.

To Lord Seymour, Baron Trowbridge, he bequeathed the Manor of Wolfhall in Wilts., also Sudden Park, Savernake Forest and lands in Easton Wootton and Great and Little Bedwin.

He asked his friends, Sir Richard How Bt. and Sir Thomas Mompesson Kt. to buy land "with all convenient speed" and the profit and rents from this shall be "for ever yearly imployed for the apprenticing of some poor children who are or shall be born within the city of Sarum." To this end he left £3,000.

He gave one year's wages to any servants with him at the time of death.

His jewels, plate and household goods and chattels he gave to Mrs Eleanor Oldfield.

He nominated as Executors "My loving friends James Mountagne of Eastham Esquire, Alexander Chistlethwaite of Winterstow, Esquire, Albertus Oldfield of Westminster, Gent, and George Johnson of Bowden Park Esquire and give to each £500.

Some years after his death the Chamberlain of the City of Salisbury was ordered to procure the picture of His Grace, the late John, Duke of Somerset, as he had been a worthy benefactor to the poor of the city and that it was to be paid for out of the Chamber Revenue. This portrait now hangs in the Banquetting Hall in Salisbury.

8   Tragedy on the Grand Tour

THE new Duke of Somerset was the grandson of Francis Seymour, the younger brother of the second Duke. This Francis Seymour, who had been the first to hear of the escape from the Tower of his elder brother William in 1611, had in the next reign loyally served Charles I and had by him been raised to the Peerage as Lord Seymour of Trowbridge. His eldest grandson, also christened Francis, had succeeded on the death of his father, to the barony in 1665 as the third Lord Seymour of Trowbridge. Now on the demise of his father's first cousin he became, at the age of seventeen, the fifth Duke of Somerset.

The Worcesters were looking for a suitable alliance for the Marchioness's daughter, Lady Elizabeth Seymour. The new young Duke seemed a most desirable match. With this in the forefront of his mind the Marquess wrote to his brother-in-law, the Earl of Essex, the young lady's Uncle —

"Badminton. 30 December 1675. Dear Brother, It is no small trouble to mee that I should bee now forced to despair of waiting on you whilst you are on this side of the seas, a thing both civility required and my inclination urged mee the most in the world. I comforted myself, till now, with the hopes of repairing my omission at London with seeing you at Coventry, but I am now disappointed of that too, by my wife's still continuing so weake, and apt to be disturbed (to the apparent prejudice of her health) at the least thought of my shortest absence and being without hopes till the spring she will bee otherwise. I should if I had waited on you, have desired your opinion in the concerne of your niece Seymoure for whom I think it is high time to thinke of a match and I finde she expects wee should. I confesse both my wife and selfe had a great persuasion to have her estate, wch comes from her family, have helped to set it up againe by matching to him that has the tytle, and whom the law makes the head of it, but you cannot imagine the aversenesse she has to it, and you know she is of an age not only of consent and dissent but to be *sui juris* so that there is nothing to bee done, but with her approbation.

My wife has proposed severall, as the Marq. of Winchester's sonne, Lord Aylesbury's and all the young men that are either of quality or estate worth considering but insisted most upon the M of W's and Ld Aylesbury's the latter of wch shee seems most inclined to. We are unwilling to begin anything of treaty without having your opinion in it, to wch end I addresse this to you by a messenger of my owne, by whom you may and we beg you would write your thoughts freely, and also that you would suggest if you can think of any other person more fit, and we will try whether shee can bee brought to it, tho by what I perceive, it will bee extreamly difficult shee having taken a liking to the young man. I desire you would please to communicate that parte of my letter which relates to your neece, to my brother Harry, that he may also if hee please, have his thoughts upon it, to whom though I writt last poste I have said nothing concerning it, not thinking fit to mention a thing of that nature in a letter by the poste. I am, Dear Brother, Yr most faithful humble, sincere and most affectionate Brother, Worcester."

The Earl of Essex was at this time Viceroy of Ireland and was presumably either on leave or on business in England, hence the reference to being on this side of the seas.

Lady Elizabeth Seymour was over twenty-one and it is understandable that she might not then be attracted to the new young Duke who was quite four years her junior, or to the son of the Marquis of Winchester, who was only fourteen. Thomas Bruce, the Earl of Ailesbury's son, was much nearer her own age. So negotiations were started between Lady Worcester and Lord Ailesbury, and the latter found her ladyship a shrewd and tenacious character. She was determined to secure a good bargain; and she emphasised the value of her daughter's inheritance and expected Lord Ailesbury to settle a lot of land on his son and heir. Rumour of this proposal must have been gossip at an early stage, for among the Verney papers there is a reference to it — "The Earl of Aylesbury's son is to be married to the late Duke of Somerset's sister, a great fortune and their wedding clothes are now a-making." That was in March 1676, but it was over five months before they were worn! The young people only met each other formally and in the presence of others, while the lawyers on both sides argued over the details of the contract. A vast legal document was at last produced and accepted on both sides and the marriage took place at Badminton on 24th August 1676, one month before Thomas Bruce's twentieth birthday. The ceremony was followed by a banquet and general celebrating went on until night time, when the bridal pair were escorted by a number of guests to their bedchamber. It was the custom of the time for some of the closest relations to see them into bed with a final kissing of the bride before pulling the curtains of the four-poster. Then they had to wait for the footsteps to disappear along the corridor before they could be sure of undisturbed privacy.

The provision of money for the young couple was not to prove easy in spite of the marriage settlement. Lord Ailesbury promoted a Bill in the House of Lords to vest certain manors and lands of Robert, Earl of Ailesbury and Thomas, Lord Bruce, in trust because of the minority of Lord Bruce. These lands which were in four counties were to be vested in trustees for the performance of marriage settlements made on the marriage contracted between Lord Bruce, a minor, and Lady Elizabeth Seymour, sister and heiress of the late Duke of Somerset. The Bill was read for the first time in February 1677 and objection to it was raised in Committee by Lady Southampton and Lady Clifford (aunts of Elizabeth) who mentioned a deed which affected them. In consequence Counsel for both parties were ordered to meet and adjust their differences. In the end the Bill was dropped.

When the young Lord and Lady Bruce left Badminton not long after their marriage, they went to live at his father's house, a common practice then, where they were allotted a suite of rooms. Then they moved to a house in the Strand. The marriage settlement proved to be of no help, and it turned out that although Elizabeth was heiress to large estates in Somerset and Wiltshire, she derived no benefit because of outstanding debts. These had been incurred by the second Duke through his financial support of Charles I and Charles II. There were still also other debts of the fourth Duke. In addition the Seymour aunts had rent charges and jointures which had to come out of the estate. Elizabeth appealed to her mother saying that what they had to live on did not maintain them. All she got in reply was equivocation but no money — "What relief I can honourably and justly give you I will being sincerely to you and yours an affectionate mother." Only when one of the aunts died did she receive any benefit. This trouble over the settlement went on for over twenty years and caused a considerable rift between the two families. In later years Thomas referred to his mother-in-law as having always been against him, saying that he had been at the mercy of the implacable hatred she felt, but adding "God forgive her".

*   *   *

Young noblemen generally obtained some experience of life by travelling abroad. The new Duke accompanied by his uncle, Hildebrand Alington, later Lord Alington, his mother's brother, went to the continent on such a tour. Due courtesies for rank were usually expected. Perhaps it was some apparent or intended insult that took place with another peer of lower precedency which prompted this gossip in a letter to Lord Roos from Lady Chaworth — "1677 Jan. . . . . A quarrell beyond sea between the Duke of Somerset and Lord Plymouth, the last wholly in fault, and the other passive and civill, and the King very angry att Lord Plymouth and says he will make him know he hath no rank but what he has given him. . ."

The following year stark tragedy lay in the path of uncle and nephew. They arrived at Lerice* in the Genoese Territory on the 20th April 1678. The Duke got into the company of some French gentlemen who were also travelling just to see foreign parts. They went into the Church of the Augustinians where some Italian ladies felt insulted by the behaviour of the Frenchmen who were said to have been guilty of some indecencies towards them. These Italians were members of the family of Botti, and when the husband of one of them was told what had taken place, he lay in wait outside the inn where the visitors were staying. The first of them to come out of the doorway was the Duke of Somerset and Horatio Botti shot him. He died instantly. This ghastly happening to the least guilty member of the party was a devastating shock. He had not been responsible for any offensiveness towards the ladies. His uncle at once notified the officials of the Republic of Genoa and demanded justice for such a crime. The news having reached England Mr Secretary Coventry wrote to Mr George Legatt, Consul at Genoa — ". . . But I am likewise by the King's command to tell you that you look narrowly that there be no connivance in it and upon any omission of justice or of search to quicken them; and in case you find any neglect, to acquaint his Ma^{ty} or me with it. Besides the misfortune of losing so hopefull

---

*Lerice, a small place on the sea coast in the bay of Spezzia about sixty miles from Genoa on the way to Leghorn.

a young Lord the damages that arise to the family are very important and though it should be forgotten in Genoa it will not be so in England." The authorities did seem to be incensed against the perpetrator of this crime. They found on proceeding to apprehend him that he had fled out of their dominion. On 14th September Mr Legatt wrote to the Hon. Hildebrand Alington to say that the Great Council met in Turin on the 10th "who gave full power & authority to the Collegio which is the Senate to passe sentence on the murtherers in the nature they shall think fit." He goes on to say that he gathered from one of the Senators that the process of law was likely to begin again *"ab integro"*.

On the last day of September Secretary Coventry wrote again fearing that "delay may arise dishonourable to the Duke so cruelly murdered, and favourable to the murderers." He had been commanded by His Majesty to make his great indignation known and to request "pressing application in his name for the immediate passing of sentence on the two homicides Botti, not only that they be put to death but that their houses be razed to the ground, their goods confiscated and a tally set on their heads with other rigorous penalties that are usually enforced." The brother of Horatio Botti was also considered to be incriminated.

Action was taken by the Genoese, who pursued the affair by naming the two men responsible for the murder, and passed sentence on them *in absentia*. Anthony de Botti was to be hanged and Horatio de Botti was to serve ten years in the galleys. Previously a plate had been fixed above the door where the murder had been committed, promising a reward for the delivery of the murderer. Now the Court ordered that the opening at which the Duke was shot should be perpetually blocked up and an inscription placed there. The murderers were hanged in effigy only. They were never apprehended.

The body of the Duke was brought back to England and he was buried at Preshute, Marlborough, on 15th October 1678.

THE Dukedom now descended to his younger brother, Charles, who was later in life to be known as The Proud Duke. After James II came to the throne he was appointed a member of his Court. He was at first a loyal supporter and at the time of the insurrection of the Duke of Monmouth he took an active part on behalf of the King. He was at Wells on 16th June 1685 and sent news from there for the information of the King, "Pray, my Lord, acquaint the King that there shall not be anything wanting in me to put a stope to this rebellion, which I hope now in ten days you will find a very great alteration for the best." Later he sent a message to say he was ten miles from Bridgwater "where the enemy now is."

The following year the King stayed with the Duke of Somerset at Marlborough. It was the subsequent intrusion of Roman Catholicism that disturbed their relationship and the crisis came when James II asked the Duke, in his capacity as first Lord of the Bedchamber, to receive the Papal Nuncio, Ferdinand, Count of Adda, Archbishop of Amasia, on his arrival at Windsor. This the Duke refused to do, and although friends pointed out to him that this action might jeopardise his future career, he stood firm and was prepared to risk royal disfavour. He could not subscribe to James's religious views. The King was angry; "I thought my Lord," he said, "that I was doing you a great honour in appointing you to escort the Minister of the first of all crowned heads." The Duke replied, "Sir, I am advised that I cannot obey your Majesty without breaking the Law." At this the King was really roused. "I will make you fear me as well as the Law; do you not know that I am above the Law?" The Duke answered, "Your Majesty may be above the law but I am not and while I obey the law I fear nothing." The Duke was then only twenty-five and his firmness and his courageous spirit was remarkable. Of course the King did not forgive him, and he lost his place at Court. Another repercussion of this conflict with James II concerned his brother's murder. Knowing that James II was a Roman Catholic and likely to be sympathetic to those of that religion, the family of Botti petitioned him to pardon the assassin of the fifth Duke. This he did, it was said, out of resentment of the behaviour of the late Duke's brother, now the sixth Duke.

When this murder was committed Charles Seymour was only just sixteen and he was then at Trinity College, Cambridge. Because most of the ducal estates had been disposed of through the female line of Seymours there was not a great deal of substance to support the title. In four years' time, however, he married an heiress, Lady Elizabeth Percy, the only child of the eleventh and last Earl of Northumberland. She was said to be the greatest match in the kingdom, and amongst other properties she owned Sion House, which had been built by the first Duke of Somerset.

When she was only twelve she had been married to Henry Cavendish, Earl of Ogle, heir to the Duke of Newcastle. He died the following year and the marriage was never consummated. Great pressure was then put upon the youthful widowed Lady Ogle by her grandmother, the Dowager Countess of Northumberland, to go through another form of marriage. When she was still only fourteen the husband chosen for her this time was Thomas Thynne of Longleat, who was one of the richest commoners in England, being known as Tom of Ten Thousand. He was just over thirty when this marriage took place in November 1681. Instead of joining her husband when the ceremony was over she escaped and fled. What a story it made for London society! Charles Bertie hastened to tell his niece, the Countess of Rutland:

"1681 November. London. I must tell you the news that our great fortune, my lady Ogle, took an opportunity yesterday as shee was at the Old Exchange to withdraw herself and immediately my old Lady Northumberland came in search of her, and some say Mr Thynne. The reason given to this resolution is the uncomfortable prospect she pretends to have of ever living happy with Tom Thynne, as report tells us, and some add that shee has betaken herself to my Lord Duke Albemarle's protection. Some say the contract shee lately signed rises in her stomach, and she shows all manner of aversion to the match with Thynne. Wee must bee allowed a little more time to learn the reason of this so surprising an action but I will write to report of the town and leave your ladyship to descant thereupon."

Here indeed was a young lady of spirit. Some days later Charles Bertie wrote again and continued the story: "The nine days wonder of my lady Ogle's amazing retreat is now over and I believe shee has left in her lover no other passion but that of indignation against the sexe." She managed to get to Holland, where she placed herself under the protection of Lady Temple, wife of the Ambassador at The Hague; and there she remained unmolested for a year. Sir William Temple must have decided to give her what help he could, and by the New Year a start was made towards obtaining an annulment of the marriage. An affidavit was made before Sir John Reresby, a Justice of the Peace, on the 2nd January 1682, concerning a pre-contract between Thynne and a daughter of Sir John Trevor*, before his marriage to Lady Ogle. Then, as now, it was the law that if consummation had not taken place, as in this case, it was possible for the marriage to be annulled. Some said that Miss Trevor had been seduced by Thynne. A copy of the affidavit was submitted to the King.

The whole affair became the talk of the town. Lady Chaworth wrote to her brother, Lord Roos, "Mrs Trevor goeing away nobody knows whither or with who, but her mother told the Dutchesse it was by Mr Thin's desire and askt leave for theire marrying which she most willingly gave and sent with the Duke to let Mr Thin know their joy of itt upon which he disownes the thinge and denyes ever any thought of marrying her or speaking to that purpose to her or her mother. So Mr Trevor sent him a chalenge on Wednesday and thiere was a duell without mischiefe, Lord Cavendish second to Mr Thin, who denies knowing where she is or her being with child by him. Yet the King says that had she staid much longer she had been delivered att St James's, yet others say she is not with child."

The betrothal of an heiress always excites attention. Tongues had probably been active over this particular case for some time. At the time of the marriage contract Chaloner Chute wrote to the Countess of Rutland, "1681 November 15 . . . I must tell you how matters stood with my lady O. when Mr T. first began his addresses to her consequently the rivals he had at that time to deale with all. The chiefest among them the Duke of S. the Earl of N. & the Earl of K. For the Duke until she came of age she had not enough money. Against the Earl of N. she was fully resolved as being a bastard & she had heard something of the Earl of K. she did not like Mr T. doubted his chances as he was not a Lord." On the next day

---

*He was Secretary of State 1668-72.

another letter to the Countess, this time from her mother, Viscountess Campden. ". . . . my lady Ogle's great fortune has brought her a great deale of ill fortune. Some say my Lady Trevers will preduse a contract from Thin to her daughter."

The case must have given rise to considerable speculation. John Evelyn in his *Diary* under date 14th January 1682, "Dined at the Bishop of Rochester's at the Abbey it being his marriage day after twenty four years. He related to me how he had been treated by Sir William Temple, foreseeing that he might be a delegate in the concern of my lady Ogle now likely to come in controversy upon her marriage with Mr Thynn."

No one could have foreseen what was to happen. On 12th February Thomas Thynne was barbarously murdered in Pall Mall at about seven o'clock in the evening. Sir John Reresby described the event — "Mr Thyn, a gentleman of £9,000 a year (lately married to my lady Ogle who repenting of the matter fled from him into Holland before they were bedded) was sett upon by three ruffyans and shot to death as he was coming along the street in his coach. He being one deeply engaged in the Duke of Monmouth's interest, it was much feared what construction might be made of it by that party, the authors escapeing and not known. I was at Court that evening when the King hearing the newes seemed much concerned at it, not only for the horror of the action itself, to which his good nature was very averse, but also apprehending the ill constructions that the anti-court party might make of it."

Sir John Reresby was to become very much involved in the matter. As magistrate, representations were made to him the same night at eleven o'clock for him to grant a "Hue and Cry", a method by which felons were caught. Once the official "Hue and Cry" had been issued, all inhabitants were embraced in the hunt for the criminal, on horseback and on foot, and word was passed from place to place.

No sooner had he agreed to that than there arrived at his door the Duke of Monmouth's coach with a page asking him to go to Mr Thynne's lodging where the Duke was. This he did and there consulted with the Duke and other lords and gentlemen. As a result he issued immediately several warrants of search for persons who might be suspected of having some knowledge of what had taken place. Two informants put the searchers on the track of the murderers: one was a sedan chairman who had that afternoon conveyed a man from a lodging in Westminster to the *Black Bull* to collect a horse, the other was, "A whoor that used to visit that gentleman." As a result the man was found in that lodging and he proved to be a Swede. He was brought before Sir John Reresby and he stated that he served a German Captain who had told him he had a quarrel with Mr Thynne. This servant then gave the addresses of various houses where his master might be found. These were followed up at once and the Duke of Monmouth with Lord Mordaunt and others, accompanied the magistrate. Throughout the night they went from house to house until at six o'clock in the morning they found their quarry in the house of a Swedish doctor in Leicester Fields. Sir John was the first to enter the bedroom, followed by Lord Mordaunt. The Captain was in bed, his sword some distance away. This Reresby seized and then arrested him. His name was Vratz and his two accomplices were also soon taken. They were all foreigners, Captain Christopher Vratz, John Stern, the Swede and George Borosky, a Polander.

It was small wonder that the Duke of Monmouth had been personally so interested in apprehending the murderers, because only a short while before Thynne was shot he had been riding with him in the coach. It was after he had descended and when Thynne was continuing on alone that the attack took place. It came out that the three men had been shadowing the coach and some time after the Duke had descended they galloped hard and overtook it. One of them then challenged the driver to stop, while another, Borosky, discharged a blunderbuss straight into Thynne's body. They had all then galloped off leaving the victim mortally wounded. It was clear there had been no design on the Duke of Monmouth.

Thynne was terribly injured by the attack and died soon afterwards. The surgeon, Mr Hobbs, who was called to him, said four bullets had entered his body and these had torn his guts and wounded his liver, gall bladder and his stomach. Both the great guts and the small guts had been severed as well as some ribs and the "great bone below". (?pelvis)

William Cole who was Thynne's servant said that he was in front of the coach with a flambeau* in his hand. At the lower end of St Alban's Street, at its junction with Pall Mall, he heard the blunderbuss go off and saw a great smoke and heard his master cry

---

*A flaming torch.

out that he was murdered. He saw three horsemen who rode away on the right side of the coach and off up the Haymarket afterwards.

What was the motive behind it all? By more interrogation it was learned that Captain Vratz had been for eight years a companion and particular friend of Count Conismark, a Swede of considerable standing whose uncle was at that time Governor of Pomerania. The Count had been in England during the previous year, and it was said had made addresses to Lady Ogle. Something Mr Thynne had done the Count resented and had felt affronted. Captain Vratz, it was contended, had taken upon himself an act of revenge. He it was who had stopped the coach while the Polander fired the blunderbuss.

More enquiries led to the questioning of a Monsieur Flaubat who kept a fashionable school for riding, fencing and other accomplishments in London. The Count's younger brother was at this academy. It was then disclosed that the Count himself had come incognito to England ten days before the murder. It was further discovered that the Count had been in disguise until the morning after the crime when he had disappeared. This, naturally, cast great suspicion upon him as having been the real author of the dastardly assault.

Eight days later one of the Duke of Monmouth's men found Conismark at Gravesend in disguise, when he was trying to get aboard a Swedish vessel. He was taken to London and the King called an Extraordinary Council to examine him. Sir John Reresby was present and recorded that Conismark "appeared before the King with all the assurance imaginable, was a fine gentleman of his person, his hair was the longest for a man I ever see for it came below his waist." After a brief examination he was handed over to the Lord Chief Justice and the Attorney-General for more questioning. He said that he was not concerned in the murder and that the reason for his being in hiding was because he was being treated "for a clapp"* and was therefore unwilling to be seen until he was cured. He said he had gone away in disguise because when his friend had been accused of such a crime, he feared that if it was known he was in England it might have reflected upon him and he might be thought to have been a party to it, not knowing our law.

---

*A slang term for the venereal disease, gonorrhea.

The trial took place at the Old Bailey, the three men charged as principals in the murder and Charles John, Count Conismark, as accessory. All three, Vratz, Stern and Borosky were convicted and sentenced to death. The Count was acquitted. Vratz maintained he acted independently and Conismark denied complicity.

Some there were who expressed concern that the Count escaped. One of these was William, Earl of Devonshire, who was firmly persuaded of Conismark's guilt. He sent him a challenge soon after the trial, which was accepted. They agreed to fight on the sands of Calais but the Count never met his adversary.

Gallows were erected in Pall Mall where the murder was committed and all three were hanged there on 10th March 1682. Sir John Reresby, who had been so closely involved from the beginning, was present at the end and put down on paper his impressions: "The Captain dyed without any expression of fear, or laying any guilt on Count Conismarke. Seeing me in my coach as he passed by in the cart to execution he bowed to me with a steady look, as he did to thos he knew amongst the spectators before he was turned off. In fine his whole carriage from his first being apprehended till the last, relished more of gallantry than religion." He was known as a man of great courage and had commanded a forlorn hope at the Siege of Mons where, out of fifty men, only he and another survived. For this exhibition of bravery the Prince of Orange had made him a Lieutenant in his Guards and afterwards the King of Sweden gave him a troop of horse.

An entry in Evelyn's *Diary* gives a similar picture to that of Reresby of the man on the day of his execution — "He went to execution like an undaunted hero, as one that had done a friendly office for that base coward, Count Koningsmark . . . Vrats told a friend of mine, who accompanied him to the gallows and gave him some advice, that he did not value dying of a rush, and hoped and believed God would deal with him like a Gentleman. Never man went so unconcerned to his sad fate."

Fourteen days later Evelyn has another entry, "I went to see the corpse of that obstinate creature Colonel Vrats, the King permitting that his body should be transported to his own country, he being of good family, and one of the first to be embalmed by a particular art invented by one William Russell, a coffin maker, which preserved the body without disembowelling or to appearance using any bituminous matter. The flesh was florid, soft and full as if the person were only sleeping. He had now been dead near fifteen days and lay exposed in a very rich coffin lined with lead, too magnificent for so daring and horrid a murderer."

To Sir Thomas Thynne, who inherited Longleat after the murder of his cousin, Sir William Temple wrote the following letter.

"Sir,   Sheen, March 29th 1682

Upon my return to Town though for two days onely I immediately endeavoured to wayte upon you; and was very sorry to lose that honour by your beeing out of Towne. I have since receaved yr commands of the 22nd from Longleat and though I have seen my Lady Ogle but once since her arrivall and keepe my resolution of having nothing more to doe with her affairs yett I would not fayle of performing that office you were pleased to desire and wch I promised you. Upon it shee assured mee that shee never intended to make any use or advantage of any such deeds if shee found them unles it should bee to defend herself against claimes of Mr Thynne's executors and since you seem assured there can bee nothing of that kinde I am confident you may reckon there will bee nothing of the other from my Lady Ogle. I am sure I shall alwaies doe my parte to hinder it as a pointe I think of so much honor. For the more formall ways of securing this intention it must bee yr parte and yr counsels to finde them out, and whenever you doe and thinke I can bee of any further service to you in them, you may very freely command mee but whenever you pleas to doe it I desire yr Secry will give mee the style of a private country gentleman for his last was too harde to a man that has quite forgot all past imployments and the styles belonging to them. I shall alwaies endeavor to deserve that of,

Sir, Yr most faythfull and most humble servant,

Wm. Temple.

I send this by a servant of mine who having been with my wife in Holland goes down to see his friends in your country and will upon his returne bring any commands you may have further for mee upon this or any other occasion."

*   *   *

Lady Elizabeth Percy*, who had been married twice, was now a widow for the second time without having lain on a marriage bed. She returned to England and her grandmother got busy again looking for another desirable suitor. Charles, Duke of Somerset, was the choice and this time everybody, including Elizabeth, was willing. They were married on 30th May 1682 when he was just twenty and she not quite sixteen.

A letter to Lord Preston says ". . . my lady Ogle was married two days ago to the Duke of Somerset to the disappointment of C. Koningsmark and others."

Within a few months the young Duchess became desperately ill with smallpox. Her mother, who is not mentioned in connection with all the matchmaking, went to her side and although she herself had never had the disease yet she remained and would not stir from her. The grandmother considered the Duchess caught the disease by going into the country and she wrote to her sister, the Countess of Rutland, "thus you may observe the country ayer will not secure from that distemper and I hope will make you less apprehentious of coming to towne."

Fortunately she survived but not without disfigurement. In September her grandmother wrote ". . . and the Dutches of Sommourset as to her health is recovered the small pox but her beauty is gon, for she is like to be extremely marked." In three consecutive letters the spelling of Somerset moves from Sumerset to Sumersitt and on to Summourset!

There were nine children born to this marriage and the eldest, Algernon, who was born in November 1684, restored the harmony with the Thynnes by marrying into that family. His bride was Frances, daughter of Henry Thynne, who was related to Tom of Ten Thousand.

The sixth Duke was in time to hold high office at Court in three reigns and his Duchess succeeded Sarah Jennings, Duchess of Marlborough as Mistress of the Robes to Queen Anne.

---

*Lady Elizabeth was previously married to Lord Ogle.

10 Cheshire and Presbyterian Roots

MARY Langham was the only grandchild of Sir Edward Alston. She was just seven when her mother died and when her grandparents died she was Sarah's closest relation. Although her father married twice more in her lifetime, and for a fourth time after her death, there were no further offspring. So the baronetcy passed to his younger brother and Mary was his heiress.

When she was seventeen she married Henry Booth, son of Lord Delamer, whose family had lived at Dunham Hall in Cheshire since the time of Sir John Booth, who was slain at Flodden Field. Henry Booth's father had been brought up by his grandfather, Sir George Booth, because he was an orphan at the age of fourteen. He was also called George Booth and thus became a ward of his grandfather who had the same name.

On the outbreak of the Civil War old Sir George supported the Parliamentarians, so it was understandable that his grandson George, then about twenty, also became active on their behalf. As with countless others who were opposed to absolute power in the hands of the monarch, young George began by upholding the right of parliamentary government. Like very many others, too, he saw, as the struggle proceeded, that one oppression was simply being replaced by another. So, as in the case of Sir Harbottle Grimston, his sympathy swung to the Royalist side as the excesses of Cromwell and his army became apparent. The execution of Charles I was a profound shock to an enormous number of people who had wished to see the King's power curtailed but not completely cut off.

Early in 1642 the struggle between the King and Parliament was approaching its final division. The armed forces were still under the control of the crown. Anything the soldiers did which disturbed the lives of the people or damaged their property, produced remonstrances in Parliament. Grandfather Sir George was one of the leading men in the county of Cheshire, through which soldiers were moved en route for Ireland. Their behaviour left much to be desired and so repercussions followed via Westminster. Mr Speaker

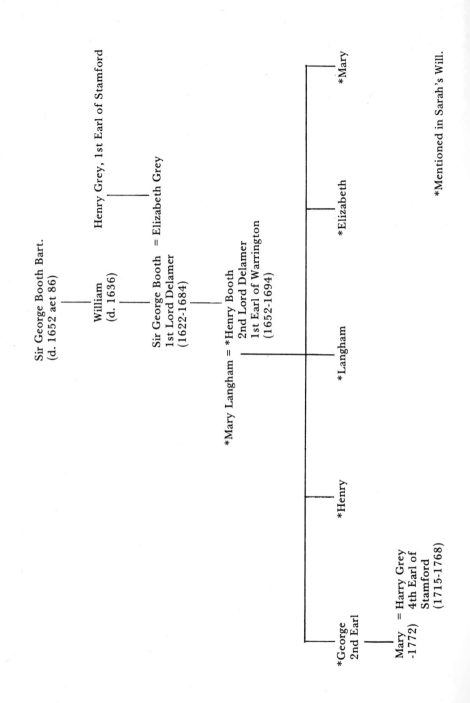

Sir George Booth Bart.
(d. 1652 aet 86)

William
(d. 1636)

Henry Grey, 1st Earl of Stamford

Sir George Booth = Elizabeth Grey
1st Lord Delamer
(1622-1684)

*Mary Langham = *Henry Booth
2nd Lord Delamer
1st Earl of Warrington
(1652-1694)

*Henry

*George
2nd Earl

Mary = Harry Grey
-1772) 4th Earl of
Stamford
(1715-1768)

*Langham

*Elizabeth

*Mary

*Mentioned in Sarah's Will.

Lenthall wrote to Sir George and the rest of the Justices of the County Palatine, as well as the Mayor and Aldermen of the City of Chester, to inform them of orders that had been issued for troops passing through, which were expected to be enforced. Complaints had been received from many sources; of damage and outrages committed when troops were billeted, that no compensation had been made, either for the soldiers or for their horses. Such irritations provided the tinder by which the conflict burst into flame. By midsummer the rift between the two sides became a gulf, although the first clash did not happen until the end of October at Edgehill.

Throughout the length and breadth of England the country was divided irrespective of class or family allegiance. Some places might be largely Royalist, like Oxford, while others exhibited a preponderance for Parliament, as at Cambridge. There was really no rigid pattern. Cheshire, like the rest, had adherents on both sides. The Parliamentary leader in the county was Sir William Brereton, but, lacking officers of experience, in February 1643 he sent from Nantwich a request for help from HQ. "We have near upon 5 troops of horse in the county, but because they are independent troops and not subject to command it was and is my desire that there may be a major sent down, an honest and conscionable man. Now that we have gathered our forces together we are at extreme way of money and therefore desire that we may benefit of the like orders for raising money, in our county as hath been already granted for Yorkshire, Bucks, Leicester, and in particular Somersetshire dated 27 January 1643 giving power also to possess malignants* estates in the said county, which if it be not granted we shall be speedily very much distressed. The names of the Commissioners I have already given who are to appoint assessors are Sir George Booth, George Booth and twelve others."

Chester itself had decided to serve the King. In September 1642, after Charles I had raised his standard at Nottingham, he visited the city. Because there had been some opposition to him, word was sent in advance to the Mayor, bidding him "to have the Trained Band ready and provision made for him and his retinue." On his arrival the King ordered a search of several houses, starting with Sir William Brereton's and including the *Red Lion*

---

*Malignants were those who had elected to support the Royalist cause.

and the *Golden Lion,* and all arms and ammunition found were to be seized for the King's use. Later Chester did, in fact, achieve lasting fame by its defence and, although besieged for over three years, resisted several assaults and the garrison was only reduced by attrition. The King's men were accorded the honours of war and were allowed to march out, and the safety of the citizens was preserved. Among the Parliamentary forces investing the place were George Booth and his uncle, Colonel John Booth, who was at one time appointed Governor of Warrington.

The overall position of troops during the Civil War must have been very fluid at times, with marauding parties of horse roaming the countryside. In North Wales and Cheshire this must have been particularly true, and such a situation is reported by Sir John Meldrum – September 1644. "The next day after my coming to Nantwich I went to see Tarvin where I found Col. George Booth, a young gentleman of great expectation, holding the place, which was not defensible and imperfectly victualled. He desired to be relieved in regard the Chester horse were plundering all Wirrell so that the garrison at Tarvin should be deprived of relief. This being so and finding that there were more of the scattered horse which had escaped from Montgomery, come over to Wirrell by fording the Dee, I desired Sir William Brereton to send his horse that night to Wirrell so that they, joining with the Yorkshire horse, might fall upon the Chester horse the next day." So the young George Booth was already recognised as a leader, and at the age of twenty-two had been made a Colonel. He had a colourful career in front of him.

This to and fro type of situation was not infrequent. A few months earlier George Booth had reported that fragments of Prince Rupert's routed army could molest them unless prevented, and he suggested that Oswestry should be victualled and manned and that Lord Denbigh should draw nearer to Chester to stop the Lancashire and Shrewsbury forces joining each other. It would also hinder the broken elements of Prince Rupert's forces and prevent them doing harm. Very soon after sending that despatch he issued an urgent appeal to the Commander-in-Chief at Nantwich. "Speed, speed, I am informed that Prince Rupert is come to Preston or verie neare it with 6,000 horse and some foot and that Lieuten'nt Gennerall Cromwell lefte the pursuit of him and is returned to York to the Leaguer, so as the enemy hath more scope and libertie to advance as he pleaseth. And therefore it will behove us of this county to stand well upon our guard and rallye our fforces for the publique safetie."

Apart from the problem of keeping forces assembled in the most advantageous places and at the best time, there was always the need for money to pay the troops and feed them; this applied equally on both sides. In August 1645 when the siege of Chester was proving arduous, Booth and others submitted their views to the Speaker of the House of Commons. They recounted the charges that had been borne by the county and added that its wealth was now well nigh exhausted. They appealed for "such timely assistance of horse and foot as you in your wisdom think fit for reducing of Chester on which depends the well being of the County, Lancashire, Shropshire, North Wales and the North part of England and also of Ireland, and that those forces be not maintained at the expense of the county." As a result of this Sir George Booth, the grandfather, and other Deputy Lieutenants were asked to send in a further report at the end of the next month: "From the leaguer before Chester . . . we found the soldiers left in a mutinous condition for want of pay and the county quite exhausted . . . . yet it hath pleased God so to render our endeavours prosperous that the County and forces are now reduced to a cheerful and obedient condition ready and capable of any proportionate design that can be presented them for the service of Parliament. . ." They must have received some money or been made handsome promises.

In October George Booth reports again to the Speaker from the Chester suburbs — "Upon Monday we so straitly begirt the town on both sides the river that none can get forth or come in to them. Yesterday we again attempted the City by storm. The most part of the day was spent in battery — after a parley of 24 hours held with them— We fell to the storm a little before sunset which continued for an hour and a half. The service was very hot, in which attempt we spent much ammunition, for which the gentlemen of the County stand engaged. The service was performed by the expense of some blood, yet no considerable man lost. Amongst the wounded Lt. Col. Venables, a gallant man, received a wound in the arm but not dangerous." He went on to plead for a speedy supply of money and thought the adjacent counties should help to provision them. He finished by saying that unless support was received "this overcharged county will be in danger to sink under the burden."

The King's forces in North Wales were still a serious threat, and in March 1646 Colonel John Booth was ordered to take a regiment that had been made up to a strength of one thousand men, together with a troop of horse and some mortar pieces, to aid Colonel Mytton in overcoming the opposition there. Soon armed resistance was to peter out everywhere.

This was followed by a period of confused political talk and bargaining, involving various religious bodies, the Scots, and Parliament, concerning the future of the King. There was much searching of heart by many men on both sides. The Booths were among those who came to realise that the victory was not producing a satisfactory state of affairs, and so in time both uncle and nephew, the two colonels, transfered their allegiance and both subsequently suffered imprisonment for it, John Booth during the second part of the Civil War and George Booth before the return of Charles II.

In April 1651, when there was a resurgence of support for the royal cause, Colonel John Booth was arrested and imprisoned in Liverpool. Later he was brought down to London and lodged in the tower. He was however, allowed some privileges, for his wife was permitted to be with him, and his sisters were allowed to visit him in the presence of the Lieutenant of the Tower. After the Battle of Worcester in September, when the danger was over, and Charles Stuart was a fugitive, he was released on bail in his own surety of £2,000, with two others of £1,000, on condition he appeared at any time before the Council of State during the next twelve months. His horses, money and goods which had been taken from him on his detention were restored. This leniency may have been due to the continued loyalty of his father, old Sir George Booth, to the Parliamentary cause. The Council of State wrote to thank Sir George for his constant demonstration of faithfulness "and readiness against the enemy whereof yourself may reap the comfort we doubt not Parliament will be duly sensible for your just advantage." When John Booth was released the Council again wrote to thank Sir George for his services and wished him "to take recognizances of his son, Col. John Booth, and to admonish him as to his peaceable carriage in the future."

Sir George only lived another year and his grandson the young George succeeded to the baronetcy at the age of thirty. He was elected to Parliament in 1654 as a representative of Cheshire. This was the first Parliament in which members from Scotland and

Ireland sat together with those from England. There were no members this time from the rotten boroughs or pocket boroughs; it was considered to be a fair representation of the people. Its views, however, did not coincide with Cromwell's, and so he dissolved it. From then on, there gathered an increasing amount of hidden support for the restoration of the monarchy, but with the country in the iron grip of the Protector dictator there was little chance of the change back taking place until after his death.

THROUGHOUT the years of the Commonwealth and particularly towards the end of it, Charles Stuart kept in touch with his adherents in England through agents and by means of cyphers. Under the pseudonym of Mr Adams he wrote to Sir George Booth on 22nd September 1654 that he was glad Sir George had been returned to Parliament, and although he knew that as an M.P. he must attend to public service, yet he hoped that his uncle and his other friends would take care of the King's "concernments".

Correspondence between agents in England and the exiled King was carried on with difficulty and much risk. Pseudonyms were freely used and were changed from time to time. The Nicholas papers give evidence of this. Earlier in 1654 Charles II is addressed as "Mr Jackson" and Booth is called "Mr Blacke", while Cheshire became "Catting".

During this time Cromwell governed by dividing the county into ten areas, each with a Major General in charge. Each had power invested in him to arrest any suspected person, and he was to take care of Royalists and papists. Those who thought differently chafed under the control. Sir George Booth was said by one of Charles Stuart's agents to have been rash enough to tell someone whose loyalty was perhaps unknown, "that the Major Generals were Cromwell's hangmen and in answer to a sharp reply said he would satisfy any man that was angry at his words with his sword". The agent felt this behaviour was imprudent.

In 1656 Cromwell summoned another Parliament, but excluded from it about a hundred members who were likely to be awkward. It is not surprising to find reference in another informant's letter to "Booth of Cheshire, one of the most considerable of 'our party' was likewise excluded". Sir George was now doing all he could to favour a Royalist revival.

During the years of the Commonwealth there had been much change. An incident recorded by Sir John Reresby, the magistrate, shows the throwing off of servility and respect. "The citizens and common people of London had then soe far imbibed the custome and manners of a Commonwealth that they could scarce endure the sight of a gentleman, soe that the common salutation to a man well dressed was "French dog" or the like. Walkeing one day in the street with my valet de chambre, who did weare a feather in his hatt, some workmen that were mending the street abused him and threw sand upon his cloathes, at which he drew his sword, thinkeing to follow the custom of France in the like cases. This made the rabble fall upon him and me that had drawn too in his defence, till we gott shelter in a hous, not without injury to our bravery and some blowes to ourselves."

At the beginning of September 1658 Cromwell died and in the next twelve months there was much jockeying for the power which had been invested in Richard Cromwell, his son. He did not want it and vacated it at the first opportunity.* After his resignation Sir George Booth was one of a committee of fourteen who were appointed by the excluded members to "go up and try whether they could find admittance to their places" in the revised Rump Parliament, but they "found such a restraint put upon them that they scarce could get into the lobby". Thereupon he became one of the leaders of the malcontents called "The New Royalists."

Many hearts were now favourable to the King and wished to see him brought back. The problem was how this should be accomplished. After a long exile Charles had learned to be patient. Those who had fought and suffered in the long struggle of the Civil War did not want to start another. Sir George Booth, however, was one of the few who had drive and energy and a pressing will to get on with the job. He was one of seven active supporters who wrote to the King on 7th June 1659 to the effect that the common talk seemed to be that there would be "no peace in England without the King", yet no one was willing to begin a war. This view is mirrored in the Verney correspondence where it is recorded that "public anxiety is growing, a terror of a new civil war seizes upon quiet people."

The enthusiasts for restoration of the Monarchy had great difficulty in co-ordinating their avowed supporters in many parts of the country. There was not only the problem of when to revolt but how to order the movements of all dissidents so that they

---

*He sent in his Abdication on 25th May 1659, and it was at once accepted by the House.

acted together. The end of July 1659 was considered propitious, and the plan embraced a number of simultaneous risings in many parts of the country. In their Declaration they were careful not to mention the King, but to stress simply the need for a free Parliament. They stated that they had determined to take arms to restore the Constitution, religion and liberty of the country and to act in "defence of ourselves and all others whoe will partake with us in vindication and maintenance of ye knowen lawes lyberties and properties of ye good people of ye nation who at present groane under illegal arbitrary and insupportable taxes and payments unknowne to our ancestors."

In the event this uprising proved to be a dismal failure. Sir George Booth, who was the leader of the Cheshire party, was the only one to cause the Government forces any trouble. Many of the plans became known before being put into action. To such a dynamic man as Sir George, the lack of cohesion and paucity of effort following months of underground work, must have been bitter. Mr Secretary Nicholas, in exile, a month later wrote, "there was great fault in some in England for not rising as they promised to join Sir G. Booth. His defeat is a great misfortune." Dr William Denton likewise put it "no considerable force, if any at all, up anywhere but with Sir G. Booth who, with others, are now proclaimed traitors." Another correspondent conveyed the information that "Sir George Booth rageth most horribly and vowse discovery of all those that promised to joine with him and most unworthily failed. I thinke few will blame, but rather pitty him to have to doe with unworthy men. But I hope our game is not wholly lost."

Following the collapse of this revolt on the part of the Royalist faction, the pattern of political life nevertheless began to change, and during the next six months the Army and Parliament increasingly opposed each other. It was, in fact, the crushing of Booth's force by Lambert and his army that gave the latter the notion that they were the all-important element in the country. The rising in Cheshire had been much better organised than anywhere else, and here is a brief account of it. By connivance of the Mayor and others, who had been approached successfully by Colonel John Booth, the gates of the city of Chester were opened at 4 a.m. on the morning of the 2nd August by one of the Sheriffs, Mr Pleyward. Sir George had then entered at once with his supporters and took possession of the city. Unfortunately this did not include the Castle, which was stubbornly defended by the Parliamentary Commander, Colonel Robert Croxton. This meant that the benefit of the garrison and magazine was denied to Sir George who, nevertheless, issued the Declaration for a free Parliament. Having secured Chester, but not its Castle, Booth left a force to hold it and set off for York, which was considered likely to welcome him. On the way he had word that the overall enterprise had misfired and that the Rump had despatched Lambert to meet him. So he turned back and took up a position at Winnington Bridge near Nantwich. At night the two forces were aligned on opposite banks of the river. With great speed early in the morning Lambert attacked and gained control of the bridge and quickly dispersed the royalists. It was said that Sir George had been defeated because his chief officers deserted him and his army did "a sudden shifftinge for themselves." Thus, by ill fortune and the instability of his officers and men he himself was compelled to escape. Major General John Lambert afterwards gave it as his opinion that Booth never appeared to have more than two thousand men, whereas he had horse and foot of over six thousand, mighty unequal odds. On Booth's side thirty were reported killed and many wounded, whereas the Parliamentary force suffered only trivial losses.

A Proclamation was then issued declaring Sir George Booth and his adherents rebels and traitors. He was on the run. His only chance lay in disguise, so he dressed himself in women's clothes and hoped to reach the coast and then cross to the continent. He reached Newport Pagnell in the company of others about seven o'clock one evening. Two of them arrived in advance at an inn and told the innkeeper they wanted a room for a gentleman and a gentlewoman who were coming along. They were shown one room after another, but none of them were considered suitable, until they looked at one of the poorest rooms which was within another. Sometime later another man arrived with "one in woman's habit"; the innkeeper being in the yard "offered the civility of helping the supposed gentlewoman down, but she refused and leapt off from the horse and went from him." Whilst supper was being prepared they sent for a barber and the three men were all trimmed by him, and then one of them taking a razor out of the case asked the barber how much he would take for it. The barber answered that to sell that one would spoil his set, but said he had a spare one at home which he would sell on being offered half a crown. He was asked to go and fetch it and return again with a washing bowl. As supper was now ready for them the maidservants came up to offer their services to the supposed gentlewoman who had all this while been in the inner room lying on the bed. She, however, refused to be helped in any way and declined assistance in putting off "her hoods, scarfs and safeguard". Supper over, they retired into the inner room after asking for "water, pipes, tobacco, wine, chamber-pot, and other necessaries." They shut the doors and placed a screen before the door of the inner room which led to a back pair of stairs. The innkeeper became suspicious of all this and was not deceived by one of the men who addressed the woman as Mrs Dorothy, and he guessed they might be about to shave her. He decided to consult a relation of his who was an apothecary in the town. Together they sought the Constables and told them the innkeeper thought he had observed a man in woman's apparel. They then summoned together over a dozen well armed men with swords and pistols, and set a guard of five men at the back stairs. The remainder then went up the front way and, knocking on the door, demanded it should be opened. After attempting to escape by the backstairs and finding that way blocked by the guard "they called for quarter". The apothecary advanced on Mrs Dorothy and set a pistol to her breast, she then "called for quarter." He demanded to know whether she was a woman or a man. She answered if he would spare her life she would tell him. "Speak the truth and I will." Thereupon she said she was a man. On being further pressed the secret was out. "I am," he said, "that unfortunate gentleman, Sir George Booth." The assault party was astonished and disarmed them all. The constables arranged for two of them to be taken to St Albans and two to Aylesbury. On the way Sir George said quite frankly that he had been misled and delivered by the gentry who had promised to help him. The next day he was taken to the Tower of London where he was made a close prisoner, and "no person be suffered to speak with him without leave of Parliament or by direction; and that he be kept from having the use of pen, ink and paper." His Uncle John and his brother Nathaniel had also been captured and shortly afterwards they were in the Tower too.

The captors were rewarded; £40 to the innkeeper, £10 to his servants, and £60 among those who brought him to London.

Newsheets had recently come into being, and the above type of news was livened up and turned into rich, salacious gossip in order to sell well. This is how it was reported in *Mercurius Pragmaticus,* a weekly intelligence from all parts, touching all affairs, designs, humours, conditions, carriages, and practices of all sorts of people.

"From Newport Pagnel

There came a more certain relation of the taking of Sir George Booth, he came into the Inn in woman's apparell. A gentleman stood by and perceiving such a bona roba*, thought by his confident carriage that he had been a courtesan; whereupon the gentleman made his applications to him by way of extraordinary curtesie, but finding him very coy and hard hearted, he resolved in heat of blood to have ravish't this seeming gallant. Whereupon he threw Sir George upon the bed and taking up his coates he saw something that he expected not to see; at first he thought Sir George had been a Hermaphrodite but being at length without spectacles fully satisfied, he presently smelt the Plot and caus'd the He Madamoiselle to be apprehended. He is now in the Tower unravelling at London what he had been so long knitting in Cheshire."

Lord Mordaunt, in explaining to the King why the rising had not succeeded, attributed it partly to the failure to take Chester Castle and its magazine, which caused Booth to leave seven hundred men there. He thought also that some were deterred by the absence of the King, the Duke of York, or any considerable person. He went on to say that he thought that Sir George had been badly served with intelligence and that in the fight at the bridge many of his men had been insufficiently armed. He gave it as his opinion that Lord Derby and Sir Thomas Middleton had "behaved modestly" which suggests that he felt their support was not sufficiently energetic. They were both taken and put into prison. Many others were also arrested on suspicion and placed in preventive custody. The Earl of Derby was captured in the guise of a serving man.

Sir George Booth and all the prisoners were, of course, submitted to much interrogation, but because of the uneasy political situation no charge was laid and so he was not brought to trial, merely being held in the Tower indefinitely. His estates were, however, sequestered. In September Lady Booth, after she had been delivered of a child, came up to London and after some days was allowed to be with her husband in the Tower.

---

*A showy wanton (Shakespeare).

In the Clarke Papers under date 6th September, 1659 is this entry — "Sir George Booth, his Lady lately sent a letter to the Lord Bradshaw, desiring his mediation to the Parliament for mercy and favour to her husband. The Council ordered his Lordshippe to send an answer that the way for him to receive favour and mercy is to bee ingenuous and confesse the whole truth of what he knoweth in the late designed rebellion."

In December Charles wrote to Sir George from Colombe. How or when he received the letter is not known.

"Your handsome and considerable engagement gave me not only full satisfaction for your former actions but a tender sence of your particular misfortune and if it please God to bless me, neither you nor yours shall ever have cause to repent it. So signall a testimony as you have lately given of your inclinations to me, make me very willing to encourage the generous returnes of misled persons and to assure them they can no sooner acknowledge their error, than I shall have a value and esteeme for them. Your good friend, my Lord Mordaunt, hath given me a particular account of your proceedings by which I clearly finde you intended my restoration, and my Kingdom's tranquillity, and this induces me to give you the assurance of my being your very affectionate friend, Charles R."

On the other side Parliament graciously bestowed upon Lambert a jewel worth £1,000, a letter of thanks, and appointed a thanksgiving day.

As autumn turned into winter, discontent in the country continued to grow, and the struggle for power in London increased. Lambert sought to dominate Parliament, but in so doing fell out with Fleetwood, his C-in-C. The former, it was thought, had come to be sympathetic to a restoration, but every move had to be conducted with great caution and some degree of secrecy. This explains why the prisoners in the Tower were gradually treated more leniently, and on 22nd February 1660 Sir George Booth was released on security and the further disposal of his estates stopped. Monck with his army in the north had been invited to come south to restore authority. After he arrived he returned the excluded members to the House, and arrangements were made for summoning a new free Parliament. In March Sir George and his fellow prisoners were all pardoned and in April the Lords resolved that "they owne and declare that according to the ancient and fundamental lawes of the Kingdom the government is and ought to bee by King, Lords and Commons."

On 1st May the House of Commons resolved that "Sir George Booth do go to the Lords to let them know that this House is ready for a conference with the Lords as they desired." He returned with the answer that "The Lords desire it may be with what speed may be." A committee was appointed by the Commons to wait upon the King at Breda. Sir George Booth was one of those chosen, and he was the first man to kiss the King's hand on reaching him.

Charles II certainly remembered those who had served him well; £10,000 was awarded to Sir George as a mark of respect for his eminent services and great sufferings. At the coronation he was raised to the peerage as Baron Delamer.

Very soon after his return the King was inundated with Petitions for rewards or recompense for suffering by innumerable persons. Some of them give a picture of what had been endured.

Petition of John Aylett for the Governorship of Chepstow Castle granted him by H.M. in 1657 but then under Cromwell. He was kept prisoner for twenty weeks on Sir George Booth's business. He had raised a hundred horse at his own charge for the late King: at Colchester (the siege of) his horses were eaten by the soldiers and he sentenced to be shot but made his escape.

Petition of John Southcott for the Office of Receiver of First Fruits in Ireland void by the death of Rob. Wadden. He had served H.M. since his youth but was discovered, his estate seized, and he outlawed by Cromwell: returning to England by H.M.'s order was taken in Sir G. Booth's business and was many months in the Gatehouse.

Similarly William Gery for the place of Commissioner of Excise. His father lost his whole estate by adhering to the late King: he himself was plundered to his shirt and imprisoned for following Sir George Booth.

Col. John Daniell for the place of Surveyor General of Customs & Excise. He served the late King in Ireland and lost his estate: he was Q.M.G. in Sir G. Booth's rising and six months a prisoner in Chester.

George Duke for the office of Secretary to the intended Council of Trade. Statement of his services. He was engaged in late wars but was taken prisoner in December 1646 and kept in the New Prison in Thames Street on pump water and potage until April 1647. He was then turned out half dead and naked into Lambeth

Fields. He made his way back to Windsor where he lived and engaged in a design which was long continued to surprise the Castle for the King: he had spies at the Council of State and Cromwell's Council and spent large sums on intelligence and holding correspondence with H.M. and his friends. He raised 500 men for Sir George Booth's rising. He had often helped the King's friends with necessaries and money and thus spent 20 years and most of his fortune having lost £3,000 purchase money and £1,200 a year by suppression of his office in the Star Chamber.

Col. John Booth also pleaded for help. He lost £2,000 and his horses when Governor of Warrington, £6,374 when he was sent to the Tower, £1,800 in Lord Wilmot's business, £3,750 value of his plate, jewels, etc. stolen by his fanatic wife and her servant when he favoured Sir G. Booth's rising. He entreated payment of part of the above to save him from his creditors or the nomination of a baronet and a lease of the Manor of Berkhampstead, Co. Herts! In July 1660 Sir John Booth was granted the offices of Clerk Pronothary, and Clerk of the Crown and Keeper of the Records in the counties of Chester and Flint.

The spirit of toleration was in the air. Lambert, himself now a prisoner in the Tower, was — on Michaelmas Day — released at the request of Sir George Booth and General George Monck (these two were called by many people the English Georges). On the day of Lambert's release, a lioness in the Tower was delivered of three whelps, which was regarded as a good omen.

Thomas Bruce, second Earl of Ailesbury, who had married Lady Elizabeth Seymour, wrote that his worthy Uncle, Sir G. Booth, the first Lord Delamer, had said that he knew by woeful experience what it was to live under a tyrannical Commonwealth, and that he hoped in God that our happy establishment should never be shaken for the second time, but that if Almighty God for their sins should so order it, he went on to express his conviction that he would rather live under one despotic King than under five hundred. Ailesbury described Delamer as being "a man of worth and great morals and a true lover of his King and the established laws." Another writer described him in a letter . . . "I have always remarked in my Lord Delamer the great sentiments of honour, virtue and piety, may God preserve him from dangers."

12   A Famous Trial

JUST as William Seymour's early adventures had followed those of his grandfather, so Henry Booth was soon to simulate his father's rebellious attitudes and actions in the nation's affairs. Henry, who had been brought up in the Presbyterian tradition, became an avowed opponent of any return towards the papacy. The people were becoming alarmed by the inroads that the Jesuits were making into the religious life of the country, and this was suddenly fanned into flame by Titus Oates, and particularly by the murder of Sir Edmund Berry Godfrey, the magistrate before whom information had been laid of a Popish Plot in October 1678. This fired off a great hunt for and persecution of Roman Catholics, who were rumoured to be planning a sort of terrorist campaign. Whatever may have been behind it, the papists received a boomerang a hundred times more fierce. All this led on to the presentation of the Bill of Exclusion aimed at denying the succession to the Throne of the Duke of York, Charles II's brother, who had openly accepted and supported the Catholic faith. One faction wished the heir to be the Duke of Monmouth, Charles II's eldest illegitimate son, and a Protestant, and so tried to substantiate that there had been a royal marriage with Lucy Walters, his mother. But Charles would have none of it, and resisted all moves to depart from the legitimate succession. The other main opposing body to the Duke of York preferred going through the proper order of claim to the throne. They wanted the Duke's daughters, Mary and Anne, who were both anti-Catholic, to be next in succession. The former was married to the Prince of Orange and she was to be named heiress apparent. Charles continued to stand firm against both propositions. He had been cautious enough to send both the Duke of York and the Duke of Monmouth out of the kingdom while the storm raged. Eventually Titus Oates overstepped the mark and his perjury was exposed. As a result some relief thereby came to the afflicted Catholics, and the Duke of York was given leave to come back.

Not uncommonly when moderate opinion is satisfied, there remains a hard core of recalcitrant force that is still obdurate. This small number planned to act desperately for the Duke of Monmouth. A party of them were to gather at Rye House on the Newmarket Road and take both the King and his brother by surprise on their return from the races. An outbreak of fire in Newmarket caused them to leave early and the plot failed. The ringleaders were arrested, among them the Earl of Essex, Lady Beauchamp's brother, who was sent to the Tower and later took his life there.

Suspicion was spread over a much wider field and many were detained for questioning. Henry Booth was one of these, and in 1683 he had his first taste of the Tower*. In the previous year during August and September there had been meetings in Chester in support of the Duke of Monmouth. A letter written to the Countess of Yarmouth at that time stated "we are informed here of the Duke of Monmouth's coming to a race and private meetings two a week by my Lord Macclesfield, Lord Delamer, Sir John Bollen, Col. Whitley's and so amongst the rest of the phanatick party. It is high time for the King to look after him and be sure to gratify his old friends that lost their lands for the service of him and his father."

The enmity between Papists and Protestants in Cheshire and Lancashire was great and the Presbyterians were gathering together to consolidate the anti-Catholic party. A little later the writer of the above letter gave an account of the Duke of Monmouth's reception at Chester in September 1682. "About 6 o'clock Sat. he came accompanied with the Earl of Macclesfield, his son, Lord Colchester, Lord Delamer's son†, Sir John Manwaring, Col. Whitley, Mr Booth and a great company of citizens where his entertainment was at the Plume of Feathers, at 5/- a piece where the Duke sat, and 2/6 at the other table . . . the fanaticks as declared by themselves have gathered 1,000 guineas for the distressed prince as they call the Duke of Monmouth; they have great banks of money, powder and all sorts of ammunition; those that are for the King and His Royal Highness are afraid to speak and all this while the King's Commission for two great counties is in the Earl of Derby's hands. They openly drink the Duke of Monmouth's health and pray in private conventicles for his prosperity."

---

*His father must have been greatly worried by this. A letter dated 21st July says, "Lord Delamer and Lady came on Wed to towne upon their son's being put in the Tower".

†Henry Booth.

These letters written to the wife of a member of the Court, the Earl of Yarmouth, who was Treasurer of H.M. Household, incriminated to some degree all those present on such occasions. It is not surprising, therefore, that Henry Booth was arrested. He was not necessarily involved, of course, in the Rye House plot and indeed, there being no definite evidence against him, he was released.

The plot caused a revulsion of feeling throughout the country and when in February 1685 Charles became seriously ill and died, the succession of his brother to the Throne was accepted. The Duke of Monmouth was, however, determined to try to wrest the Crown from James II. With a plan concocted on the Continent for landings in Scotland and England, he accomplished the latter and landed at Lyme Regis. The rising in Scotland failed and although Monmouth got a following of a few thousand men, in a month he was defeated at Sedgmoor by the prompt action of James in sending trained troops against him. After a few days the Duke of Monmouth was captured and sent to the block.

Now began another great hunt, not only for supporters, but for any suspected sympathisers. The Bloody Assize of Judge Jeffreys was the result. Henry Booth had succeeded to the title of Lord Delamer on 8th August 1684 when his father died at his home, Dunham Massey. He was buried at Bowden Church in the family vault. Henry was already known as a staunch Whig, and following Monmouth's defeat, a Proclamation was published requiring him to appear within ten days before the Privy Council. On 26th July 1685 he was arrested and sent again to the Tower to await trial for High Treason. The special charge was that he had gone secretly to Cheshire with a view to inciting a rising in the North.

He was kept in the Tower without any further move being made against him. He wearied and on the 14th November he petitioned the Lords, but they were unable to order his trial as no bill had yet been found against him. A fortnight later he appealed by Habeas Corpus and with Sir Robert Cotton and John Crew Offley Esq. for want of prosecution they were admitted to bail. This was in the sum of £10,000 for four persons each and £20,000 in their own surety individually; a very great amount.

Eventually the trial took place in Westminster Hall in January 1686 before Jeffreys, presiding as Lord High Steward, and thirty peers who were all officers in the King's Household or Army or Lord Lieutenants. Lord Delamer must have felt his life in peril.

For some years Henry Booth had been violently opposed to Jeffreys who at one time was Solicitor-General to the Duke of York. In 1679 when the Exclusion dispute was raging Jeffreys who was now Recorder of London was as far as the Whigs were concerned persona non grata and as they held a majority in the City they strove to oust him from his office. Although Jeffreys was appointed Chief Justice of Chester in the spring of the following year he held on to the Recordership. This still further angered the Whigs, and a petition was submitted for his removal. That November Henry Booth spoke against him in Parliament. He wanted to unseat him in Chester as well as in London and he was very outspoken. "The County of which I serve is Cheshire", he said, "which is a County palatine; and we have two Judges peculiarly assigned to us by His Majesty. Our puisne judge I have nothing to say against, he is a very honest man for aught I know; but I cannot be silent as to our Chief Judge; and I will name him because what I have to say will appear more probable. His name is Sir George Jeffreys who I must say behaved himself more like a Jack-Pudding than with the gravity which becomes a Judge . . ." He went on to complain of his behaviour towards witnesses and of the delays caused by irregular Assizes in Chester.

Now six years later he was arraigned before this same man who had been advanced still further in the legal profession.

Thomas Bruce, Earl of Ailesbury, was the only peer of the King's Bedchamber who was not chosen, for the particular reason that James had not named him because he was Delamer's cousin. The King remarked that "he imagined it would not be an agreeable thing to sit on blood". Lord Delamer's mother and Lord Ailesbury's mother were sisters, and these two cousins had never seen things the same way. Ailesbury remained a most faithful servant of James and described Delamer as "a person of implacable spirit against the King and of a most sour temper of mind", others described him as a man of generous and noble nature.

Judge Jeffreys was said on this occasion to have "kept himself better than usual in bounds as to his tongue; however, he launched out sometimes". In this trial he and the Solicitor General*

---

*Heneage Finch.

insisted on a new piece of law not practised before; that if there was but one positive evidence to any one fact of high treason which was clear, that other evidence though it were but circumstantial concurring with that, was sufficient to find the prisoner guilty.

Delamer conducted his own defence throughout and sturdily stood up to Jeffreys, exhibiting considerable dexterity and ability.

The trial began by the Clerk of the Crown calling upon the Serjeant-at-Arms to make proclamation which he did thus: "O Yes! O Yes! O Yes! My Lord High Steward of England, his Grace doth straitly charge and command all manner of persons to keep silence and to give ear to the King's Majesty's Commission to his Grace my Lord High Steward of England upon pain of imprisonment."

The Commission was then read, his Grace, and all the Peers standing up bare-headed.

Then the Staff being carried between Garter, King of Arms, and the Gentleman Usher of the Black Rod, was with three reverences delivered upon the knee of his Grace and by him re-delivered to the Gentleman Usher of the Black Rod to hold during the service.

The Proclamation was then read by the Serjeant-at-Arms. This was followed by the delivery of the Writ by Sir Edward Lutwyche, one of his Majesty's Serjeants-at-Law and Chief Justice of Chester.

After the Lord High Steward (George, Lord Jeffreys) had taken his seat, the Peers by whom Henry Booth, Lord Delamer, was to be tried, were each summoned individually. One by one they then stood up, uncovered and answered "Here" and made reverence to the Lord High Steward. Apart from The Lord High Treasurer (The Earl of Rochester), The Lord President of H.M. Privy Council (The Earl of Sunderland), The Earl Marshal (The Duke of Norfolk), The Lord Chamberlain of H.M. Household (The Earl of Mulgrave), The Comptroller of H.M. Household (Lord Maynard), the Major-General of H.M. Ordnance (Lord Dartmouth), The Lord President of Wales (The Duke of Beaufort), The Treasurer of H.M. Household (Viscount Newport), there were also two Dukes, twelve Earls, one Viscount and four Barons. The trial began by the Lord High Steward addressing the prisoner:

L.H.S.　My Lord Delamer, the King being acquainted that you stand accused of High Treason, not by common report or hearsay, but by a Bill of Indictment found against you by gentlemen of great quality and known integrity within the County Palatine of Chester, the place of your residence, has thought it necessary in tenderness to·you, as well as justice to himself, to order you a speedy trial. My lord, if you know yourself innocent, in the name of God do not despond, for you may be assured of a fair and patient hearing, and in your proper time a free Liberty to make your full defence: and I am sure you cannot but be well convinced that my noble Lords, that are here your Peers to try you, will be as desirous and ready to acquit you, if you appear to be innocent, as they will to convict you if you be guilty. But, my Lord, if you are conscious to yourself that you are guilty of this heinous crime, give Glory to God, make amends to his vice-regent the King by a plain and full discovery of your guilt, and do not by an obstinate persisting in the denial of it, provoke the just indignation of your Prince, who has made it appear to the world, that his inclinations are rather to shew mercy than inflict punishment. My Lord, attend with patience and hear the Bill of Indictment that hath been found against you.

Then he called upon the Clerk of the Crown to read it. Before doing this he called out "Henry, Baron of Delamer, hold up thy hand."

There followed the first exhibition of the stuff he was made of, for Lord Delamer appealed at once to Lord Jeffreys and the following exchange took place —

Lord Delamer   My lord, I humbly beg your Grace would please to answer me one question, whether a Peer of England be obliged by the Laws of this Land to hold up his hand at the Bar, as a Commoner must do; and I ask your Grace this question the rather because in my lord Stafford's case it was allowed to be the Privilege of the Peers not to hold up their hands.

L.H.S.   My lords, this being a matter of the Privilege of the Peerage, it is not fit for me to determine it one way or the other, but I think I may acquaint your Lordships that in point of Law, if you are satisfied this is the Person indicted, the holding or not holding up of the hand is but a formality which does not signify much either way.

Lord Delamer   I humbly pray Your Grace's direction in one thing further, whether I must address myself to your Grace when I would speak or to your Grace with the rest of these noble Lords, my Peers?

L.H.S.   You must direct what you have to say to me, my Lord.

Lord Delamer   I beg your Grace would please to satisfy me whether your Grace be one of my Judges in concurrence with the rest of the Lords?

L.H.S.   No, my Lord, I am Judge of the Court but I am none of your triers. Go on.

The Clerk of the Crown then delivered the Indictment that Henry, Lord Delamer "a false traitor against the most illustrious and most excellent Prince James the second etc." had disturbed the "common tranquillity" and stirred up war and Rebellion to depose the King from the Throne. It was said that on 14th April in the first year of his reign he had conspired with other traitors "rebels in the County of Chester" to an Insurrection against the King. It was said he agreed to raise sums of money and numbers of armed men to take the Castle at Chester and its magazines. That he left London on 27th May for Cheshire and on 4th June did excite and persuade subjects against their duty of allegiance to the King at Mere in Cheshire.

At the end of the long Indictment he was asked "How say'st thou Henry, Baron of Delamer, art thou guilty of this High Treason whereof thou standst indicted and hast been arraigned, or not guilty?" He then showed his ability to match the lawyers in their wordy battles. "My Lord," he said, "I humbly beg the Indictment to be read again." Let it be read again, said Lord Jeffreys. At the conclusion Lord Delamer then spoke, "May it please your Grace, I humbly beg the favour to be heard a few words before I plead to the Indictment." To this Jeffreys replied that he must plead before he could say anything further, to which Delamer then said that he had something to offer for consideration which was a matter of Law. Further argument ensued in which the L.H.S. again stated that now was not the time for him to speak but to plead. Lord Delamer persisted and eventually was allowed to present a Plea which was read by the Clerk of the Crown. This was that as Parliament had only been prorogued and not dissolved he should not be tried or proceeded against for High Treason, except in the House of Peers and before the whole body of Peers there because of the Right and Privilege of the Peerage of the Realm. After lengthy reasoning he ended, "may it please your Grace and your noble Lords, I do not offer this Plea of any difference or distrust in my cause, nor out of any dislike I have to any of your Lordships that are here summoned to be my Triers; I cannot hope to stand before any more just noble, nor can I wish to stand before any others but your Grace and my Lords will pardon me if I insist upon it because I apprehend it a Right and Privilege due to all the Peerage of England, which, as it is against the duty of every Peer to betray or forego, so it is not in the power of anyone, or more, to waive it or give it up without the consent of the whole body of the Peers, every one of them being equally interested." Lord Jeffreys said, "What say you Mr Attorney?" Sir Robert Sawyer, Attorney-General, then gave his opinion that after a prorogation the Proceedings were properly before the High Steward by Commission. "Besides, my Lord," he proceeded, "Your Grace sees it is a Plea in paper and in English without any Counsel's hand," and he asked that it be over-ruled. Whereupon Delamer requested that a counsel might be assigned to him to put the Plea in form.

Further argument and time was then consumed between the L.H.S. the prisoner and the Attorney General about the privileges of Peers and cases appertaining to them. Finally Lord Jeffreys said, "If your Lordship have any mind to have counsel heard and your counsel be ready, we will hear them." Delamer answered, "If your Grace require of me to produce counsel presently and they to argue it immediately I must acquaint your Grace I cannot do it, for I have none here." The Plea was then definitely overruled and to the Charge being put to him for the third time Lord Delamer pleaded Not Guilty.

The Recorder, Sir Thomas Jenner, then outlined the case which was that Delamer had conspired with others to raise sums of money and numbers of armed men to make Rebellion against the King, which conspiracy had started in April at Mere in Cheshire, and that subsequently on 27th May he took a journey from London to Mere to accomplish these treasonable intentions.

The case rested on the activity of agents of the Duke of Monmouth, and it was said that he had looked upon Cheshire as one of his main supports and upon Lord Delamer as one of his chief assistants there. Lord Delamer was known to have taken himself out of town on 27th May, to have used the name of Brown, which was a pseudonym known to all his confederates, and to have made the journey by byroads.

The whole case, in the end, revolved round the credibility of one witness, an obscure fellow by the name of Thomas Saxton. He swore that about the time of the Duke of Monmouth's landing having been recommended by Lord Brandon to Lord Delamer, he met him at his house in Cheshire on the 4th June with Sir Robert Cotton and Mr Offley also present. The talk was about the rising there to aid the Duke, and Lord Delamer was to muster ten thousand men but had not yet the money to do so. All the other evidence was circumstantial. There was therefore just this one witness to be discredited. By examining a number of witnesses Delamer was able to prove that Sir Robert Cotton and Mr Offley were not in Cheshire at the time. Further, he was able to show that Saxton had himself been taken prisoner in the rebellion and was at that time in Newgate and might be swearing to save his own life. What Delamer still had to do was to explain his own movements which cast considerable suspicion upon him.

He admitted riding a devious route to Cheshire on the 27th May under the name of Brown, which he said was done because he had been summoned to the sick bed of one of his children and he had assumed the name of Brown because he had been told there was a warrant out for his arrest. To support his explanation for the hurried journey to Cheshire he was able to produce witnesses to confirm the illness of his child, including his mother, the Dowager Lady Delamer, who had sent for him. He had ridden by way of Hoddesdon where he spent the night of the 27th, and then to Hitchin and eventually reached his house at Dunham Massey near Altrincham by the 31st May. He still had to reveal why he could not have been at the supposed meeting with Saxton on 4th June. His account was that after only a short stay at home he was sent for to return to London because his other son, who was there with his wife, had also fallen seriously ill and she had perforce to ask him to come back. By 2nd June he was on the road again, this time making the journey via Coventry, on both occasions on horseback, with one servant and two friends. By 3rd June he was once more in the capital. To substantiate all this he called a physician, Sir Thomas Millington, who said he found the child very ill on the 28th May and he gave his opinion to Lady Delamer that he thought the child might "not escape". He had also told Sir James Langham, who was his neighbour in Lincoln's Inn Fields, and he was also called upon to confirm, but it was decided there was no need to hear him. Lord Delamer's two brothers, Vere and George, both testified he was in London from the 3rd to the 10th June. Then a Mrs Kelsey said she had received letters from Lady Delamer and from Mrs Vere Booth to say that Lord Delamer had arrived back in London on the night of the 3rd. When he was asked why he had gone by byroads and come back on the post road, he replied that when his wife summoned him to return she had also said that there was no warrant out for him. It all now hinged on the evidence of Saxton. Delamer was able to bring forth other witnesses who showed that Saxton was untrustworthy and deceitful. That settled it, and the Lord High Steward, in the final paragraph of his summing up said, "And if you do not believe the testimony of Saxton, whose testimony hath been so positively contradicted by divers witnesses of Quality, the Prisoner ought to be acquitted of this indictment. If your Lordships please, you may go together and consider it."

The Peers thereupon withdrew in their order according to Precedence with the Serjeant-at-Arms before them. After about half an hour they returned in the same order, and seated themselves as before. Once again they all had to answer their names by standing up, uncovering and saying "Here". Lord Jeffreys then asked, "My Lords, are you agreed on your Verdict?" The answer came back, "Yes." The Lord High Steward then took the Verdict Seriatim beginning with the puisne Peer in this manner —

"How say you, my Lord Churchill, is Henry, Baron of Delamer, guilty of High Treason whereof he stands indicted and hath been arraigned or not guilty?" The Lord Churchill stood up, uncovered, and laying his hand on his breast answered, "Not guilty, upon my Honour." And so did all the rest of the Peers. The Lord High Steward then addressed the prisoner at the Bar, discharging him. Finally the Serjeant-at-Arms called out, "O-Yes! My Lord High Steward of England, his Grace, straitly willeth and commandeth all manner of persons here present to depart hence in God's peace and the King's, for his Grace my Lord High Steward of England now dissolves the Commission. God save the King."

At which words his Grace, taking the White Staff from the usher of the Black Rod, held it over his own head and broke it in two, thereby dissolving the Court.

There was no doubt that according to the evidence and the law he was rightly acquitted, but there were some who felt otherwise of his actions. The Earl of Peterborough, one of the Peers who tried him, and a man of hot and fiery temper, when he had given his verdict as those had done before him, whispered aside to his neighbour "Guilty, By God!"

The next day the King declared that Saxton should be indicted for perjury and then hanged for high treason. To Lord Ailesbury James said, "Well, my Lord, your cousin escaped narrowly; he may see how fair a trial he hath had and by the Grace of God I shall never be for taking away the life of the least of my subjects by indirect ways, and they shall have as fair a game for their lives as your cousin hath had; and this depend on, and tell it to all as you have occasion."

After the acquittal Lord and Lady Delamer returned to Dunham Massey, their home in Cheshire. She had cheered him constantly throughout this time, and while he was in the Tower, she had stayed with him when permitted to do so. For a time he lived quietly in the country enjoying his family life, but it was not long before he was again in the limelight.

Abdication of a Sovereign

FOR the next two and a half years James endeavoured to reward Roman Catholics with patronage by promoting them to positions of importance such as Lord Lieutenants, senior officers in the Army, and of course political appointments. For example, in August 1687 he visited Chester and made Lord Molyneux, who was a popish recusant convict, his Lord Lieutenant of Lancashire, displacing the Earl of Derby. He antagonised all other shades of Christian belief so that they became more closely welded against him. When on top of this, because they had refused to countenance the reading of the Declaration of Indulgence in all churches, he proceeded to charge seven Bishops, including Archbishop Sancroft, with seditious libel, there were few supporters for the King. The Bishops' acquittals aroused such acclamation everywhere that it became evident that James would be sustained in his actions by only a very few. He certainly had a large trained army, but its loyalty in such circumstances might be equivocal. When the crunch came in the autumn of 1688 defections were quickly apparent. James, indeed, was left with only a handful of truly loyal servants, like the Earl of Ailesbury.

The trial of the Bishops would seem to have been a real turning point and so, from the end of June 1688, approaches were made to William of Orange to come to the rescue of the nation. The future had become darker still for all sections of the population who were opposed to Roman Catholicism when the Queen gave birth to a son, for there was a real fear of a papist succession. The great political and religious ferment that had been aroused by the designs of James, particularly against the Protestants, now agitated Lord Delamer's conscience. He was disturbed by the introduction of Jesuits and Roman Catholic priests into the country, and he feared that it would be committed to Popery. His father had always subscribed to the principles of Presbyterianism; he himself had joined the Church of England and was truly alarmed at the possibility of the Church of Rome becoming dominant.

At this point James at last realised he had gone too far in supplanting worthy men in important offices by Roman Catholics for no other reason than to exert Catholic influence, but it was too late. In desperation the King began to reverse many of these appointments and the Earl of Derby was asked in October to resume his position of Lord Lieutenant for Lancashire and Cheshire in the place of Lord Molyneux, the ardent papist.

This invitation called for a careful appraisal of the situation because already there had been correspondence with William with a view to ensuring a Protestant monarchy. Lord Derby was advised by his friends to consult with Lord Delamer and others about the re-acceptance of the Lieutenancies. They decided it would be a sensible thing to do as both counties were pestered by papists and were the main route for Irish Catholics to enter the country.

By the end of October plans for William to come over were well advanced, and Lord Derby met Lord Delamer secretly to co-ordinate arrangements. There had, however, been a slight hitch in the appointment of the former to the lieutenancy because the actual Commission for it had not arrived, the Earl of Sunderland, displaced as Secretary of State, having left the country for Holland. Lord Derby then communicated with the new Secretary, Lord Preston, but the actual document from which only he could command authority did not reach him until the 8th November, and he was not sworn in before the next day. Much had happened in the meanwhile.

Prior to that the two peers, Derby and Delamer, had made a secret arrangement that when William landed Delamer should declare for him and quickly gather a following around him. Derby was then to raise the militia, with his authority as Lord Lieutenant, and to quarter some of them near Delamer's house to protect his family. It was also agreed that Lord Derby would not take action until Lord Delamer had moved, in order not to alarm the half-hearted.

The Prince of Orange having reached Torbay landed at Brixham on the 5th November. How long it took for news of this to reach the North is conjecture. A letter from London dated 13th November to the Earl of Derby at Knowsley gave the information that "the western letters tell us that the Prince of Orange landed but 16,000 men and 5,000 horse and those were numbered by some persons of discretion; that the Earl of Shrewsbury, the Earl of Macklesfield, and Lord Wiltshire came to Exeter on Wednesday, but the Prince of Orange did not come thither till Friday and lodged himself at the Deanery." The letter-writer continued by saying that the horse were pretty good but the foot very ordinary; that some of the troops had reached Honiton and Tiverton and were thought to be heading for Bristol where they hoped to obtain 7,000 pairs of shoes and a similar number of yards of cloth. There was more news too showing that all was not well with the King's forces, for Lord Colchester, with a troop of Guards and other officers, including a Brigadier, were absent and supposed to have gone to the Prince of Orange.

There were stories too of civilian uproar, of a rabble trying to pull down the "Popishe chapel at St James'", and of priests removing their goods being set upon and two cartloads of their belongings burnt on Holborn Hill and in Smithfield, "whereupon the guards were sent to suppress them and with orders to fire with bullet, which they did and killed 4 or 5 and forced the rest to retreat."

On the 14th November a letter from London to Roger Kenyon, Lord Derby's agent, displayed anxiety about what was happening in the North. . . ". . . and we have been in expectation of his calling the militia together every day. Now, good cousen, we desire to be informed by you of the truth in that matter, and what you doe conceive that his Lordship does design to doe, for we doe apprehend the consequences of sitting still at the time to be as fatal as those of doeing something, provided always that a man have but the good luck to doe that little thing that he does wisely; but hit or miss, we are at his Lordship's devotion and if we may be thought worthy to understand his mind, nobody shall be more ready to the utmost extent of our power to serve him than we."

On the 15th Lord Delamer let Lord Derby know he was rising and told his tenants and all the others who followed his lead "that Lord Derby would go the same way." Derby, however, had not yet intimated to his Deputy Lieutenants how he proposed to act, and this premature release of his intention startled several D.L.'s making them averse to helping to raise the militia.

Then Lady Delamer let it be known on the 19th November that Lord Derby had promised part of the militia at Altrincham to be put in defence of their house. This was regarded by Lord Derby as a disclosure of a secret pact between them. The militia was not raised until the 21st and on the 24th word was sent to Lady Delamer by Lord Derby to assure her of his "constant care for her safety." Two days later he quartered several companies of foot five miles from Dunham with secret orders that if any force were observed approaching that property, they were to defend it and he would then follow with his troops.

Uneasiness was increasing everywhere. Colonel Gage, who commanded a Romish Regiment in Lancashire, decided to move into Chester. They arrived in the city at night and were put into the Town Hall. All the regimental quarters were already occupied by the recently raised Militia, which had been summoned together by twenty-nine newly appointed Deputy Lieutenants, all of whom were Protestant. In due course all these troops declared for the Prince of Orange. Then, in early December, wild rumours spread throughout the county of Cheshire of burnings and killings committed by Irish papists, and Lord Derby sent word to Lady Delamer assuring her that he would send a force for her protection if needed.

What had Lord Delamer been doing during this time? From Cheshire he had marched his followers to Nottingham, and then on to Birmingham, where on the 26th November his force was increased by five hundred horse, all well armed. They went to Edgbaston Hall where they seized a great quantity of arms. It was no doubt difficult to keep abreast of what was happening elsewhere, but early in December Delamer must have received a disturbing report of how things were going in Cheshire. Indeed, what he heard made him furious and he wrote his mind in no uncertain terms:

"For the Earle of Derby at Knowsley in Lancashire.

December 10th

My Lord,

Had I foreseen how backward your Lordshipp is in doing your part, I should have told your Lordshipp that it was not worth the while to mention your name to the Prince; for you cannot forgett you promised to raise the militia immediately and to quarter Bucklow Hundred at Altrincham, and that if, in case the Papists committed an outrage, or rose in armes, that then you would fall upon them and leave neither foot nor branch. How far have you made this good, your Lordshipp can best tell but I hear on the 3rd instant, no militia of Bucklow Hundred was up, and though the Papists made an attempt to burn my house, yet I don't hear of any resentment your Lordship has expressed against it. Your Lordship must think you cannot be esteemed by the Prince, or those with him, as a man that has given any assistance to the cause and I believe the nation will have the same opinion of you. But God be praised, we need none of your help, or if we be distressed, we shall not seek to you for succor. Thus you have the opinion off,

Your humble servant,

Delamer.

P.S. Just now I hear you have suffered the Papists to possess themselves of Chester."

One can feel his ardent spirit seething with anger. Lord Derby's answer was that no papists were at any time near Lord Delamer's house, which was not burnt at all; that the papist regiment never possessed Chester Castle or governed the City, but were merely quartered there for a fortnight and three days and were then taken prisoners by the Governor and Militia.

Was the threatened incendiarism just rumour or had some real intent taken place? Lt. Colonel W. Fleming wrote to his brother that "Squire Mullinax was going with two companies to burn Lord Delamer's house but the country rose to the number of 4 or 5,000 men with such arms as they had, to defend the house, and Mr Mullinax turned home again." Could this be Lord Molyneux, the papist, the former Lord Lieutenant?

The cautious approach to the problem of containing the popish regiment adopted by Lord Derby would not have been in accord with Lord Delamer's dashing temperament. He had already been in action before he tore off his diatribe and he had received a slight wound in the hand in a skirmish with a party of Lord Ashton's soldiers.

Meanwhile, William of Orange moved slowly and steadily forward on his march to London. He had written to Lord Delamer on 2nd December and addressed the letter to Gloucester.

"My Lord,

I have heard so worthy a character of you that I am glad to find you so frankly embarked in the same design with me; and you may depend on me to show you all the kindness in my power. If your occasions will allow of it I shall be glad to see you at Hungerford next Friday night; but you must send me notice of your coming the night before your arrival that I may direct quarters for you and your troops, and that my out-guards may let you pass to me.

I am your most affectionate friend,
Prince d' Orange."

The King's Army at Salisbury was exhibiting signs of being a broken reed. It was inexorably borne in upon James that he could call on none for help. The citizens of London wondered what was going to happen; they were laying in large stocks of provisions as if either in fear of some siege or for a free entertainment of guests. As the Prince of Orange progressed he issued Proclamations, and the third one was read by a merchant at the Exchange, a copy of which was given to the Lord Mayor who let the King know of it. The main substance of it was to require all Roman Catholics to lay down their arms and vacate their offices on pain of receiving no quarter. No wonder the King had little sleep except for some induced by opiates.

There had been very little actual fighting apart from some isolated skirmishes occurring here and there. Near Bruton a party of horse and dragoons belonging to the King met some of the Prince's foot. The Commanding Officer of the horse troop and three others were killed, while nine foot soldiers succumbed, seven were taken prisoner, three were wounded and one, the sole survivor of a party of twenty, escaped.

William exercised a stern discipline over his troops and did not hesitate to make an example of any case of disobedience. Two of his men were hanged for stealing a chicken, and he told the rest that they had money enough and the only time to steal was when they were in need of it. It is not surprising to read a report that stated "His soldiers are mighty civil." They needed to be.

Lord Delamer's force continued to grow in size as more and more elected to ride under his banner. There were risings elsewhere in the county. Lord Preston, the new Secretary of State, "wished His Majesty could spare troops to put a stop to the progress of my Lord Delamer and those who join with him."

By the middle of December James was in a hopeless position. The Prince of Orange had reached Windsor and on the 17th December he sent a message to the King, who was still in London, advising him to go to Ham to the Duchess of Lauderdale's house, couched in these words: "it is thought convenient for the greater quiet of the city and for the greater safety of his person that he doe remove to Ham, where he shall be attended by guards who will be ready to preserve him from any disturbance." This letter was delivered between one and two a.m., the Earl of Midleton being lighted into the Bedchamber by a Page of the Backstairs to tell the King that three Lords desired to speak to him. They were the Marquis of Halifax, the Earl of Shrewsbury, and the Lord Delamer, who had been chosen by William for this task. The King's reply was that the Duchess was in Scotland and the house was very cold and uninhabited and he would rather go to Rochester. That was the end of any resistance from James.

Delamer's part in this mission must have been carried out with dignity and courtesy because the King was later heard to remark "that the Lord Delamer whom he had used ill treated him with so much more regard than those to whom he had been kind and from whom he might better have expected it."

King James II finally left the shores of England on the 23rd December. The Revolution had been almost bloodless.

14   Panegyric for Two Brave Souls

A FTER the accession of William and Mary, Lord Delamer was made a Privy Councillor in February 1689. The feud which had developed between him and the Earl of Derby was to continue because in May Delamer was appointed Lord Lieutenant of Cheshire, Lord Derby having previously held both the Lancashire and Cheshire Lieutenancies. Greatly slighted by this, and so upset and resentful, he resigned the Lancashire office. Those who spoke on his behalf held the view that he had done many things which in others would have been regarded as meritorious, but that he had been badly treated by Lord Delamer. It was emphasised that the House of Derby had held these appointments for a very long time and both were held by Lord Derby at the accession of James II, so rather than hold Lancashire alone he preferred to have neither. In June Lord Brandon was appointed to Lancashire in his stead. This was greatly disliked by the people of that county, and a Petition was in consequence submitted — "It will not easily be forgott in Lancashire that Lord Brandon has had two pardons — one for murder, another for high treason* — and that after the late Kinge had forgiven him, he was a violent asserter of that King's dispencing powers to the highest degree in that county and in that raigne when he was a Deputy Lieutenant to the Lord Mollineux, a grand papist . . . In the late Revolution this Earle of Derby acted his part and was in his place much more instrumentall than any for the accession of their present majesties to the Crown. There is no blott in his ancestor's escutcheon; they have born the office of Lord Lieutenants of Lancashire and Cheshire about two hundred years except in the time of the horrid rebellion in which the Earle's grandfather for his loyalty lost his life and so a great part of his estate. And what has this Earle of Derby done soe much to demeritt as to be turned out of these Lieftenancies?" Lord Brandon had been condemned some years before for breaking a boy's neck in a drunken fit, but obtained the King's pardon. He

---

*Following the Rye House plot Lord Brandon had been tried for treason and found guilty. The sentence of death was deferred and eventually he was set free and pardoned. At an earlier date he had been convicted of murder "for breaking a boy's neck when he was in his cups"

was also a partisan of the Duke of Monmouth and was tried and condemned but reprieved in December 1685. He was the son and heir of the Earl of Macclesfield.

Very early in the new reign trouble came from Scotland and Ireland. Troops were despatched beyond the border and any that could be spared were sent to Ireland. The Army was indeed scattered because William had formed the Grand Alliance against France and John Churchill was already abroad with an English brigade serving alongside the Dutch on the Sambre.

Lady Chaworth* kept her brother† abreast of the news, "1689 May 11. This day came out the Proclamation of war with France. Lord Delamer went yesterday with some say 1,000 others 2,000 men for to goe horse for Scotland and thence to Ireland. Others say only to settle the militia in his counties." At this time in Ireland the Protestants had been forced to withdraw into Ulster by the Catholic Earl of Tyrconnel, who had raised a large army for James who was already in that country, having landed at Cork. With the aid of French money to sustain his followers, the deposed King made his way to Dublin where he was acclaimed. His Irish adherents' chief design was to rid themselves of the Protestants and English overlords who had all withdrawn to the north and had become beleaguered in Londonderry, which they defended desperately. The siege lasted for one hundred and five days, causing very great hardship, some having died of hunger and others of malnutrition and fever. With only two days' supply of food left relief came, and a ship from England broke through the blockade. It had needed a stern Governor and Commander to hold out, and at one time he had erected a gibbet in the middle of the town and hanged nine who were for surrendering. When the garrison had been revictualled and revitalised they attacked the encircling force with such determination that the Catholic troops were driven back to Dublin.

There is a further reference to Lord Delamer in a Newsletter but it is not clear where he was at the time. It may be he was in Cheshire organising the militia and supplying reinforcements and receiving prisoners from Ireland. It states "One Mr Donneller, an Irishman, formerly of the Middle Temple has brought several

---

*Daughter of the eighth Earl of Rutland, married to third Viscount Chaworth.

†John, first Duke of Rutland. He supported the 1688 Revolution and was created a Duke in 1703.

letters, one to Lord Delamer, to request an exchange of prisoners and several other trifling complaints but being supposed to be a person sent to attempt some dangerous design, he is taken into the messenger's hands."

Lord Delamer continued to be very active in support of William and Mary and was regarded as a leader of substance. His service was recognised and in April 1690 he was created Viscount Delamer and Earl of Warrington, with limitation to the heirs male of his body. In view of the expenses incurred by him he was given a pension of £2,000 and a grant of all land discovered in five or six counties belonging to the Jesuits.

Religious intolerance which had been the cause of the change of royal allegiance, could not be cleared away at once. William made attempts to alter the liturgy of the Church of England, to reform its ecclesiastical courts, and to take away all penal laws from non-conformists, but the Church party was opposed to too much leniency. However, he obtained for the Protestant dissenters permission to hold separate gatherings, but they had to profess their belief in the Holy Trinity. This helped the position of all except the Socinians* (Unitarians) who then began to disseminate their views anonymously through the press. This aroused the papists to incite a popular outcry against the Act of Toleration which was regarded as satisfactory by Presbyterians and moderate Churchmen.

The alarm felt by this caused the Earl of Warrington as Lord Lieutenant of Cheshire to make a speech in Chester in April 1692. He regarded the act of indulgence as a prudent, necessary and pious work, and referring to earlier times said, "The laws against dissenters have ever been stretched and executed beyond their genuine and natural intent or construction; several laws have been put into execution against them, which were plainly and directly made for other purposes, by which the laws themselves have suffered violence; while more diligence and care has been employed to punish people for non-conformity, than to reform their lives and manners." He then gave his view that any who spoke against the ordinance should be regarded as sowers of the seeds of division in the state.

---

*A sect formed by Laelius and Socinus, two Italian theologians in the sixteenth century, who denied the divinity of Christ.

This speech is said to have had a profound effect in Cheshire and Lancashire and the rising tumult there began to subside, the Protestant dissenters being allowed to meet together in tranquillity.

*   *   *

In the year after his elevation to an Earldom a grievous blow fell upon Lord Warrington. His wife died. She, the only niece of Sarah, Duchess of Somerset, had supported him in all his troubles and for a time shared his confinement in the Tower. Now he was bereft of her ever-present help and when she passed away in 1691 he must have been profoundly affected.

The funeral of the Countess of Warrington took place at Bowden Church and the Warden of the Collegiate Church, Manchester, the Rev. Richard Wroe D.D. preached the sermon.

Barely three years later, early in January 1694, the Earl of Warrington died. It must have been a severe winter. Alice Kenyon wrote to her husband Roger, who was a Member of Parliament, on the 12th January, when he was at Westminster. She felt he would suffer much in London from the cold weather and prayed that he would keep as warm as he could, suggesting that he took "something in thy pocket to the House to supp off". She had heard that Mr Nathaniel Hilton had died and that his body "comes along" with Lord Warrington's. She then adds as a postscript "Cosin Hilton was telling me he heard you are doeing something about clippers; hee says hee thinks the best way to lessen the number of them would be to abate the value of clipt moneys. He remembers it was so when he was a boy; a shilling went but for 9d and halfe a crown for 18d."

On 15th January the Rev. Dr Richard Wroe also wrote to Roger Kenyon, M.P. "My Lord Warrington's corpse will be brought to Bowden tomorrow in the night and a friend of his is to say something of him there on Sunday which you may imagine I am at present very busy with having a hard task both through short warning and a very critical subject." He did pay a tribute in an address of considerable length, during which he said of Lord Warrington, "His honour was the jewel he most highly prized, which he could not be tempted to forfeit or prostitute; and I doubt not to affirm, that his conscience was the rule and measure of it, which two, when joined together, render a man truly great, honourable and noble. For men to pretend honour

) Sir Harbottle Grimston, second Baronet.
Engraving from Harding's Biographical Mirror, 1796, from picture by Lely.

(x)   Henry Booth, second Lord Delamer and first Earl of Warrington.

By kind permission of the Earl of Stamfor

(xii)   Lady Delamer, wife of the first Lord.   *By kind permission of the Earl of Stamfor*

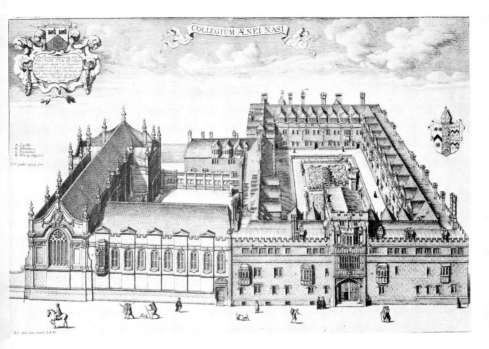

(xiii)   Brasenose College, Oxford.   *From a print by D. Loggan in Oxonia illustrata, 1675.*

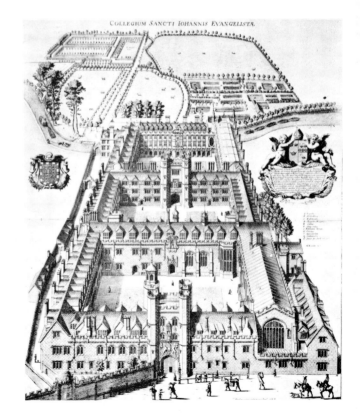

xiv)   St John's College,
        Cambridge.

*From a print by D. Loggan
in Cantabrigia illustrata,
1690.*

(xv)   Tomb of Sarah, Duchess of Somerset.   (xvi)   Tomb of Thomas Thynne.

Both from John Dart's Westmonasterium, c 1723.

(xvii)   St Margaret's Hospital or Green Coat School.

From a drawing of 1812 by courtesy of the Archivist, City of Westminst

xviii)   The Somerset Hospital and the Old Bath Road, Froxfield.
By courtesy of the Rev. P. E. Bird, Vicar of Froxfield.

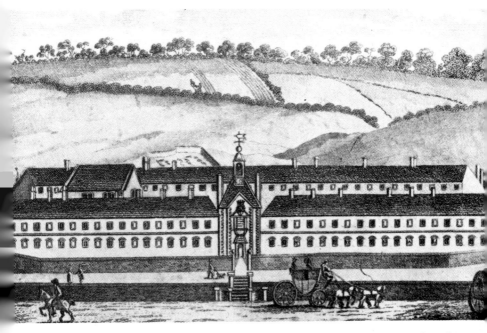

ix)   The Somerset Hospital at Froxfield.   *By courtesy of the Rev. P.E. Bird, Vicar of Froxfield.*

(xx)   The Grammar School at Tottenham, engraved by W. C. Walker.
By courtesy of W. S. H. Ashmore, F.I.A., Controller of Libraries, Borough of Haringey.

without conscience is to sacrifice to an idol of their own setting up; but when honour is guided by conscience, it becomes sacred and venerable." After further exposition along similar lines he continued, "But to come closer to my subject, with which I must hasten, lest I injure your patience; and this I should hazard, were I to trace him through all his commendable qualities and praiseworthy accomplishments." He went on, "I leave it to his servants and domestics, who best know him, to proclaim him the best of masters, and honour his memory as they ought, with a due testimony of his freedom, affability, and kindness to all that were dependents or retainers to him. It is a part of the imperfection of this state, that we learn the value of most things more by the loss than the enjoyment of them; which will be verified doubtless, in them who have lost an indulgent master, a courteous patron, an obliging benefactor. I appeal to all the neighbourhood, and as many as had the honour or opportunity to resort to Dunham, for the greatness of his hospitality, his generous reception, and obliging entertainment; a quality, I must needs say, the less to be wondered at in him, since it has been so long hereditary to that family, that it now pleads prescription, and is become an usage immemorial:— May it remain and be continued as a mark of honour to that noble house and the lasting character of its posterity! I appeal to his country, for his courage and resolution to venture himself for the good of it, when he thought it in apparent danger; and leave the world to judge of the hazard he underwent to his person, estate and family, and all that was near and dear to him. That love to his country which was so remarkable in all parts of his life appeared very particularly at the time when he was to be tried for imputed treason. For when there seemed need of the advice of many of the best lawyers to help him to fence against the arts of the counsel employed against him, he absolutely refused the assistance of any lawyer who had been blemished with any accession to the calamities of the times. Indeed his own wonderful defence of himself superseded the use of any lawyer at his trial; and I may appeal to written evidence of his ability in speaking and managing that cause (of the highest nature and concern that could befall him, which often confounds men's intellect) when he defended himself to the great joy and satisfaction of his friends, the envy and surprise of his enemies and the wonder, if not astonishment, of all that heard him. Yet did he not, in all this, sacrifice to his own net, or ascribe the success of his release and deliverance to his own wit and policy, to his parts and management, but GAVE THE GLORY TO GOD, and paid the annual tribute of praise and thanksgiving to Him for it, by setting apart that day as a day of grateful memorial, which he solemnly and religiously observed with his family every fourteenth day of this month of January; this very day which now by the providence of the All-Wise Disposer, is become the day of his obsequies, as if prophetically chosen for a remarkable vicissitude that which was before a day of jubilee must now be written in black letters, and made a day of sadness and mourning and so become doubly observable to his honourable posterity.

His gratitude to God was rightly accompanied with charity to men and he solemnised that day, not only with prayer and praises, and other offices of devotion to God but also at the same time clothed and fed twenty seven poor people, according to the number of peers that acquitted him that he might increase his own rejoicing and gratitude with the joy and refreshment of the poor and indigent."

Dr Wroe then mentioned that his charity was not limited to an annual distribution for "almost every day was a dole-day at his door; but particularly every Friday in the year when a larger distribution was made to the poor and necessitous."

Richard Wroe was Vicar of Bowden from 1674-1684 and so must have known the family intimately for both Lord and Lady Warrington were deeply religious. The day on which he was buried was not only the anniversary of his deliverance in Westminster Hall, but was also the day after what would have been his forty-second birthday. His wife died when she was only thirty-eight. The title passed to his eldest son, George, who lived on till 1758, when the Earldom became extinct, but his daughter Mary married Henry Grey, fourth Earl of Stamford, and that family thereby inherited Dunham Massey.

Just as Sir Harbottle Grimston had left an exhortation on the conduct of life for his son so in similar manner did the Earl of Warrington write at some length advice to his children.

It was addressed to "My dear Sons" and went on "Having lived in an Age where a few months has produced great Revolutions and Troubles the mischievous effects of which having fallen very heavy as well upon my own person as upon my family. For before I was nine years old I saw my father a close prisoner in the Tower seven months for his Loyalty to his King and Country and by little less than miracle thence delivered; and having but just passed over my thirty fourth year, for the next day (after having been a close prisoner in the Tower three times) I was tryed for my Life for adhering to the Interest of my Country. And now in my thirty seventh year perceiving a boisterous storm to approach by which I may probably expect to be swept away in the common calamity and consequently, must leave you all very young; I think it to be the best thing I can do for you to advertise you of the rocks and precipices which by means of my troubles and sufferings I have discovered. And to that end it is that I recommend to you the following discourse".

It is a lengthy document. His deeply rooted religious convictions are evident throughout. The day was to begin and end with God — "Let not any business prevent you from spending sometime in private devotion both morning and evening".

He recommended that before entering into public service his sons should be sure that they were in good measure qualified for it, and he insisted that it should be undertaken for God's glory and the good of the country and not in order to gratify ambition. He also counselled them that they should "be easie of access".

Lady Bountiful

W HEN Sarah became a widow for the second time she was forty-three. Although she had been estranged from her husband for some time she must have become attached to the Seymour family and presumably enjoyed the dignity conferred by the title. A month before Charles, sixth Duke of Somerset, was married, her position was made certain. She was granted by Royal Warrant licence to enjoy the precedence of a Duchess "notwithstanding any marriage she may hereafter contract". When the new Duke married on 30th May 1682 she was at once identified by the style and title of Sarah, Duchess of Somerset.

It may be that she was already contemplating remarrying before the Royal Warrant was issued. Henry Hare, the son of the first Lord Coleraine, had succeeded his father in October 1667. He became a widower on the death of his wife in 1680. From the Verney papers it appears that his name had been linked with hers before she married Lord John Seymour. Now they were both free again and in July 1682, when she was fifty, he became her third husband and she his second wife. In the following year she cautions her husband in a letter, "not eat too much musmillion* — Lord Conway has just died of a surfeit of it".

Henry Hare's father, the first Baron, had inherited a considerable fortune from his great uncle, Sir Nicholas Hare, who had been the Master of Requests and Master of the Rolls, and also from his Uncle Hugh, who was Master of the Court of Wards. The first Lord Coleraine's mother, on the death of his father, had married the Lord Chief Justice, the Earl of Manchester, as his third wife. This gave the young Hare, as he was then, entry to the Court where he became a favourite. He was a man of accomplishment, good at languages, fond of travelling, and a classical scholar also. In 1625 he purchased the manor of Tottenham and he married the second daughter of his step-father by his first wife. Of this marriage Henry Hare was the eldest surviving son and he became much

---

*Muskmillion, i.e. Muskmelon, originally an oriental melon with a musky scent but later applied to the Common Melon grown in England (O.E.D.).

attached to Tottenham. He wrote an account of the place, and the manuscript is now in the Bodleian, and was added as an appendix to the *History and Antiquities of the Parish of Tottenham High-Cross* by Oldfield and Dyson 1790.

He must have induced a similar enthusiasm for the place in his second wife, Sarah, because she supported Tottenham Grammar School with her beneficence and so enlarged its influence. In 1966 this school was joined to another, the Rowland Hill School, to become comprehensive under a new education pattern. The combined school now rejoices in the name, Somerset School, in her honour.

The marriage lasted just over ten years, when Sarah died leaving Lord Coleraine a widower for the second time, and later he took a third wife. Luttrell, under date 15th October 1692, records "Dutchess Dowager of Somerset lies very ill." She died ten days later and the same diarist estimated she was worth about £50,000 which, in our present currency, would be in the region of one million pounds or more.

She did not postpone making her Will until the onset of serious illness, but had already considered and settled this over six years before her death. Two thoughts may have induced her to do this in 1686. The first would be the reservation made in her marriage settlement that she had power to dispose of her own estate, and secondly her desire to lay out this considerable fortune for the benefit of the poorer part of the community by way of education for the young and relief of hardship for the old. This she did while yet providing for and remembering surviving relations, friends and servants who all benefited in greater or lesser degree by her care and thought for them.

The Will is a massive document of over sixty pages and it commences in the approved style of those times.

"In the name of God. Amen. I Sarah Dutchess Dowager of Somersett late wife of the Right Noble John, Duke of Somersett deceased and now the wife of the Right Honourable Henry Lord Coleraine being in good health of body and of perfect mind memory and understanding (praise be God) yet knowing the certainty of death and the uncertainty of the time thereof and haveing in and by my marriage agreement with my now husband Henry Lord Coleraine and in and by the conveyances and settlement of mine estate made in pursuance thereof reserved to myselfe a power to dispose of mine estate reall and personall (although under coverture) do this seventeenth day of May in the year of our Lord God 1686 and in the second year of the raigne of our Soveraigne Lord James the second by the Grace of God, King of England Scotland and Ireland Defender of the Faith, make and ordaine this my last Will and Testament in writing and manner and forme following. First and principally I recommend my immortall soule into the hands of God who gave it, assuredly trusting by and through the merritorious death and passion of Jesus Christ my blessed Saviour and Redeemer to receive full pardon and full remission of all my sins and a glorious Resurrection amongst the just, My body I leave to the earth from whence it came to be interred in the Abbey Church at Westminster" . . .

She then referred to a Tripartite Indenture made in the reign of Charles II between herself, Lord Coleraine and Sir Harbottle Grimston whose place in it after his death had been taken by his son Samuel.

She directed that her executors should expend £800 good money on her funeral expenses and in erecting a tomb for her. She wished not more than £300 to be spent on the funeral and if a less amount then what remained was to be added to the remaining £500 and laid out with it upon the tomb.

Theophilus Hastings, seventh Earl of Huntingdon, who had at one time been considered as a possible suitor for Mary Langham, the Duchess's niece, was in 1698 in touch with Grinling Gibbons about a monument to be erected to himself. In a letter to the sculptor he expressed his opinion strongly. "I desire you to forbear carving the arms till you have finished the rest of the monument. . . I like not your painting of the arms on Sir Humphrey Ferrers at Tamworth, Mr Poole at Radborn, nor the Duchess of Somerset at Westminster, which were all your work." From this and also on stylistic grounds Professor J. D. Stewart* felt her monument could be safely ascribed to Gibbons.

She bequeathed sums of money for building an almshouse in Froxfield, Wiltshire, and this is considered separately in a chapter headed The Somerset Hospital. Certain lands were left to apprentice boys born on her Wiltshire estates "to some honest trade or calling". This was the Broad Town Charity.

---

*Some unrecorded Gibbons monuments", *Burlington Magazine*, March 1963.

Further manors were given to Brasenose College, Oxford, and St John's College, Cambridge, for scholarships. These are dealt with in more detail in subsequent chapters.

£1,000 was to be expended for the benefit of the poor widows of Westminster and £100 for the Green Coat boys.

For Westminster Abbey she set aside £200 for Communion plate and for a similar purpose at St Margaret's she gave £100, as well as Communion cloth and cushions.

£250 for placing and binding apprentices (to sound honest trades) 40 poor male children born and living in the Cities of London and Westminster, and the liberties of Westminster whose parents are very poor and not able to do it — some from St Margaret's.

Additional building was to be provided at a cost of £250 for the School House at Tottenham and over £1,000 for buying land to maintain it, so that the children of poor Tottenham parishioners would be taught free.

Tottenham Church was to receive Communion plate and the pulpit and Communion Table were to be upholstered in crimson or purple velvet; the pulpit cloth was to have a deep silver fringe at the bottom and a narrow silver fringe at the top and sides. There was a further bequest for the poor women of Tottenham.

Her personal legacies were great and covered a wide field of relationships and servants —

£200 and mourning to each of her executors, Lord Delamer, Sir Samuel Grimston and Sir William Gregory.

£300 to the children of Richard Skynner, late of Sudbury, Suffolk, to be divided equally between them.

£50 to Sarah West, daughter of Francis and Hestor Browne of Worlingsworth, Suffolk.

£10 to Mrs Mary Martin, former servant.

£10 to the god-daughter of the above.

£20 to Anne Knapp, former servant.

£30 to Crow and Knapp to assist executors in discovering and finding all her moneys, jewels and other goods (to the laying and placing of several parts and particulars whereof they were privy). Elizabeth Crow was her waiting woman.

£20 to Mrs Elisabeth Guilbert in guiney gold, (her aunt).

£100 to Mrs Elizabeth Coke, daughter of the above, her husband not to intermeddle.

£20 to Sir Joseph Alston in guiney gold.

£10 to his wife.

£20 to his eldest son, Joseph Alston, in guiney gold.

£20 to the other sons and his daughter, Mrs Mary Clayton.

£100 to Joseph Alston "my godson" son of Isaac Alston.

£10 to Thomas Knight "lately my page to bind and place him as apprentice in honest trade.

£20 to John Cooke if in her service at her death "also for apprenticing and when he had served it and reached age of 21".

A year's wages to every servant who had not had a particular legacy.

£30 to Lydia Skinner, wife of Richard Skinner.

£10 to Margaret Webb, daughter of her former servant, Mrs Elizabeth Holmwood.

£4,000 to Elizabeth Booth.

£3,000 to Mary Booth and Japan Cabinet and other furniture, as well as necklace of largest pearls "five and forty in number" and locket with "nine and twenty" diamonds.

100 guineas to Charles, Lord Bruce, George Booth, Lady Lukin and Capell Lukin, her son.

To Elizabeth, Countess of Ailesbury (niece of the Duke) one silver gilt pierced work cup and salver weighing "four score and eight ounces".

To Frances, Viscountess Weymouth (niece of the Duke) one great silver basket.

To Lady Delamer "Her twylight plate (being part of my chamber plate) bought from Mr Scrimshaw, goldsmith, to use and enjoy during her life and after her death to Elizabeth Booth her eldest daughter immediately upon her mother's death if she is 21, if not to be held until she is. Remainder for use of Lady Delamer and her other daughter, Mary Booth" (her god-daughter).

To Sir Samuel Grimston, a large table diamond ring and gold enamelled watch with gold chain and pair of silver candlesticks and silver gilt pot and cover weighing 60 ounces.

To Sir William Gregory, large silver "bason" and largest silver "chiest".

There were legacies for the Keepers of her Courts and her Manors —

William Thomas and Warner South of Gray's Inn with Edward Ryder of Wilton as well as James Gregory of Gray's Inn who looked after her Courts in Hereford.

To Langham Booth, lands in Little Ashley, Co. Wilts, and Cherrington and Clinton farms.

To Lady Grimston a silver gilt salver of 60 ounces.

To Lady How (sister-in-law) necklace of pearls.

To Mrs Mary Brideoake, widow of Dr Ralph Brideoake, Bishop of Chichester, a legacy.

To Charles, Duke of Somerset and successors, the Manors of Pewsey and Titcomb cum Oxenwood and other properties "out of regard for supporting the honour of the Dukedom of Somerset".

PART II

THE Duchess of Somerset's Hospital at Froxfield, Co. Wilts., is the full title given by the Charity Commissioners in their documents. In her Will dated 17th May, 1686 Sarah, Duchess of Somerset bequeathed £1,700 to build an Almshouse in two certain acres of land in "ffroxfield" near to the village and church, for thirty poor widows.

The Almshouses were to be in the form of a quadrangle with a chapel in the middle of the court; both houses and chapel were to be built of brick. The houses were each to have a ground room and a chamber above with a hearth in each room but to be without cellars or garrets.

She ordered that £200 was to be spent on tables, bedsteads and "such durable furniture" as well as seats in the chapel and cushions. Bibles for the Minister and similar necessaries were also to be provided.

*As soon as the hospital was finished and fit to be inhabited, her trustees and their heirs were to place therein thirty poor widows. No widow possessing lands or tenements worth £20 a year or more to be eligible. Each widow was to have an equal share from the maintenance fund. The thirty widows were to be "poor but honest and such as lead a good life" and chosen thus — five and twenty from the Counties of Wiltshire, Berkshire and Somerset, ten of whom should be Ministers' widows and ten at least of whom should be from her Manors in Wiltshire. The other five were to be the widows of Ministers from London or Westminster. These ratios were also to be maintained in the filling of vacancies.

They were to enjoy their rooms and maintenance only during widowhood. If they should marry the rooms were to be forfeited.

Cloth gowns, all of the same sort and colour, were to be given to the widows at Christmas, not exceeding £1. 6. 8. each.

---

*"And I do hereby direct and appoint that so soon as the said Almshouses shall be built and made fitt to be inhabited, they the said Henry, Lord Delamere, Sir Samuel Grimston and Sir William Gregory and the survivor or survivors of them my heirs shall make choice and place therein thirty poor widows that are poor but honest and such as lead a good life."

The Minister at Froxfield was to receive £10 per annum for saying daily prayers.

For the maintenance of the widows and the almshouse for ever she conveyed her farms at Milton and Fyfield and all lands thereto belonging previously to Thomas Kellway, gent. She also gave her Manors of *Froxfield, Huish (Hewish) and Shaw for this purpose.

Furthermore, in order to advance the endowment she directed that when leases expired they should not be renewed for longer than twenty-one years and at improved rents. By this and other restrictions on copyhold estates she intended to increase the income, so that the almshouse lodging could be augmented to care for twenty more poor widows. When the income allowed, a Chaplain for the almshouse was to be appointed to read prayers daily with the widows and to preach to them every Sunday as well as visiting the sick. He was to be paid £30 a half year.

Of these additional twenty widows five were to be from London and Westminster and the other fifteen from any part of England that was not above a hundred and fifty miles from London and not in the counties of Wiltshire, Berkshire and Somerset for whom she had already made provision. She also wished five of this twenty to be Minister's widows. All were to receive the same benefits.

It was also stipulated that rents and fines which were received after her death but before the almshouse was built should be kept in bank or stock for the poor widows. To this fund to be established she added £500 and wished the total sum then to be divided into ten equal parts, one of which was to be divided yearly for ten years amongst the widows.

By a Codicil dated 10th February, 1692, she gave to the Trustees the perpetual advowson patronage and right of presentation of and to the Church of Huish,† and said that the Chaplain to the almshouse, if fit and capable, was to be presented to that

*The Manor of Froxfield was granted to the first Duke of Somerset. It was one of the twenty presented to him by Henry VIII after his marriage to Jane Seymour his sister. He was then Sir Edward Seymour but Henry created him Viscount Beauchamp and gave him a yearly pension of twenty marks (the English mark was then worth thirteen shillings and fourpence).

†Crockford now shows Wilcot and Huish together and the patronage is recorded as Bishop of Salisbury two turns, Froxfield College one turn and Archdeacon of Wiltshire one turn. The living is now worth £1,074 and the population is five hundred and ninety-eight.

Church when void after her death, and from thenceforth the Chaplain's stipend and salary shall cease. Thereafter the Minister or Incumbent of Huish Church and his successors were for ever to be Chaplains to the almshouse without additional salary. If this could not be well secured by law then the provision she had previously made for the Chaplain's maintenance was to stand.

In this Codicil she appointed the Manor and farms of Cherrington alias Chinton with the appurtenances, for the better support and increase of the upkeep of the poor widows and she gave a further £500 towards the building and £100 more towards furnishing the almshouse and chapel.

The Duchess died in the autumn of the following year in which she executed this Codicil. One of the Trustees, the Earl of Warrington, expired early in 1694; another, Sir Samuel Grimston, refused the trust and so Sir William Gregory undertook the task and caused the almshouse and the chapel to be built and placed thirty widows therein.* Sir William was well qualified to undertake this duty as he was one of the Judges of the Court of the King's Bench.

The building was completed in June 1695 and the inscription above the Hospital entrance reads:

THE
SOMERSET HOSPITAL
FOR TWENTY CLERGY
AND THIRTY LAY WIDOWS
FOUNDED AND ENDOWED
BY THE LATE MOST NOBLE
S A R A H
DUCHESS DOWAGER OF SOMERSET
A.D. MDCXCIV

Sir William Gregory then caused a conveyance to be drawn up for Sir Samuel Grimston to convey the Charity Estate to persons fitly qualified and living near the Almshouse as Governors and Trustees but he died in May 1696 before anything further was done, leaving his wife Elizabeth Gregory executrix and William Gregory his grandson and heir. They objected to act further in the Trust or to pay the money received by Sir William for the use of the poor widows without the sanction of the Court of Chancery.

---

*Mr. William Bailey was appointed Receiver of the Rents and Profits of the Estate.

Now Sir Samuel Grimston, in whom the Charity Estate was still legally vested, refused to convey it to Trustees without the direction of the Court. So a Bill in Chancery was exhibited by the King's Attorney-General on behalf of Mary Farwell and the other poor widows in the Almshouse, against Sir Samuel Grimston, Lady Gregory and William Gregory, Esq. to compel Sir Samuel to act in the Trust or convey to other Trustees, and for an application of the profits of the Estate for the benefit of the poor widows.

The Cause was heard before the Lord Chancellor on 21st December, 1697 and he decreed that Sir Samuel Grimston should attend Sir Richard Holford, a Master in Chancery and declare whether he would accept the Trust or not, and should give authority to a Receiver to receive the profits of the Estate to be applied to the relief of the poor widows. He also ordered that the defendants, the Gregorys, should account before the Master for what was received by Sir William and the Duchess's Will and all Deeds relating to the Charity Estate should be left with the Master who was to certify what number of persons were proper and who were fitting to be Trustees, and who was fit to be Steward and Receiver. The Master was further ordered to prepare a Conveyance to the Trustees to be ready for Sir Samuel Grimston to execute in case of his resignation.

Sir Samuel did formally refuse to act as stated in the Report of the Master dated 3rd June, 1698 and Mr Alexander Thistlethwaite was appointed Receiver with the Master's approval. The Gregorys accounted for all the money held by them and it was considered that nine was a sufficient number of Trustees to take over. The Master then nominated the following as fit persons living in the neighbourhood and settled that five of them should be a quorum:

Alexander Popham	of	Littlecott
Edward Seymour	of	Easton
Francis Stonehouse	of	Great Bedwin
Francis Goddard	of	Standon
Lovelace Bigg	of	Chilton
Samuel Whitelocke	of	Chilton Lodge
Thomas Fettiplace	of	Fernham
John Hippesley	of	Lambourn
John Blandy	of	Unglewood all Esquires

Finally, Warner South, Esquire, who held the Duchess's Courts was appointed to continue as Steward thereof.

The Somerset Hospital has been modernised in recent years and the residents now enjoy a measure of comfort that the early inhabitants can never have known. Its rules and regulations have been adjusted to the changing society in which we now live. Over all such establishments the charity Commissioners exert a paternal control through the Trustees whose membership still reflects the interest of prominent people in Wiltshire and the Seymour family continue to be represented in the person of His Grace The Duke of Somerset who is the Chairman.

BY HER Will and Codicil the poor widows of Westminster were to benefit with particular reference to the poor of St Margaret's Parish. Particular thought was to be given to aged poor women, or those with many children or who "were burnt out by the late dreadful fires."

She also left £250 for placing and binding apprentices. Forty poor male children born and living in the Cities of London and Westminster and its liberties were thus to be provided for and some were to be from St Margaret's. In addition £1,000 was to go to the Hospital of Green Coat Boys towards the maintenance of the "said Green Coat boys for ever."

A further £1,000 was for the purpose of buying land to support the poor of St Margaret's, Westminster. In addition she left money for the provision of velvet cloth for the pulpit and Communion Table and for velvet cushions all with gold and silver fringes for St Margaret's Church. A sum of £100 was to be spent on Communion Plate for St Margaret's and £200 for a similar purpose at Westminster Abbey. With the £100 two medium large flagons, Silver Gilt, weighing 60 ounces each were purchased. These were 11½ inches high but are not now in regular use but are displayed in St Margaret's on the occasion of the Patronal Festival. There is also a Silver Gilt Paten of the same year, 1693, which may have been part of the gift.*

The following information has been extracted from a Return made of the Endowed Charities of the County of London in 1901. It gives some idea of the fortunes through which the bequests have passed.

There was difficulty for a number of years in getting release of the various monies from the Executors. Eventually the Attorney-General "at the relation of Nicholas Onely, Rector of St Margarets and other parishioners with the Governor and Treasurer

---

*I wish to thank Canon Michael Stancliffe (now Dean of Winchester) for these details.

of the Hospital of the Green Coat boys" obtained a Decree in the Court of Chancery that the several sums mentioned should be paid out of £7,000 which the Court was holding on behalf of the Estate of the late Duchess. The matter was then to be referred to a Master of that Court to compute the interest due upon the various amounts. He was also to see that these were then laid out and applied according to the Will. By this time it was March 1701 and the Master who dealt with the business decided that the interest due on the £1,000 given for the poor of the parish, should be £318. 3. 4., making a total of £1,318. 3. 4. Exactly the same applied to the equivalent amount given for the Hospital. Then there were two sums of £200 and one of £100, the former were for apprenticing Green Coat boys and also for helping them when the contract was completed; the latter was to increase the stock of the Hospital. The interest on these was £30. 18. 9. for each £100. The money had, as far as the recipients were concerned, been lying untouched for nine years.

The Charity Commissioners in 1881 issued a Scheme for administering the Charity afresh. It was to be known as "Sarah, Duchess of Somerset's Charity" and there were to be fifteen Trustees who must reside in the City of Westminster or within seven miles of Westminster Abbey measured in a straight line on an Ordnance Map. Additional Trustees were to be appointed by the Continuing Trustees, but no appointment was to be valid until approved by the Charity Commissioners. Meetings were to be held four times a year and five trustees should form a quorum. The Charity from then on was to be for the benefit of poor persons of good character, being either married couples or widowers or bachelors or widows or spinsters not less than sixty years of age, who shall have resided in the united parishes of St Margaret and St John the Evangelist in the City of Westminster, or one of them for not less than five years and not have received poor law relief during that period. They should be unable to maintain themselves by their own exertions, either from age or ill health, accident or infirmity and preference was to be given to those who shall have become reduced by misfortune from better circumstances.

The number of pensioners was to be determined by the trustees and the amount was to be not less than £5 nor more than £10 in any one year. It need not be distributed in money, but as thought fit for the pensioner. Pensioners must reside in

Westminster. If in any one year the entire net income could not be spent for want of proper objects, the remainder was to be held over until the amount reached £50, when it was to be invested in the name of the Official Trustees of Charitable Funds.

There were to be five representative trustees of the Charity appointed by the Vestry of the united parishes of St Margaret and St John the Evangelist, and each appointment was to be for a term of four years. The Trustees in 1899 were —

Co-optative: George Howard Trollope, John Ferguson, Rt. Hon. John Gilbert Talbot M.P., David Verity, Francis Young, Henry Arthur Hunt, George Taverner Miller J.P., Thomas William Davies, John Benjamin Barnes.

Representative: Walter Bonwick, Dr James Edward Sinclair, George John Chappel, Charles Spencer Smith, William Henry Pendlebury.

Mr Lewis Herbert Winckworth of Messrs. Trollope and Winckworth, Solicitors, was Clerk to the Trustees.

The distribution consisted of thirty-three recipients of £10 a year and thirty-seven of £5 p.a. The pensions were paid by the Clerk quarterly — pensioners were appointed at properly constituted meetings and qualifications prescribed were duly observed. At that time there were always a large number of applicants, so a form was filled up giving details of age, married or single, whether ratepayer or in receipt of poor law relief, children living, state of health, whether any assistance from other charities and so on. It had to be supported by recommendations from three persons who were to testify to need. It is interesting to note that an income from private sources not exceeding £15 was not regarded as a disqualification.

At the present time Mr Peter Winckworth (Messrs Winckworth and Pemberton) is Clerk to the Trustees of this and other charities and I am indebted to him for much of this information. The pensions are now £10 per annum payable quarterly on the first Tuesday in the months of January, April, July and October. The beneficiaries are poor people from the united parishes and there are fifty-five of them. The conditions are still as outlined above, and the pensioners are paid at duly convened meetings held at St

Stephen's Church, Rochester Row, S.W.1 at 12 noon on the days mentioned. The number of Trustees is fifteen, of whom five are appointed by the Westminster City Council, the remainder by the Board.

*   *   *

In 1633 following a desire by several inhabitants of the City of Westminster to provide a House and Hospital for maintaining poor orphans and instructing them in manual arts the above-named School came into being and receiving support from Charles I was also called the Hospital of St Margaret. It was to have a governing body of twenty residents of the City and they were to purchase land in mortmain to the value of £500 per annum.

After the restoration of Charles II it was given fresh life by benefactions of the King and others, particularly Sarah, Duchess of Somerset. The school was kept for the benefit of orphan children in the parish of St Margaret and was situated in Tothill Fields.

This was the first of four schools in Westminster all established on similar lines and for the same purpose. The Black Coat School was founded in 1656, The Blue Coat School in 1688, and the Grey Coat School in 1706.

The Green Coat School* consisted of a building in the shape of a large quadrangle and the master's house stood in the middle of the playground opposite the entrance and was ornamented by a bust of Charles I. It also had the Royal Arms which were only preserved from destruction in the time of the Commonwealth by a thick coat of plaster. In the Board Room there were portraits of Charles I and Charles II.

The boys wore a long green skirt with a red leather girdle similar in pattern to the attire of the boys of Christ's Hospital. Those supported by the Duchess of Somerset's endowment were distinguished by yellow caps.

The Duchess lived in Dean's Yard for many years and was a good benefactress to St Margaret's Church and the poor of the parish. For her kindness she was excused paying the poor rate.

---

*The building has been demolished and on its site now stands the Army and Navy Stores

Tottenham Grammar School, now The Somerset School

IN HER Will Sarah left £250 for additional building to the school house at Tottenham and £1,100 for the buying of lands for the support of it, so that children of poor Tottenham parishioners should be taught free.

Her interest in the school derived from her third husband, Lord Coleraine, who was Lord of the Manor and lived in Bruce Castle. He was a governor of the school and was said to have asked his wife "to be kind to the parish of Tottenham the place of her abode when in the country." This she did in her Will and the appropriate part of it read "also I do give and appoint the sum of two hundred and fifty pounds to be expended, paid and laid out by mine executors, in and for the making an additional building to the school house at Tottenham near the High Cross in the County of Middlesex, for the enlargement thereof, whereby it may be made capable to receive a greater number of scholars. Also I do give and appoint the further sum of eleven hundred pounds . . . for the buying and purchasing of lands, rents, or other hereditaments, in fee simple, and they to settle the same for the support and maintenance of the said school and the master and usher of the said school for ever. . ."

Further detail showed that she wished the schoolmaster's salary of forty pounds a year and the usher's of ten pounds, to be forthcoming out of these provisions and that there should be free education for "the children of all such people, inhabiting within the said parish of Tottenham, as shall not have estates of their own, of free or copyhold, of twenty pounds per annum." The master could, however, admit fee paying scholars.

The following has been taken from the Tottenham Vestry Book:

At a vestry held on 23rd July 1693 it was unanimously agreed "that as the late Duchess Dowager of Somerset, being the Rt. Hon. Henry Lord Colerane's Lady, did by her will leave to the parish of

Tottenham a considerable sum of money for an additional building to a house now standing on the waste, to make a more convenient schoolhouse, and also to endow the same as a Free School for the benefit of this parish; and it being found convenient to take in a piece of the waste on the South of the present tenement for the additional building, and one other piece of the common or waste lying on the north of the garden already enclosed for the use of the present tenement; we do hereby wholly relinquish and quit claim to any right or interest of herbage or otherwise which as tenants of the manor we might or ought to have in the soil, whereon the present tenement standeth, as also the yard, garden and appurtenances already appropriated to the said tenement and all right, tithe or interest, we have or might have in the two pieces of common or waste beforementioned, now to be enclosed for the benefit of the said school, and we humbly make it our request to the Rt. Hon. Henry Lord Colerane that he would be pleased to surrender and grant to the executors of the Duchess of Somerset the interest and title his lordship hath in the present tenement and appurtenances; as also the right title and interest his lordship hath (as Lord of the soil) in the two pieces of common or waste beforementioned, to the aid of the aforesaid premises, which may be erected into a Free School for the benefit of the parish; and we do desire Mr John Woodhouse to signify this our request to his Lordship".

The following exhortation was probably drawn up by the Trustees of the Duchess and they show the strong religious background that existed at that time.

DIRECTIONS TO BE READ TO EVERY SCHOLAR UPON HIS ADMISSION INTO THE FREE GRAMMAR SCHOOL AT TOTTENHAM HIGH CROSS

First you must rise early in the morning, and when you are dressed, you must fall on your knees and give God thanks for the preservation of you the night past; and beg his blessing upon your endeavours that day, to increase in knowledge, wisdom and virtue.

In the next place, ask your parents' blessing, and bid them good morning; then wash yourself, comb your hair and make haste to school.

In your way to and from school, you must not be rude and unmannerly, but you must pull off your hat and make a bow to those you meet and know. When you are come to school you must first bow to your Master, and then sit down in your place, where you are to make no noise, but to apply yourself diligently and peaceably to learn what you are required to do.

When you are from school, and have leave to play, let your play be such as is free from blame; and you must not use any evil words, neither must you sware, or lie, or in any way deceive or impose upon your play fellows, but your behaviour must be such as shows that you have the fear of God before your eyes; and that you are conscious that God knows all your thoughts, words and actions, and therefore, you will carefully avoid whatever will displease Him.

And, in the last place, you must be particularly careful how you spend the Lord's day: you must not spend it in idleness or any diversion; but you must go to Church, and that early that you may be seated in your proper place before the minister begins, and then you must be attentive to him; take out your Common Prayer Book, and make such responses as are required, but they must be made with a low voice, that you may not disturb the congregation; and when the minister goes to the pulpit you must mind his text, and if you have your Bible with you, turn to it and as soon as you go home get it by heart, that you may be able to repeat it on Monday to your Master, and what else you may remember of the sermon, and when Church is done, you must stay in your seat till the principal part of the congregation is gone out, then go out quietly and return home peaceably.

But your business is not yet finished — as you begun, you must end the day with prayer; before you go to bed you must pray to God to defend you from all the perils and dangers of the night, and to return him thanks for his protection from all accidents the day past, and that he would give you grace so to lead your life here, that you may be qualified for his eternal inheritance hereafter. These are the particulars that you are required to comply with, and I hope you are determined to do what lies in your power, faithfully to perform them all.

And then the Scholar was to answer: "I will, God being my helper."

It was some time before the terms of the Will were carried out, but in 1704 about sixty acres of land at Farncombe near Godalming was bought with the £1,100. The last of this land was sold by the Governors in 1927.

Although the school had been in existence prior to the Duchess's endowment yet 25th October, the date of her death, is kept as Founder's Day at the school. Every year a party of boys attend at Westminster Abbey for the ceremony of laying a wreath on her tomb. The order of service which takes place at the tomb follows this pattern — Opening Prayer by the Headmaster:

"As scholars, master, and governors of the Old Foundation of the Tottenham Grammar School, we come again on the occasion of the anniversary of the death of Sarah, Duchess of Somerset, whose charity created out foundation, to pay our annual tribute to the memory of this illustrious lady. As we stand before her tomb, we thank God for the long and valuable life in which so much was done for Education and Charity. Amen."

A wreath is then laid by the Captain of the School.
A boy then reads the Latin inscription on the Tomb.
Another boy reads the translation —

"Here lies Sarah, lately the distinguished Duchess of Somerset, well known for her continual kindness towards the poor; who founded the Tottenham Grammar School for boys in the County of Middlesex; she considerably furthered the growth of the Green Coat Hospital at Westminster; she endowed for all time the colleges of Brasenose at Oxford and St John's Cambridge for the promotion of young men of good promise in godliness and literature; she was also concerned for the training of others in technical skills; in her concern for old age she caused a Hospital to be built and endowed to keep thirty widows at Froxfield in the County of Wiltshire; she set up a perpetual fund for the better support of the poor of the Parish of St Margaret's at Westminster; she handsomely adorned some churches, apart from this, with fine fittings. She died on the 25th day of October in the year of our Lord 1692."

In accordance with her wishes the school was enlarged early in the eighteenth century. Just over a hundred years later it was found that the funds of the school were sufficient for the education of twice the number of pupils, which was then eighty. The main schoolroom was in poor repair and it was decided to raise money for rebuilding it by public subscription. This was successful and a new schoolroom was built of similar design and the coat of arms of the Duchess was placed over the porch, and an inscription "Free Grammar School founded by Sarah, Duchess of Somerset" was later amended to "endowed by".

In 1865 one of H.M. Inspectors was invited to make a report about the school. He found that conditions were not entirely satisfactory and so a new scheme for the administration of it was prepared by the Charity Commissioners. This was approved in 1876. Under this free scholars were no longer to be admitted to the school, and those already on the register were to be transferred to a public elementary school and their fees paid by the Governors. The Headmaster of the old Free School resigned and was awarded £400 compensation for the loss of his position. The school was then closed for a short time and completely re-organised. It was re-opened in January 1877 as a middle class secondary school. The Master's House was demolished and a new one built, which was destroyed during the Second World War.

In 1906 the school had about two hundred pupils and by 1920 there were three hundred. Between these years the old school was pulled down and a new one built at a cost of £10,000. This building is now used as offices by the Greater London Council. After the end of the first war the school expanded greatly and in 1938 the present school was erected to accommodate four hundred and fifty boys. This was put up on an island site in White Hart Lane. A tablet commemorating the opening of this new school building was unveiled by the then Duke of Somerset, maintaining the family's connection with the school.

After the Second World War further expansion took place and in 1960 a new wing was added containing sixth form rooms, additional laboratory and workshop accommodation and other rooms. The latest change occurred in 1967 concomitant with the re-organisations of the schools under the Greater London Council, the successors of the Middlesex County Council. Tottenham Grammar School and the Rowland Hill School (named after the famous Postmaster-General who founded the penny post) were amalgamated into a comprehensive school for boys under the name The Somerset School, thus perpetuating the Duchess's Endowment. The school is under the voluntary control of a

Board of Governors who represent the Local Authority and the Foundation Governors. They have control still of certain endowment funds which can be used to provide amenities for the school and to award grants and assistance to worthy pupils for further education. These are now in the region of one thousand pupils.

So the old tradition has been absorbed by the latest change in the school's history and homage will continue to be paid on the 25th October to the noble lady who supported the early foundation and helped to sustain and advance the education of the young.

Brasenose College

THERE can be little doubt that it was in memory of her first husband that Sarah endowed scholarships to Brasenose. George Grimston was admitted to the College in 1649 at the age of eighteen and he remained at Oxford for three years before proceeding to Lincoln's Inn. He died in 1655 leaving Sarah a widow when she was barely twenty-four.

Her gifts to the college began in her lifetime by her composition in 1679 when she settled lands in the parish of Iver, Buckinghamshire for maintaining four Scholars at Brasenose College. They were to be called "Somerset Scholars". This benefaction was regulated by a Deed made by the Duchess with Dr Yate the Principal of the College dated 17th February, 1679. The lands when the Deed was executed were let to three different tenants for £25, £18, and £17 making a total of £60 per annum clear of all taxes whatsoever, and the arrangement was that the Principal and Fellows were to use all diligence to preserve the lands and improve them. These lands called Woodhill and Bramley Moor in the parish of Iver remained in the care of the College until 1869 when part of the estate was sold and the remainder was disposed of in 1894.

These four Scholars were to be elected by the Principal and six fellows out of Manchester School within forty days after any vacancy, and they were to be born in the Counties of Lancaster, Chester, or Hereford. If nobody from that school was considered fit then they were permitted to choose a boy in any of the said counties from any other school. From their admission into these scholarships they were to receive five shillings per week each for seven years (£13 per annum) but they were not tenable with Fellowships. They were also to have a chamber or chambers and four studies provided, for which the Duchess paid £50, by that was meant one chamber with four studies or four chambers.

At their first admission the College was to provide them each with a Cap and Gown which would be replenished at the end of their third year and again at the end of their fifth year. For this purpose, £5 was to be allowed. Caps and gowns must at that time have been worn almost continuously. It was laid down that the Cloth Gown was to have open sleeves like the students at Christ Church, and Square Cap but without tassels while they were undergraduates. These scholars were to be exempted from paying Caution Money, but if they exceeded in their Battels (the name given for the Kitchen and Buttery accounts) and did not pay in fourteen days their names were to be crossed and their allowance stopped 'till the arrears were paid. There was one further condition to be filled by these Scholars and that was that they should speak Latin with one another under penalty of two pence per default.

A particular clause in the Deed ordered that if the Principal and Fellows should misapply the premises and after admission continue to do so, then the Duchess's heirs might seize the rents and employ them to the uses mentioned, either in Brasenose College or any other College in Oxford.

The Bishop of Lincoln was appointed Visitor of the Scholarships and he was to determine all questions and differences relative thereto.

Finally the Duchess proposed a Commemoration on the day of the Foundation, 17th February, and for this £2 was to be allowed to the Principal, Fellows and Scholars, but the Principal was to have a double share! On this day one Scholar, in rotation, was to make a Latin speech to commemorate the Benefactress (this was later discontinued). The money for this feast was to be deducted from the rents of the Iver Estates. If there was a failure to accomplish a Latin oration, there was to be a fine of twopence. Further, the distribution of the forty shillings was to be done at prayers.

During her lifetime the Duchess was to nominate the Scholars personally but refusal was allowed by her to the College. After her death the choice was to be made by the Principal and six Fellows. Some of the original nominations signed by the Duchess are in the College Archives. The early SOMERSET (IVER) SCHOLARS were:

1680	May 25	John Whitfield
		Roger Cooper
		Jethro Brideoake
		Thomas Prescot
1681	Feb. 4	Thomas Mallory
1684	March 28	Charles Barkley
	Nov. 26	Samuel Hunter
1685	April 4	Samuel Ffranners
1686	Dec. 2	John Adee
1689	April 6	John Astley
		Thomas Wilkinson
	July 22	John Hallywell
1691	July 17	John Hyde
	Sep. 24	Thomas Smith
	Dec. 26	John Meare

In her will the Duchess bequeathed her Manor of Thornhill, Wiltshire, to support a further number of Scholars over and above the Iver Scholars. All these additional Scholarships were to be of the same value as the earlier ones except six of them which were specially mentioned and are referred to later.

She expressly stated that no lease was to be granted for more than twenty-one years so that rents could be altered to the advantage of the College, if possible, but they were not to exceed by more than one third the previous amount. She then wished that of the new rents one fourth should go to the Scholars and three fourths should be invested for the benefit of the Trust. The lessees were to pay all taxes and keep their premises in repair.

These additional (Thornhill) Scholars were to be chosen from three schools, Manchester, Hereford and Marlborough by turn in that order. In all other respects the election was to be the same as for the Iver award, and they were also to be known as Somerset Scholars.

Whenever a vacancy occured, the College was to notify the master of the School from which the next Scholar was to be chosen within thirty days. If the College failed to do this it would forfeit the privilege of the election of any such Scholar for seven years and the Heirs of the Executors would then be entitled to nominate a Scholar during that time.

It was conceived that as the rents from the Manor improved, it should be possible to add one additional Scholarship for every extra £30 of income received, and perhaps as the endowment fund increased then it might be after every additional £15 received from the Thornhill Manor. Of the fines paid for renewing Copyhold Estates three quarters was to go to the College and the remaining quarter was to be expended on providing books for the additional Scholars.

At the time of the bequest all the farms within the Manor were in Lease under small old rents and the income was only £160 per annum. It was felt that when the Leases fell in the income could be increased considerably, it was hoped up to £560. When this happened then six new Scholars could be chosen in the same manner as already from the three particular schools. The boys to be chosen were to be the most indigent and those who intended taking Holy Orders. If after election any Scholar was absent above three calender months on any pretence whatsoever, he was to forfeit his Scholarship.

In the Codicil of her Will the Duchess gave the Advowson of Wootton Rivers, Wiltshire, alternating for presentation by Brasenose College, Oxford and St John's College, Cambridge to Somerset Scholars "that hath been bred up in that College, whose turn it is to present".

At the time of her death the Duchess also gave to her four existing Scholars in Brasenose College (The Somerset Scholars) £100.

Since the last century, the awards have shrunk tremendously, from four Somerset (Iver) Scholars and eighteen Somerset (Thornhill) to only one Iver and two Thornhill Scholars, in 1968. This has been due to the increasing scale of the Subvention of undergraduates by local authorities, which led to an agreement among all Colleges to reduce the annual value of Scholarships to this figure. The current value of the Somerset Scholarships is £60 per annum.

*   *   *

There is a portrait of Sarah, Duchess of Somerset in the Hall at Brasenose above the door. The canvas is 49in. x 39½in. It is a three quarter length portrait. The Duchess is seated slightly to the right with the head almost facing the spectator, her brown hair is in curls and she is wearing a pearl necklace with ear-rings. She has a blue cloak lined with ermine over a low necked brown dress trimmed with lace, and full white sleeves. Her right hand holds a fold of her mantle, her left on a coronet which rests on a table.

Among the College papers are two that concern this picture: "April 12th, 1728. Received then of the Reverend Doctor Shippen for a Halflength Copy of the Dutchis of Somerset the sum of twelve pounds twelve shillings in full of all demands. Received by me Thomas Gibson".

"For a rich carved and gilt frame with a Coat of Arms and shield £58. 8s. 0d., case and nails 10s., portage 1s., July 23rd, 1728. R. L. West."

An engraving was done of the original portrait by G. Vertue in 1736 and it was then ascribed to T. M. Q. This has led to the suggestion that the original may have been painted by Jan Maurits Quickhardt but this painter was not born until 1688. It is possible that it was painted by his father.*

In the eighteenth century it was the custom and rule that every Somerset Scholar should purchase one of Vertue's prints for two shillings.

The original picture showed a large parchment scroll held by its upper part under the coronet and a book and then displayed in front of the table. On this scroll is a long Latin inscription commemorating the Duchess and her charities, which translated into English would read:—

M. S. P.

In sacred Memory of
the most illustrious Sarah, late Duchess of Somerset
most famous for her everlasting kindess towards the poor
who
for the benefit of BOYS
founded a School of Grammar at Tottenham in the County
of Middlesex
greatly increased the growth of the Westminster Green Coats
for the advancement of YOUNG MEN of excellent
promise in piety and letters
she endowed in perpetuity
the Colleges
of Brasen Nose at Oxford
and of Saint John at Cambridge

---

*Catalogue of Oxford Portraits by Mrs. Reginald Lane Poole.

And also looked to the training of others in the
Mechanical Arts
out of concern for the AGED
She caused to be built and endowed an Alms House
for the support of thirty widows
at Froxfield in the County of Wiltshire
for the NEEDY of the Parish of Saint Margaret's Westminster
she established a perpetual fund
whereby they might be better supported
Furthermore Sundry Churches
she splendidly embellished
with truly magnificent adornments
She died 25 October 1692.

St John's College

AS AT Oxford, Sarah began her gifts to St John's College, Cambridge during her lifetime. She executed a Deed with Dr Gower, Master of the College, dated 12th July 1682 and the Bishop of Ely was to be the Visitor. For the purpose of founding these scholarships she gave her estate at March with lands at Doddington in the Isle of Ely. At the time of the grant it was producing an income of about £160 per annum, but it was hoped that when the current leases expired it would eventually provide an income of over £500.

Her father had been a member of the College and after having endowed the first Somerset Scholarship at Brasenose in 1679 she must have felt a keen desire to do the same for Sir Edward Alston's Alma Mater.

While she was alive the Duchess could make her own nominations to the foundation, which was for the maintenance of five scholars. Unless the "posers and lecturers" refused them they were to be admitted within three days of presentation. The first four scholars did not go up until January 1683 and they were followed by a fifth in April. These scholarships were to be awarded to boys from Hereford School if of required standard and arrangements were to be made similar to those at Oxford; they were to have one or two chambers with five studies, neither ground chambers nor garrets, they were to wear gowns of cloth with open sleeves and square caps without tassels. There was also to be a commemoration once a year "upon ye day of ye foundation" and there was to be "a speech to be made in ye Hall in Latin by ye scholars in turn." The special dress and the other customs applicable to Somerset Scholars ceased when the Statutes of 1860 came into force.

In her Will there was a further endowment as at Brasenose, and for this she bequeathed her manor of Wootton Rivers. It was for the same three schools as at Oxford but in reverse order, that is

Marlborough, Hereford and Manchester. Otherwise the conditions were the same for both Colleges.

As at Oxford the number of awards in recent times has fallen considerably. New Statutes came into force in 1860. The number of Somerset Scholarships was then 27. These were converted into Exhibitions and in the latter part of that century there were only 12 of them. These fell still further and between 1959 and 1969 no awards were made as at that time it was decided to pool the income from various sources. So the uninterrupted line of Somerset Scholars and Exhibitioners from 1683 was then broken. This was not in keeping with the Duchess's wish that her name should be always associated with the recipients of the income from her estates at March and Wootton Rivers. The former position has now been restored and again there are Somerset Exhibitioners to continue the sequence.

There is a portrait of Sarah, Duchess of Somerset, in the Hall of St John's. It is dissimilar to the one at Brasenose. It came into the hands of the College in 1701 and there is no signature or date. Some have attributed it to Sir Peter Lely, but this is on style and there is no evidence to support it. The details are— painted on canvas 4' 1" x 3' 4½". The Duchess is wearing a buff silk dress with arms bare from the elbows, blue cloak lined with white fur over left arm which rests on a stone vase, holding a wreath. A coronet is on a table on her right. She has a pearl necklace and pearl eardrops as well as pearls on the bodice. The hair is light flaxen and is in ringlets. The eyes are grey and she is looking to the left of the picture which is of three-quarter length.

In the Master's Lodge there is a portrait of her husband John, fourth Duke of Somerset. He is painted on a canvas 4' 1½" x 3' 5". He is bareheaded with a brown flowing wig, and is clean shaven. He is wearing a steel corselet over an embroidered brown jerkin with white cravat. At his side is a sword shank on twisted scarlet baldrick. His left hand points forward with forefinger and thumb, with laced lavender coloured sleeve and ruff at wrist. The portrait is three-quarter length displaying three-quarter face.

The Three Nominated Schools

MANCHESTER GRAMMAR SCHOOL

FOUNDED in 1515, this school was the first choice of the Duchess when she decided to found Somerset scholarships. By a Deed dated 17th February 1679 she set apart the Manor of Iver in Bucks for the maintenance of four scholars for seven years to be elected from the Free School of Manchester. Those boys who came from the counties of Lancashire, Cheshire and Herefordshire were to be preferred. The scholarships were to enable them to proceed to Brasenose College, Oxford.

Grammar Schools at that time eased to some degree the growing class prejudice because they were open to all. The success they achieved in increasing knowledge did, however, raise some opposition from those who felt that this was a privilege of the upper classes. Between 1660 and 1730 a large number of new Grammar Schools were established and about fifty old ones received fresh endowments.

How did Sarah come to choose Manchester? It must have been largely through her Booth connections, and there were probably a number of influences. Sir George Booth, who was the father-in-law of her niece, Mary Langham, was a feoffee for fifteen years. The governing Body of the school consisted of twelve feoffees and Mary's husband, Henry, second Lord Delamer and first Earl of Warrington, was also elected one in 1676. He was the leader of the Whig party in the North of England and took a great interest in education. He may well have put before his Aunt the need of poor scholars. Then there was the Rev. Preb. Richard Wroe, D.D.,* who had been Vicar of Bowden where the Booths worshipped. He became Warden of Manchester College and was also a feoffee.

There was yet another who may have been consulted by the Duchess about her charitable leanings. He was the Revd. Doctor Ralph Brideoake, who had not only been educated at Manchester Grammar School, but had also at one time been High Master and

---

*(1641-1718) His discourses were of such quality that he was known as "Silver-tongued Wroe".

furthermore was a B.N.C. man. His mother was born a Booth and he must have been well known to Sarah for she left his widow a legacy in her Will. Another appointment Brideoake held was Chaplain to the Earl of Derby, and when the latter was captured after the Battle of Worcester, he went to London and pleaded with Speaker Lenthal for the Earl's life and did not desist until it was hopeless. He was of the Booth mould in religious matters and was appointed one of the Commissioners (by Act of Parliament) in 1659 for the approbation and admission of Ministers of the Gospel after the Presbyterian mode. When Charles II was restored to the Throne he became one of his Chaplains and was installed Canon of Windsor. In 1667 he became Dean of Salisbury and was nominated Bishop of Chichester in 1674. Four years later he died on a visitation of his diocese. He was interred in St George's Chapel, Windsor, where his widow erected a magnificent monument.

The additional proviso that natives of Lancashire and Cheshire should be specially considered would follow from all the associations of the Booth family in those parts. The addition of Herefordshire to the preferential list must have been partly due to the Duchess's connection with that county through her first husband's family, for the Grimstons had been Lords of the Manor of Eardisland in that county. How Caple in Herefordshire was also the home of the Gregorys, and Sir William Gregory was one of her executors, and a member of that family had been Steward of her Manors there which she had inherited from her second husband.

The early scholarships were much augmented by her Will when further awards were instituted and the new ones were to embrace the three schools, Manchester, Hereford and Marlborough. Because of the deaths of the original executors and legal difficulties, it took a few years for the bequest to be implemented.

Previous to the Duchess's benefaction the majority of scholars had gone to Cambridge. With the help of this and another bene-faction (Hulme scholarships), the proportion of the school's representation at the two universities was altered. Between 1660-1690 thirty went to Oxford and sixty to Cambridge. From 1690-1727 Oxford gathered ninety-one while only thirty-three went to Cambridge.

The school still supplies its allotted candidates for the Somerset Scholarships, but no boy is eligible unless he has been at the school for two years.

THE origin of the Cathedral School at Hereford is shrouded in medieval mist. The date of foundation is simply accepted as being before 1381. There is some evidence that it may have existed at a much earlier time. An Edict of the Lateran Council in 1179 directed that a school should be set up in every Cathedral town. Shortly afterwards Simon de Fraxino, who was a Canon of Hereford, mentioned that "Trivium et Quadrivium" was being taught there. There are also Deeds of the thirteenth century in the Cathedral Archives which refer to the "Old Schole Strete" which ran north east of the Cathedral. The first record of a Headmaster is that of Ricardus de Cornewaille, who was appointed by Bishop Gilbert to govern the boys "cum virga et ferula" (with birch and rod).

In the ensuing centuries the school was referred to variously as a Grammar School, Free Grammar School, Free School, College School, Collegiate School and Cathedral School. In those days a Grammar School meant that Latin and Greek were the main subjects, and a Free Grammar School was where those subjects were taught free, the master being entitled to charge for other subjects.

The Duchess of Somerset's interest in the school must have arisen from the possession of land in the county. It came about in this wise. The manors of Ross Borough and Ross Foreign belonged to the Crown until 1588 when they came into the possession of Robert Devereux, Earl of Essex. After his execution and attainder the manor of Ross Foreign was granted to Thomas Crompton, Esq., and the manor of Ross Borough to Sir Henry Lindley. In 1603 the Countess Dowager of Essex purchased both manors for £7,000. These were then assigned to Trustees for her own benefit for life and after her death to her son and his heirs, and in default of issue to her two daughters, and their descendants. The elder, Lady Frances Devereux, married Sir William Seymour, later Marquess of Hertford and second Duke of Somerset; the younger, Lady Dorothy Devereux, married Sir Henry Shirley, Bart, whose grandson was created Earl Ferrers. In 1663 Frances, Duchess of Somerset, obtained control from the Court of Delegates. In an amicable division of the property between herself and the children of her deceased sister, the manors of Ross Borough, Ross Foreign, Bodenham Devereux, Byford, Eardisland, Fownhope,

Lyonshall, Moor Court, Pembridge and Weobley were part of the moiety assigned to the Duchess.

On the marriage of Lord John Seymour with Sarah, widow of George Grimston, the manors of Ross and Fownhope were conveyed to Trustees for the benefit of the parties, and of the survivor, with the proviso that in default of issue these manors were to revert to the right heirs of Frances, Dowager Duchess of Somerset. She by her Will devised all her estates in possession and reversion to her three executors, Sir Orlando Bridgeman, Sir William Gregory, and Sir Thomas Thynne, who were directed to make a tripartite division of them for the benefit of her grand-daughters. After the death of the fourth Duke, Sarah's husband, the manors were held by her until her decease in 1692.

Sir William Gregory's father, the Rev. Robert Gregory, became Rector of Fownhope in 1619. William was born there in 1624 and was educated at Hereford Cathedral School, and subsequently had a most distinguished career. He was called to Bar in 1650 (Gray's Inn), became Recorder of Gloucester 1672 and to the dignity of the Coif in 1677. He was M.P. for Wembley in the following year and became Speaker of the House of Commons in 1679 in succession to Sir Edward Seymour. On taking the Chair, he said "I humbly thank you for your good opinion of me; but when I consider the weight of your debates, which require a person of the greatest experience and parts, my time of sitting here has not been above a year, and my experience so little, that you may suffer in your affairs, and I come with the greatest disadvantage imaginable to succeed a person of so much experience — pray consider of it, and choose a more experienced person". James Gregory of Gray's Inn who is mentioned in Sarah's Will as looking after her courts in Hereford was Sir William's son but he did not live long enough to benefit from it because he died a year before the Duchess. Sir William lived on another five years and when he died his grandson William had not yet come of age, a cause of further problems in the execution of the Will.

It seems very likely that the Gregorys may have exerted some influence on the choice of Hereford Cathedral School being nominated for the Scholarship awards.

In 1679 there is a record of a Court Baron at which in view of the frank pledge of Sarah, Duchess of Somerset, Lady of the Manor of Ross Foreign, the jurors presented inter alia two widows as common scolds upon whom a fine of 3/4d. was imposed. The copyholders fined for non-appearance were Sir John Scudamore Bart, George Bond, gent., Daniel Kerr, gent., Rev. John Darell, Jane Baynham widow, John Kyrle Esquire, Martha Stratford widow, Edward Yemm gent., and Richard Clark, gent.

MARLBOROUGH GRAMMAR SCHOOL

THIS school was founded in 1550, only a few years after Manchester Grammar School, and the appointment of the Schoolmaster was vested perpetually in the head of the Seymour family. The family at that time owned the Mansion of Wolfhall, where Henry VIII married Jane Seymour, and the Castle of Marlborough.

It is not surprising, therefore, that Sarah, with her second husband's family connections with Marlborough and her Wiltshire manors, would include within her ambit for educational help, this Grammar School. Her husband had also been M.P. for Marlborough when he was Lord John Seymour.

Much of the land that belonged to the Seymours passed into the Bruce family on the marriage of the third Duke's sister to Thomas Bruce, later Earl of Ailesbury. This included Savernake Forest, and because the vesting of the appointment of Schoolmaster had been in the hand of the Seymours because he was the Hereditary Ranger Warden or Seneschal of the King's Forest of Savernake, now on transference to the Bruce's the nomination of the Master of the School rested with the Earl of Ailesbury.

Some time later the Master was allowed to admit boarders, and this increased the School's prestige and reputation. It was decided that "the schoolmaster shall from time to time be at liberty to teach the children of foreign dwellers out of the said town as well as those of the town, provided that the children of the town be not neglected thereby." Soon boarders came, whose parents had learned of the benefit to be obtained from the scholarships established by the Duchess, and of the opportunity to gain thereby a university career for their sons.

This raised later the question of the length of stay a boy should have before being eligible for such an award. In the Charity Commission Report in 1835 it noted that the present Master of Marlborough Free Grammar School had only sent boys to Oxford, and observed that provided they had been three years in the school boys were eligible without regard to whether they were free scholars or boarders.

BY THE middle of the sixteenth century apprenticeship had become the most usual way of entering a trade. If a father wished his son to learn a trade other than his own, which he could teach him unbound, he had to find some master willing to take the lad apprentice. At that time the master had to be a freeman of his Gild, and the length of service was a minimum of seven years. It was part of the agreement that the lad should live in his master's house and be entirely under his control. He received no wages but was given instruction in the particular craft and was fed, housed and clothed. In the Indenture he would promise to be of good conduct, to abstain from games such as dice and cards, and to eschew the haunting of taverns.

During the Civil War the number of apprentices fell, owing to their enlistment in the forces. When Charles II returned a large number of the Gilds or Companies passed bye laws dealing with apprenticeship, and it was enacted that men were forbidden to work as journeymen until they had served seven years as apprentices.

The system worked well and the country was provided with skilled workmen, most of whom had also benefitted by the overall character training provided by firm masters. It is not surprising therefore that the apprenticeship of poor children became a fairly common form of philanthropy. In the reign of Elizabeth I the churchwardens and overseers of the poor had been empowered to bind any children whose parents were not able to support them. The small premium involved in such cases was drawn from the poor rate. The recipients of apprenticing charities were not necessarily paupers. Indeed, it was sometimes mentioned in such benefactions that the money was not to be used for relieving the poor rate burden of the parish. In the second half of the seventeenth century it was thought that about one person in five was obtaining some form of public relief dispensed on a parish basis. It may be assumed that the trustees of apprenticing charities chose the better masters as well as the better poor boys. As a result, the parish-apprenticed pauper might be placed with less satisfaction. On this subject William Bailey wrote in 1758 "many of those who take parish apprentices are so inhuman as to regard only the pecuniary conditions and having once received that, they, by ill usage and undue severity often drive the poor creatures from them and so leave them in a more destitute condition at a riper age for mischief than they were when first they became the care of parish officers." This arose, because any man who wanted a few pounds might obtain them by taking an apprentice, without much enquiry as to his circumstances or character or suitability for being a master.

Sarah, Duchess of Somerset, had no doubt seen the benefits of such a method of training when properly administered. In addition to some provision of this kind for the Green Coat Boys of Westminster she provided in her Will for similar help to be given to poor boys in Wiltshire.

An estate at Cotmarsh, in the parish of Broad Hinton, Wiltshire, was given by Sarah, Duchess of Somerset in trust for ever to employ the rents and profits thereof in apprenticing to some honest trade or calling four male children, born in some of her manors of Broad Town, Thornhill, Froxfield, Wootton Rivers and Hewish.

In addition, the Manor of Broad Town with all the lands and hereditaments belonging to it was bequeathed for the same purpose of apprenticing poor male children born in the county of Wiltshire and actually living in it.

She laid down that after her decease the leasehold farm or tenement in Broad Town Manor should not be leased on lives, but the lease then in being should be suffered to expire, after which the farm should be leased for no longer term than twenty-one years and that no fine should be taken upon any new lease, but that it should be let at the best improved rent that could be gotten for the same. It was further proposed that when any copyhold estate should be renewed, no fine should be less than one-third of the improved yearly value, and rents should be two-thirds of this sum, and were to be paid half-yearly.

The rents and profits and fines were to be applied towards binding the apprentices — no poor boy was to have more than £20 to bind him, and if parents should have £20 a year freehold estate their children were ineligible.

Apprenticeships ceased about 1956 and in lieu thereof the money is used to provide boys born in Wiltshire or who have resided there for at least five years prior to application, with tools. Any monies not so used are put to general purposes of education.

The Trustees can vary in number between nine and seventeen and they meet at Marlborough about every four months.

Appendix I

Will of Sarah, Duchess of Somerset

SCHEDULE

dated 17th May 1686.

"These goods I give in trust to my niece the Lady Delamer, one rich Crimson bed with mixed silver gold and vestoone great fringe upon the vallens the bed lined with white satin and embroidered suitable and white satin inward vallens, eight crimson velvet covers for chairs two of which are elbow chairs, eight chairs the frames carved and japanned and gilt, four large velvet tops and four plumes of white feathers for the top of the bed, one crimson sarcenet* case to draw over the bed and all things that belong to the said crimson velvet bed, one new suite of tapestry hangings about 8½ feet deep containing five pieces being the story Moses and the Apostles, one other suite of tapestry hangings about 9 feet deep containing five pieces being the story of Tarquin and Lucretia, one large Persian carpet, two lesser Persion carpets suitable, two white damask window curtains, one great tortoise shell cabinet embossed with silver in the inside and frame to it suitable, one ebony strong box with gilt bars cross over it, one great walnut tree trunk lined with scarlet satin, two high stands carved and gilt, one great looking glass the frame of it carved and gilt, one large ermine mantle to lay over a great bed the said mantle being lined with white satin, one large silver gilt salver weighing about 60 ounces, one silver bason narrow brimmed all the outside being wrought in several flowers, six silver trencher plates having my former Lord's and my arms engraved thereon and a Duke's coronet, one large silver pair of silver snuffers, one gold clock-watch with a black frame of ebony, one rich carved gilt new coach lined with crimson and gold colour wrought velvet and four gold coloured damask curtains and a great vestoone silk fringe on the inside of the coach and six great glasses belonging to the said coach and two yellow cloth horse-

---

*A very fine and soft material made both plain and twilled in various colours. (O.E.D.)

cloths bordered round with crimson and gold colour wrought velvet and what else belongs to the said coach and six brass harness gilt and finely wrought. I would have my niece Delamer leave these things to her eldest son to remain in the family as they will last."

To the eldest daughter of her niece Lady Delamer she gave — "One ring set with nine diamonds, one necklace of small pearls of three rows, one fine Holland twilight laced round with broad Flanders lace and one Flanders broad laced Holland border to go round the bottom of the bed suitable, four little fine Holland pillowbers laced round with broad bone lace, about 1½ yards of pure fine broad new point de Venise being for a handkerchief or shape for the neck and one pure fine very narrow point de Venise for one pair of cuffs suitable, one pocket handkerchief set round with broad point de Venise all which points are looped thick, 22 yards of black farrendine, 12 yards of new black morella tabby, one new mantle of mixed red and white venetian wrought silk stuff wrought like large leaves lined with sarcenèt (no lace upon it) and about 5 yards of the same new venetian wrought silk stuff suitable, one fillimote mohair furniture for a great bedstead lined with sky colour sarscenet and one laced quilt to lay over the bed, six chairs of fillimote mohair suitable to the bed containing four curtains vallances basis head piece, head board tester, and inward vallances 4 cups and 4 spriggs for the top of the said bed, one scarlet satin large quilt lined with sarscenet to lay over a great bed, one cloth of silver mantle wrought in little flowers of mixed scarlet and black lined with scarlet sarscenet, one cherry colour morella tabby twilight laced with a very broad ground work tape lace, one silver warming pan, nine silver knobs of wrought plate for two hooks for a chimney and for one fire shovel and tongs, two more larger round knobs of wrought plate for a fire grate, one sad cloth furniture for a large bedstead containing four cloth curtains vallance with a deep silk fringe on it of the same sad colour the bed lined with cherry colour sarscenet containing also inward vallance head piece, tester and a large quilt to lay over the bed of cherry colour sarscenet, one little picture set in gold of my former husband, John, Duke of Somerset, one hair broad bracelet for the arm curiously wrought in flowers with hair of several colours, one little tortoise shell box filled with gessimine glasses, one large strong water case embroidered all over with gold and silver of the outside and lined with red satin and all the glasses having silver tops and silver cup and handle in the middle of them."

Then to her niece Delamer's daughter, Mary Booth, her god-daughter she gave the following —

"One large silver writing standish, my late husband the Duke of Somerset and my arms engraved thereon and a Duke's coronet, nine silver knobs of wrought plate finer wrought than those before mentioned being for one fire shovel and tongs and for two hooks for a chimney, two larger silver knobs made higher for a chimney grate, one little tortoiseshell cabinet finely inlaid with ivory and ebony and the drawers lined with red sarscenet, one scarlet velvet mantle laid with a broad silver and gold lace, one scarlet brocade satin cloak mantle being bordered round with ermine and lined with scarlet sarscenet, one new pink colour satin twilight set round with a broad silver lace and four silver tassels one at each corner, one Holland twilight set round with broad point de parry, one Holland border for to go round the bottom of a bed laced with broad point de parry, about one yard and a half of pure fine broad point de venise being for a handkerchief or shape for the neck the said point being now never washed, one new fine broad point de Venise set round an apron being now never washed, one more pure fine point de Venise handkerchief or shape for the neck being wrought in several long leaves. All which points are looped thick. One new lemon colour plain satin petticoat laced with a broad rich silver lace and set down before with loops made all of silver wire, one mixed pink colour and white new plain satin gown laced with a broad rich silver lace, one sky colour cloth of silver petticoat, one new broad rich silver lace to set upon a petticoat, 18 yards of black new velvet, 28 yards of black new silk crepe, about 5 yards of new crimson velvet, 20 yards of mixed grediline and white broad new lute string. One great pear tree black cabinet that opens with doors and is well carved on the inside containing in all about 35 drawers and one black frame it stands upon and "my mind and will is that when the said cabinet is delivered to my said niece Mary Booth she shall then give to her brother Langham Booth the black ebony cabinet that I lately gave her and the frame to it", one brockedell furniture for a large bedstead of mixed colours, gold crimson and white wrought in flowers the bed lined with crimson and white striped India satin and striped satin quilt headpiece and tester suitable, 4 long curtains and basis for round the bottom of the bed, 18 silk tassels of the same mixed colours to tie up the curtains, 4 cups and 4 spriggs for the top of the bed, 8 brockedell cushions for chairs suitable, 11 yards of mixed colours new brockedell the same as my brockedell bed, one green wrought upon white dimity furniture for a great bedstead containing 4 curtains, counterpane vallance, headpiece basis and covers for some chairs being all suitable, the said bed being wrought silk lorrells and white calico lining to the said bed, one large rich sable muff and one large rich sable tippet, one white quilt to lay over a bed stitched with white silk all over, one large silver salver having abrought brim wrought, 19 yards of new white damask for window curtains, one silver little watch made in scholop fashion and silver case to it, one sedan chair lined with crimson velvet."

To her cousin, Elizabeth Cole, she gave —
"One sable tippet the shortest and worst of my two tippets, one new black velvet cloak mantle lined with black wrought satin, one pink colour wrought silk mantle wrought in little flowers lined with pink sarcenet, and one pink wrought silk large sweet bag suitable no lace on either of them, one scarlet velvet little dressing box with a looking glass in it."

To her waiting woman, Elizabeth Crow —
"One green satin petticoat embroidered with gold and silver, one white morella tabby petticoat no lace on it, one white wrought silk mantua gown striped with gold stripes and lined with cherry coloured spotted lute string, one new cherry coloured morella tabby under bodice and sleeves, one new fine black cloth gown (not laced), one petticoat, one black wrought striped satin long gown, one white sarcenet petticoat laced broad with black lace, one ash coloured sarcenet and laid with silver gold and silver fringe."

Then again to her said god-daughter, Mary Booth, and her sister Elizabeth Booth, "all my several point de Venise and all my pure fine broad Flanders lace wearing linen and all my fine household linen that I do not give away and bequeath elsewhere to be equally divided between them."

To her niece Delamer's younger son, Langham Booth, she gave —
"One silver bason of plain plate with a brim, one great silver tankard having my former Lords and my arms engraven thereon but no coronet, one great silver chaffing dish, one emerald ring

set between two diamonds, one India wood large writing standish having one great drawer in it and the outside of the wood being of a reddish colour and inlaid with black, five silver trencher plates having broad brims and one silver trencher plate having a narrow brim. Morning gown with silk, one plain satin mantle lined with white sarcenet, one lemon colour plain sarcenet petticoat, one scarlet satin petticoat (not laced), one white lutestring mantua gown lined with blue sarcenet, one tape point coif not gimped and cornett for the head suitable both of Holland and laced with the said tape point, one pocket handkerchief laced with point Holland all the said points being looped thick, one silver porringer and three silver spoons and one trencher salt and one little silver pot with handle all to be of the oldest most used plate."

She remembered Ann Knapp who was lately her servant with the following goods —

"One new black watered mohair long gown and petticoat both of them laced with a broad black lace, one mixed gredeline white and buff colour new wrought tabby long gown having slashed sleeves, one black wrought lutestring long gown laced with black lace, one fine new black cloth long gown and petticoat, one new coloured sarcenet wadded petticoat, one black crape long gown and petticoat, one cherry colour tabby petticoat laced broad with white gimp lace phillamot wrought tabby cloak mantle lined with ash colour wrought satin, one pink colour sarcenet petticoat, one green wrought satin mantle of a small work and four green wrought satin sweet bags suitable, one white cloth of silver petticoat, one white antereen stuff mantua gown and petticoat, one tape point cornet for the head being all point and gimped over and one Holland coif with tape point on it gimped suitable, one pocket handkerchief set round with tape point gimped all of the said tape points being looped, one silver porringer and three silver spoons and the least of my silver tankards, one trencher salt all to be of the oldest most used plate."

It ended — "In witness whereof I have to this schedule containing seven sheets of paper all written with my own hand subscribed my name to every one of the said sheets."

Probably because her niece, the Countess of Warrington (Lady Delamer in the Will) had died early in 1692 and as it was also nearly six years since Sarah had made her Will, she added a Codicil of some length dated 10th February 1692. The main items were —

Ten guineas to Philip Berwick, Doctor in Physic, "if by letter left with him I commit to him some care concerning my body when I am dead."

The legacy to John Cooke was revoked "he having left my service."

There was £500 more to Lady Lukyn and another £500 more for Lady Howe.

To her brother-in-law, Sir Samuel Grimston, 120 shilling pieces of "broad gold".

£3,000 to Henry Booth, son of "my niece the Countess of Warrington deceased" to buy land with.

Devise of Cherrington and Clinton to Langham Booth was revoked but £2,000 instead to be laid out in buying land. The manor of Cherrington was now given in support of the Almshouses.

100 guineas to Henry, Earl of Warrington, as well as a gold watch with steel case studded with gold and a ring set with seven diamonds and a silver gilt salver of about sixty ounces.

To Lady Elizabeth Booth 100 pieces of broad twenty shilling pieces of gold.

To Lady Mary Booth 100 pieces of broad twenty shilling pieces of gold.

To George, Lord Delamer, 100 pieces of broad twenty shilling pieces of gold.

To her god-daughter, Lady Katherine Seymour, daughter of Charles, Duke of Somerset, 200 guineas to buy plate.

£20 to Sir Joseph Alston, Bart, grandson of Sir Joseph Alston of Chelsea, Bart, deceased.

£20 to his brother, Edward Alston.

£1,000 more for the Hospital of Green Coat Boys at Westminster to buy lands.

To Lady Elizabeth Booth a great Japan cabinet.

£20 to Mary Wittewronge, grandchild of Sir Joseph Alston, Bart, deceased.

The £300 given in the Will to Richard Skynner's children was altered to £100.

£500 more was to be spent on building almshouses and £100 more on finishing the Chapel there.

Owing to the death of Lady Delamer, Countess of Warrington, her two daughters and two younger sons were appointed residuary devisees and legatees equally.

Legacies to Mary Crew revoked as she "is finally departed out of my service."

Appendix II

A Note of the Masters ffuneral charges

(SIR HARBOTTLE GRIMSTON)

	£	s.	d.
To the Searchers.		5	0
Ffour fflamboys.		18	0
Paid the groom's bill for the line of four horses expenses on road to Gorham.	1	16	0
To Mr Cole five guineys.	5	7	6
More to him the forfeiture to the poor for burying in Linnen.	5	0	0
To the Bearers.	2	0	0
To the Clarke.	1	0	0
To Joseph Carter for his work at the valt.		10	0
To Robert Bradwine for his work there.		10	0
To the Sexton.		2	0
To Mr Reeves the Apothycary his Bill.	11	0	0
Pd for making Mrs Mantor and pettycoate.		8	6
Pd Mr William Bennetts Bill.	11	7	0
To Mr Lee in leiu of mourning for his children.	4	0	0
To Mr Reeves the apothycary for his attendance in the Ma^S sicknesse.	3	4	6
To the Hosier his Bill.	3	16	6
To the Sadler his Bill.	3	0	0
Pd for making 5 mantors & pettycoats for the maids.	1	15	0
To Mr Hobart his Bill.	10	18	0
Pd for Ye Black Gown Capp & Slippers.	3	0	0
To Mr Wiseman his Bill for probate of ye Will.	2	6	0
To Edw. Downes His Bill the charge of the horses.	4	14	7
To Mr Page his Bill the charges at Gorhambury & other things on ye road.	3	11	6
To Sir Wm. Luckyn in leiu of mourning for his children.	4	0	0

To Mr Smith in leiu of mourning for her children.	4	0	0
To the Mercer his Bill for crape.	23	14	0
Pd for James (Mr Grimston's footboys) mourning & Jack's Black coat.	2	5	0
Pd Mr Saunders the Herald painter his Bill.	32	0	0
To Mr Pennice the Woollen Draper his Bill.	270	0	0
To Mr Sherl the Taylor his Bill.	25	0	0
To Mr Smithsby the Woollen Draper his Bill.	247	13	0
To Mr Russell his Bill for the coffin etc.	64	0	0
To the Gentlewomen for makeing up the Gowns & Mantors.	6	19	0
Pd for wax Candles.	5	2	0
To the Coachmaker his Bill.	55	0	0
	£810	4	0

Bibliography

PRIMARY SOURCES

Wills   —   Sarah, Duchess of Somerset
              Frances, Duchess of Somerset
              William, 2nd Duke of Somerset
              William, 3rd Duke of Somerset
              John, 4th Duke of Somerset
              Sir Edward Alston, M.D.

Archives —   Brasenose College, Oxford
              St John's College, Cambridge
              Gorhambury Collection (Herts. Record Office)
              Seymour Papers (Longleat)
              Thynne Papers (Longleat)

SECONDARY SOURCES

Historical Manuscript Commission—

    MSS of Marquess of Ailesbury, College of Arms,
    Marquess of Bath, Duke of Beaufort, Lord Braye,
    Sir H. J. L. Bruce, Duke of Buccleuch, Earl of Denbigh,
    Reginald Cholmondeley, Lord de L'Isle and Dudley,
    George Wingfield Digby, Marquess of Downshire.
    Emmanuel College, G. E. Frere, Sir Frederick Graham, Bart.,
    Duke of Hamilton, R. R. Hastings, House of Lords,
    Sir Henry Ingilby, Bart., F. H. T. Jervoise, Lord Kenyon,
    Le Fleming, G. A. Lowndes, Earl of Mar and Kellie,
    College of Physicians, Duke of Portland, J. J. Rogers,
    Duke of Rutland, City of Salisbury, Sir H. Verney,
    Mrs Stopford Sackville, Captain Stewart of Alltyrodyn Llandyssil,
    Duke of Sutherland.

Calendar of State Papers (Domestic) 1611 — 1690
Calendar of Treasury Books 1660 — 1675
Calendar of Clarendon State Papers
Calendar of Committee for Compounding
    The Pell Records (James I)
Reports of The Charity Commissioners
Proceedings of the Suffolk Institute of Archaeology Vol. XV
Wiltshire Archaeological Magazine Vols. XVIII, XX, XXVI, XLIV.
Notes & Queries 11th October 1913 (Material discovered by Bertram Dobell)
Account of The Murther of Francis Seymour, Duke of Somerset, by
    Hildebrand Allington

Mercurius Pragmaticus 30th Aug — 6th Sep. 1659
Abstracts of Wiltshire Inquisititione Post Mortem by G. S. and E. A. Fry
A true narrative of the taking of Sir George Booth, 1659.

Oxford

Alumni Oxoniensis by J. Foster
Calendar of Muniments, Brasenose College Vols. 27 — 35
Register of Brasenose College
Brasenose College Quatercentenary Monographs

Cambridge

Alumni Cantabrigiensis by J. & J. A. Venn
University Register
History of St John's College by Thomas Baker
Portrait of a College by Edward Miller
St John's College History by J. B. Mullinger
Founders and Benefactors of St John's College by A. F. Terry
Collegium Div. I Johannis Evangelistae (1511 — 1911)

Gray's Inn

A Prospect of Gray's Inn by Francis Cowper

Lincoln's Inn

Register
Record of Lincoln's Inn Vol. III of Black Books

Royal College of Physicians

History of the Royal College of Physicians by F. J. Farro
The Roll of the Royal College of Physicians by W. R. Munk

Schools

Short History of Hereford School by W. T. Carless
History of Marlborough Grammar School by Stedman
Manchester Grammar School by A. A. Mumford
History of Manchester School by W. R. Whatton
History of Tottenham Grammar School by H. Godfrey S. Groves
Endowed Grammar Schools by Nicholas Carlisle

Family Histories

Stemmata Alstoniana by Lionel Cresswell
The Seymour Family by A. Audrey Locke
Annals of the Seymours by H. St Maur
Memoirs of the Verney family, by Margaret Lady Verney
Memoirs of Thomas, Earl of Ailesbury
Life and Loyalties of Thomas Bruce, 2nd Earl of Ailesbury by Earl of
    Cardigan
Lives from the Clarendon Gallery)
Lives of Friends of Clarendon   ) by Lady Theresa Lewis
The Duppa-Isham Correspondence
Memoirs of Sir John Reresby
Granger's Biographical History
British Family Antiquities by William Playfair

County Histories

Duncumb's History of Herefordshire
Manors of Suffolk by W. A. Copinger
Able Men of Suffolk 1638 ed. Charles E. Banks
Records of the County of Wiltshire by B. Howard Cunnington
Memorials of Old Cheshire by Ven. E. Barber
Memorials of Old Wiltshire by Alice Dryden

Other Histories

History of Marlborough by James Waylen
History and Antiquities of Tottenham by W. Robinson
London, Past and Present by Henry B. Wheatley
London in the Time of the Stuarts by Sir Walter Besant
History of the Collegiate Church in Manchester by Dr S. Hibbert
The Siege of Chester by Canon R. H. Morris
An Account of the Somerset Hospital at Froxfield by John Ward 1786
Old Froxfield by Rev. A. G. Bailey
Annals of St Helen's, Bishopsgate by Rev. J. E. Cox
History of His Own Time by Bishop Gilbert Burnet
Crosby Hall by C. F. W. Goss
History of the Civil War by S. R. Gardiner

Diaries

John Evelyn's Diary
Narcissus Luttrell's Diary
Samuel Pepys' Diary
Diary of Henry Machyn
Diurnal of Thomas Rugge

Personal Papers

The Clarke Papers
The Essex Papers
The Nicholas Papers
Letterbook of John, Viscount Mordaunt
Memorials of the English Affairs by Bulstrode Whitelocke

Biographies

Life and Times of William Laud by J. P. Lawson
Life and Acts of John Whitgift by John Stype
The Standard Bearer by Peter Verney
The Stranger's Son by J. J. Keevil
Arbella Stuart by P. M. Handover
Judges of England by Edward Foss
Fuller's Worthies
Portraits of Illustrious Personages by Edmund Lodge
Oliver Cromwell by John Buchan
Oliver Cromwell by S. H. Church
Two Tudor Portraits by Hester Chapman
The Tudor Princesses by Agnes Strickland
Lord Chancellor Jeffreys and The Stuart Cause by G. W. Keeton

General Reading

Ashley, Maurice	England in the Seventeenth Century
	Life in Stuart England
	The Stuarts in Love
Burton, Elizabeth	The Jacobeans at Home
Davies, Godfrey	The Early Stuarts
Dunlop, O. Jocelyn	English Apprenticeship
Durrant, Horatia	The Somerset Sequence
Godfrey, Elizabeth	Social Life under the Stuarts
Ogg, David	England in the reign of Charles II
Trotter, Eleanor	Seventeenth Century Life in a Country Parish
Wedgwood, C. V.	The King's War

Standard Books of Reference

Dictionary of National Biography
Burke's Peerage
The Complete Peerage by G. E. Cokayne
State Trials

Index to Part I

A

Adams, Alderman, 29;
—Mrs, 64.
Adda, Court of, 122.
Adventure, H.M.S., 64.
Ailesbury, Lord, 118—9, 146, 150, 157—8.
Albemarle, Duke of, 97, 100, 123.
Albert, Archduke, 66—8.
Alington, Hildebrand, 120—1.
Alston, Arthur, 19;
—Edward, 17, 19—25, 27, 37, 41, 108, 131;
—Elizabeth, 19;
—Isaac, 176;
—John, 17;
—Joseph, 19;
—Margaret, 19;
—Mary, 21, 23, 27, 36;
—Sarah, 21—4, 41;
—Susan, 23—4, 37;
—Thomas, 19;
—William, 17.
Altrincham, 155, 160—1.
Amesbury, 80, 89, 114—5.
Anabaptists, 77.
Argent, Jo, 66.
Arlington, Lord, 107, 110.
Ashton, Lord, 162.
Awdry, Lady, 83.
Aylesbury, 142.
Aylett, John, 145.

B

Bacon, Ann, 51;
—Francis, 51;
—Nathaniel, 51.
Badminton, 113—4, 117—9.
Bagshot, 88.
Bastille, 42.
Bath, 115;
—Lord, 83.
Batten, barber, 64.
Baynes, Capt., 79.
Beauchamp, Lord, 55, 59, 63, 71, 87—93, 95—7, 114;
—Lady, 88, 90—93, 113, 148.
Beaufort, Duke of, 83, 93, 151.
Beaumont, Mr, 106.
Bedford, Earl of, 98—9.
Berkeley, Lord George, 99.
Berkhampstead, 146.
Berkley, Mrs, 52.
Berry, Lord, 74.

Bertie, Charles, 123;
—Lady Mary, 99.
Birkenhead, Edward, 47.
Birmingham, 161.
Biron, Mr, 106.
Bishopsgate, 36.
Black Rod, 151, 156.
Blackfriars, 56.
Blackheath, 33.
Blackwall, 57.
Bollen, Sir John, 148.
Booth, Elizabeth, 176;
—George, 131, 133—6, 155, 170, 176.
—Sir George, 82, 131, 133, 135—6, 138—46;
—Henry, 38, 131, 147—51;
—John, 131, 134, 136, 140, 142, 146;
—Lady, 143;
—Langham, 177;
—Mary, 170, 176;
—Nathaniel, 142;
—Vere, 155—6.
Borosky, George, 126, 128.
Botti, Anthony, 121;
—Horatio, 120—2.
Bowden, 116, 149, 168, 170.
Bradfield, 42—3.
Bradshaw, Lord, 144.
Bramston, Francis, 105.
Brandon, Lord, 155, 165.
Braunston, 37.
Breda, 145.
Brereton, Sir William, 133—4.
Bressey, Mr, 52.
Brideoake, Dr Ralph, 177;
—Mrs, 177.
Bridgeman, Sir Orlando, 96, 98, 111—2.
Bridgewater, 122.
Bristol, 160.
Brixham, 159.
Brooke, Mr, 73—4.
Browne, Francis, 175;
—Hester, 175.
Brownists, 77.
Bruce, Charles, 176;
—Thomas, 118—9, 146—50.
Bruges, 57, 69.
Brussels, 57, 66—7, 69, 93.
Bruton, 163.
Buckingham, Duke of, 99;
—Duchess of, 22.
Buckinghamshire, 25, 133.

Hare, Henry (2nd Lord Coleraine), 21–2, 172;
—Sir Nicholas, 172.
Harrington, Sir James, 29;
—Mr, 25.
Harwich, 42–3.
Harvey, Dr, 23.
Hastings, Lady Elizabeth, 38;
—Lady Mary, 106.
Hawkins, Capt. Richard, 42.
Haymarket, 127.
Hazelwood, Sir Anthony, 34.
Hearst, Dr, 93.
Henry, Prince, 66.
Herbert, Lord, 93, 95, 97–8;
—Lady, 95–8.
Hereford, 112, 177.
Hertford, County of, 146.
Hertford, Earl of, 55, 58–64, 70–4, 93, 116;
—Marquis of, 55, 76–82, 84, 88, 90, 92, 95, 115;
—Lady, 93, 96, 106;
Hewish, 107.
High Treason, 29, 59, 90, 149, 151, 153, 156–7, 165.
Hilton, Mr Nathaniel, 168.
Hitchin, 155.
Hobart, Anne, 22.
Hobbs, Mr, 126.
Hoddesdon, 155.
Holborn Hill, 160.
Holland, 33, 124–5, 129, 159.
Holles, Mr, 22, 46, 48, 50;
—Lady Penelope, 38.
Hollis, Lord, 100.
Holmwood, Mrs Elizabeth, 176.
Honiton, 160.
Hopton, Sir Owen, 63.
Hospital, St Bartholomew's, 25.
House of Commons, 43, 46–8, 50, 71, 76–7, 81, 135, 145.
House of Lords, 20, 30, 71–3, 81–2, 97, 99, 119, 144–5, 149, 153.
How, Sir Richard, 116;
—Lady, 177.
Howard, Lord of Effingham, 63.
Howard, Viscount of Bindon, 63.
Howell, Mr William, 109.
Hudson, Christopher, 21.
Hue and Cry, 125.
Hungerford, 101, 163.
Huntingdon, Earl of, 38, 107, 174.
Hussey, Susan, 21.
Hyde, Edward, 91–3;
—Sir Robert, 96.

I

Independents, 50.
Indulgence, Declaration of, 158.
Ipswich, 42.
Ireland, 112, 118, 131, 135, 137, 145, 166.
Italy, 87.

J

Jeffreys, Judge, 149–54, 156.
Jenner, Sir Thomas, 154.
Jennings, Sarah, 130.
Jesuits, 66–7, 147, 158, 167.
Johnson, George, 113–4, 116;
—Mr, 25.
Joyce, Cornet, 46.

K

Kelsey, Mrs, 155.
Kent, 79.
Kenyon, Alice, 168;
—Roger, 160, 168.
Kettleburgh, 18.
Kings:
—Charles I, 22, 46, 72, 74, 79, 87, 103, 117, 119;
—Charles II, 19, 23, 32, 48, 55, 81–3, 89, 91, 95, 97, 110, 119, 131, 133, 136, 138–9, 144–5, 147, 149;
—Edward I, 17, 27;
— Edward VI, 49, 55, 59;
—Henry VIII, 17, 56, 59, 80, 95;
—James I, 56, 66–7, 103;
—James II, 53, 122, 149, 150, 157–9, 163–6, 174.
—William III, 159, 164–7.
King's Lynn, 23.
Knapp, Anne, 175.
Knight, Thomas, 176.
Knowsley, 159, 161.

L

Lambe, John, 18.
Lambert, General, 140–1, 144, 146.
Lambeth, 145.
Lancashire, 134–5, 159, 161, 165, 168.
Langham, Henry de, 27;
—Edward, 37–8;
—James, 21, 27, 33, 36–8, 155;
—John, 20, 24, 27, 29–37, 82;
—Mary, 23, 36–8, 131, 174;
—William, 20, 27, 39.
Laud, Archbishop, 44.
Lauderdale, Duchess of, 164.
Leggatt, George, 120–1.

Index to Part II

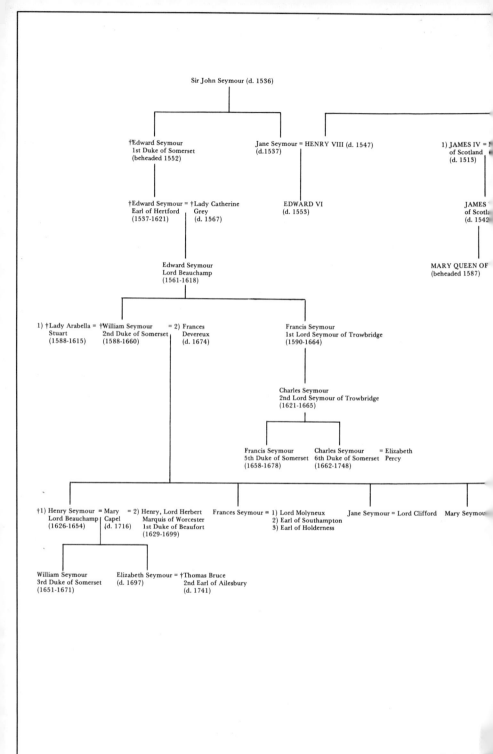

Sir John Seymour (d. 1536)

†Edward Seymour
1st Duke of Somerset
(beheaded 1552)

Jane Seymour = HENRY VIII (d. 1547)
(d.1537)

1) JAMES IV =
of Scotland
(d. 1513)

†Edward Seymour = †Lady Catherine
Earl of Hertford   Grey
(1537-1621)   (d. 1567)

EDWARD VI
(d. 1553)

JAMES
of Scotl
(d. 1542

Edward Seymour
Lord Beauchamp
(1561-1618)

MARY QUEEN OF
(beheaded 1587)

1) †Lady Arabella = †William Seymour   = 2) Frances
   Stuart   2nd Duke of Somerset   Devereux
   (1588-1615)   (1588-1660)   (d. 1674)

Francis Seymour
1st Lord Seymour of Trowbridge
(1590-1664)

Charles Seymour
2nd Lord Seymour of Trowbridge
(1621-1665)

Francis Seymour   Charles Seymour   = Elizabeth
5th Duke of Somerset 6th Duke of Somerset Percy
(1658-1678)   (1662-1748)

†1) Henry Seymour = Mary   = 2) Henry, Lord Herbert   Frances Seymour = 1) Lord Molyneux   Jane Seymour = Lord Clifford   Mary Seymou
   Lord Beauchamp   Capel   Marquis of Worcester   2) Earl of Southampton
   (1626-1654)   (d. 1716)   1st Duke of Beaufort   3) Earl of Holderness
                                (1629-1699)

William Seymour   Elizabeth Seymour = †Thomas Bruce
3rd Duke of Somerset   (d. 1697)   2nd Earl of Ailesbury
(1651-1671)   (d. 1741)

† = At variou